Drug Decriminalization and Legalization

Recent Titles in Health and Medical Issues Today

Medical Tourism, Lydia Gan
Organ Donation, Sarah Boslaugh
Food Inequalities, Tennille Nicole Allen

Drug Decriminalization and Legalization

Aharon W. Zorea

BLOOMSBURY ACADEMIC
NEW YORK • LONDON • OXFORD • NEW DELHI • SYDNEY

BLOOMSBURY ACADEMIC
Bloomsbury Publishing Inc, 1385 Broadway, New York, NY 10018, USA
Bloomsbury Publishing Plc, 50 Bedford Square, London, WC1B 3DP, UK
Bloomsbury Publishing Ireland, 29 Earlsfort Terrace, Dublin 2, D02 AY28, Ireland

BLOOMSBURY, BLOOMSBURY ACADEMIC and the Diana logo are trademarks of Bloomsbury Publishing Plc

First published in the United States of America 2025

A catalog record for this book is available from the Library of Congress.

ISBN: HB: 978-1-4408-8062-9
ePDF: 978-1-4408-8063-6
eBook: 979-8-7651-1062-1

Series: Health and Medical Issues Today

Typeset by Newgen KnowledgeWorks Pvt. Ltd., Chennai, India
Printed and bound in the United States of America

For product safety related questions contact productsafety@bloomsbury.com.

To find out more about our authors and books visit www.bloomsbury.com and sign up for our newsletters.

This book is dedicated to my siblings—Avraham and Aimee, Isaac and Wendy, Nathan and Mary, Gabriel and Phaidra, Estee and Nic, and also Sandi and James, Michael, Andy and Rebecca, Josiah, and Petia

Contents

Series Foreword

Every day, the public is bombarded with information on developments in medicine and health care. Whether it is on the latest techniques in treatment or research or on concerns over public health threats, this information directly affects the lives of people more than almost any other issue. Although there are many sources for understanding these topics—from websites and blogs to newspapers and magazines—students and ordinary citizens often need one resource that makes sense of the complex health and medical issues affecting their daily lives.

The Health and Medical Issues Today series provides just such a one-stop resource for obtaining a solid overview of the most controversial areas of health care in the twenty-first century. Each volume addresses one topic and provides a balanced summary of what is known. These volumes provide an excellent first step for students and laypeople interested in understanding how health care works in our society today.

Each volume is broken into several parts to provide readers and researchers with easy access to the information they need.

Part I provides overview chapters on background information—including chapters on such areas as the historical, scientific, medical, social, and legal issues involved—that a citizen needs to intelligently understand the topic.

Part II provides capsule examinations of the most heated contemporary issues and debates and analyzes in a balanced manner the viewpoints held by various advocates in the debates.

Part III provides case studies that show examples of the concepts discussed in the previous parts.

A directory of resources and a glossary provide additional reference material and serve as the best next step in learning about the topic at hand.

The Health and Medical Issues Today series strives to provide readers with all the information needed to begin making sense of some of the most important debates going on in the world today. The series includes volumes on such topics as stem-cell research, obesity, gene therapy, alternative medicine, organ transplantation, mental health, and more.

Preface

A lot has changed in America's drug laws over the past thirty years. It usually takes at least that long to see how our social experiments impact society. New laws pose new challenges, which lead to new public reactions, and after a time, the new laws are slowly revised and adapted to address new social conditions. We saw major changes in our drug laws and have also seen many of the first reactions to those changes. The final resolution is probably still to come.

The story of drug decriminalization and legalization of marijuana began in the late 1990s but did not reach its maturity until the 2020s. A wave of states decriminalized marijuana for medical use or legalized it entirely for recreational use during the 2010s. By the end of the decade, some highly experimental forms of decriminalization were introduced at the state and local levels—especially in Oregon, Washington, California, and British Columbia (in our Canadian neighbor to the north). However, by the mid-2020s, many of these experiments were revised after disturbing urban conditions sparked strong public reactions. No state chose to recriminalize marijuana, but the rules of recreational drug use were modified—in some cases, dramatically.

What we saw over the past thirty years is a gradual division among state policies. Most of those states that wanted to legalize marijuana legalized it. Those states that did not want legalization did not—and both sides seem willing to keep the status quo for the time being. It is at the national level where we see the strongest debates over the wisdom of decriminalization, and there does not appear to be any national consensus emerging in the near future. At the state level, however, we have seen some general consensus within regional districts.

This book does not attempt to make an argument for or against decriminalization or legalization. Instead, we outline the issue as a matter of differing legal, medical, and moral viewpoints. It is important to recognize that drug policies, like any other law, reflect public values. Our nation has not demonstrated strong consensus over many cultural priorities in the twenty-first century, so it is understandable that those same cultural debates naturally carry over into our drug policies.

It is tempting to tell the story of marijuana legalization as if the old and outdated ideas of the drug war have been overcome by modern enlightened ideas of decriminalization and harm reduction. The problem with that sort of story is that it assumes a level of cultural consensus that simply does not exist. Opponents of marijuana legalization continue to oppose recreational drug use, even after the laws change. Supporters of decriminalization do not find that they are immune from harsh criticism. The various groups seem to have coalesced around particular ideological preferences, but there is not a lot of shifting from one group to another.

In part, the evolutionary story of cultural transformation is based on the idea that each successive generation is a little more open to new ideas than the previous generation—therefore, the modern young people of today must all want to legalize drugs. That does not seem to be true. In our case, the Baby Boomer generation had an unusually powerful impact on influencing social and economic priorities from the 1960s to the 2020s, but baby boomers can be found among all ideological groups. The current digital social media generation certainly shares many characteristics, but they are also just as divided on cultural priorities as any previous cohort was, and it is not always clear exactly what they believe in. Recreational drug use and the associated social and psychological problems of drug addiction impact people of all age levels and socioeconomic backgrounds. The quest to legalize (or criminalize) certain drugs is not a generational movement. There is no guarantee that experiments in drug policy that were initially launched during the 2010s will continue to be supported by later generations of the 2030s or 2040s. Ideological views play a more important role than age in politicized drug-policy debates.

This book is original in that we explain drug decriminalization and marijuana legalization in terms of sincere and honest cultural debate. We do not criticize those who supported (and continue to support) the war on drugs and the ideals of a drug-free society. Nor do we condemn those who support (and continue to support) drug decriminalization, legalization, and other harm reduction policies. We examine historical trends in an effort to explain how and why these various supporters and opponents grew into what they became in the 2020s. Each perspective reflects sincerely held ideological views, and each side is genuinely interested in helping to relieve the very real problems experienced by others. We assume that both supporters and opponents believe that their policy priorities are best for society. We hope that readers will evaluate the differing ideological presumptions according to each group's separate expectations and not on predetermined judgments. In this way, readers can best recognize and identify the strengths and weaknesses of policy approaches and make judgments based on how these reflect their own values and priorities.

This book is organized into three main parts—the first two are more or less equal in length, and the third is much shorter. The first part provides an overview of the foundational concepts that are necessary for really understanding the complexity of drug decriminalization proposals. We look at our political system, legal history, the history of drug use and criminalization, and the long tradition of penal reforms. These concepts are compared to international examples that place the United States within a larger global context where recreational drug policies have long been debated. Specific decriminalization and legalization proposals of the 2000s are then introduced as a culmination of national and global trends that date back hundreds of years. This first part also introduces three ideological perspectives that are used throughout the book to help distinguish differing viewpoints. For ease of reference, these are labeled libertarian, social welfare, and traditional conservatives.

The second part adopts a more topical approach. Drug decriminalization and the legalization of marijuana is considered in terms of its impact on society relative to health and crime. We consider specific risks to individual physical health, the collective health of communities, and the potential changes that normalization of recreational drug use may cause for our mental and emotional well-being. Since the interpretation of quantifiable data is always subjective to ideological interpretation, we consider these effects according to the presumptions of our three different ideological perspectives. We then shift from health to crime and consider the potential, expected, and actual changes that occur in cities and states after drug-decriminalization policies are implemented. Entirely different conclusions are drawn from the same data points depending on differing ideological presumptions. We consider each in turn.

Lastly, the third part presents five case study scenarios from which the reader can consider more personalized perspectives on decriminalization and legalization. These are narrative stories that describe the experiences of individuals living in rural or urban communities that adopted new drug decriminalization or legalization policies. The specific characters used in each story are fictional, but the circumstances in which they are set are all strictly factual. Each case study story includes two individuals who have different perspectives from shared experiences in the same community. In some cases, these different viewpoints lead to opposing opinions on drug decriminalization and marijuana legalization. In other cases, the two characters arrive at the same general conclusions, though for differing reasons. These case studies provide readers with more relatable context for understanding issues that are often complex and generally much more nuanced than we would expect if we reduced the conflict down to a simple matter of being "for" or "against."

The full story of drug decriminalization and legalization has not yet ended in our culture. We achieved a sort of stasis at the state level, which is likely to continue at least for the next decade. However, the potential long-term benefits or harm that may result from our current drug policies are still being debated. The economic, social, and cultural consequences of any policy are always subject to differing ideological interpretations. These ideological differences over recreational drug use will continue. We do not intend to change anyone's deeply felt ideological views. However, this book should help readers to better consider and examine how and why they prefer some policies over others. More importantly, since our cultural debates will necessarily continue, it is crucial that we strive to understand with compassion the reasons, arguments, and expectations of those who may disagree with us.

Acknowledgments

I would like to thank my editor, Maxine Taylor, for suggesting a topic that fits so neatly into my continuing research into public policies related to medical health. We moved from contraception to steroids to anti-aging to marijuana, and this topic of decriminalization seems to cap off a culmination of discussions over policy debates that balance therapeutic potential with the risks of individual preference.

I also need to thank the thousand or more community members who helped me to contextualize the question of drug decriminalization within larger social issues related to addiction. For the past two years I have been blessed with a half dozen public forums where we discussed the dangers and predominance of digital addiction and its impact on our students, our schools, and our businesses. Special thanks go to Father John Del Priore of the UW-Platteville Catholic Pioneer Newman Center; Monsignor Roger Scheckel of St. Mary's Parish and School in Richland Center; Father Robert Letona and Edward Paloucek of Providence Academy in La Crosse; Deacon Mark Grunwald and his wife Ann from the Prairie du Chien Public School District; and Father Christopher Padilla along with the very energetic ladies of Life Guardians in Boscobel, especially Heather Kramer, Theresa Brewer, Pat Dearth, Dale and Rosemary Hall, Emily Hall, Christine Colley, Shawna Walz, Maya Saudia, and Mary Turner. There were far more people who helped organize these forums, and they are all appreciated.

As usual, this project required a little more than 500 books collected from libraries all across the state—some of which lived in my office for more than a year. I would like to thank the helpful attention (and patience) of Todd Roll, Le Suong Cina, and Sara Winger at the Miller Memorial and Karrmann Libraries on the University of Wisconsin—Platteville campuses.

Finally, my friends and family members who willingly listen to and contribute to discussions that seem to range over very wide fields. For law, my attorney father Moshe Calberg Zorea (and Rivka), my two attorney brothers Isaac Zorea (and Wendy) and Avraham Zorea, and my attorney friend Bill Cook (and MaryAlice), all of whom help protect me from any gross errors— as did my law students Levi Machovec and Joseph Jarrell, as well as Derek, Sierra, and Simon Zorea. For biomedicine and chemistry, Doctors Michael Kloess, Brad Walker, and John Hayes. For general cultural debates, Carol Sander, Nathan, and Mary, Gabe and Phaedra Zorea, Nic and Estee Abrams, Roxanne and Brandon, Jerry and Margie Morgan, Tim and Amy, Randy and Jaime, Michelle and Jason, and Chuck and Madelyn, with Virginia, Emma and Stephen Weigel, Laura, John-Paul, and Rachel, Julia, Justin, Jakob, Joseph, James, and Jane-Marie Kloess, Jim and Gail Rebhan, Stephanie, Mary, and Joe Rebhan, Michael Sander, Dorothy Thompson, Phil and June Nee and John Thompson.

Most especially, I thank my family for their general help and understanding—Jacob and Raelyn, Jonah, and my very supportive and patient wife, Emily. She is the perfect writing companion, with whom I test-drive most of my ideas and to whom all my books are always dedicated.

Part I

Overview

1

Why Criminalize Anything? Why Legalize (or Decriminalize) Anything?

This book tells the story of how and why laws are passed to prohibit the purchase, sale, and use of certain drugs without strict guidelines (called "criminalization"). It also tells the story of how new laws are made to allow these same drugs to be manufactured, bought, and sold with little or no guidelines at all (called "decriminalization").

In a democratic society like the United States, all of our laws—including the drug laws—must serve specific purposes. Before we explore the details of criminalization and decriminalization, we need to first remember why we have any laws at all. What purposes do our laws serve? How do the laws that criminalize (or decriminalize) drugs serve those purposes?

Criminal laws are set in place primarily to protect society by ensuring safety and civil peace among its citizens. As society develops over time, the purposes behind certain laws change, and there is much public debate over whether those changes are good or bad or effective or ineffective. Also, multiple layers of political jurisdiction create wide variations in the numbers and kinds of laws and the manner in which they are enforced. Such debates add complexity to the stories of criminalization and decriminalization of drugs and drug-related behaviors.

Basic Legal Theory

The history of American law owes its roots to English traditions. In 1689, an English philosopher, John Locke, wrote,

> The commonwealth seems to me to be a society of men constituted only for procuring, preserving their own civil interests ... therefore is the magistrate

> armed with the force and strength of all its subjects in order to the punishment of those that violate any other man' rights. *Two Treatises of Government,* p. 308fn3

In plain language, Locke believed laws were created by people who wanted to protect their individual rights. Almost a hundred years later, in 1776, the American Revolutionary Thomas Jefferson borrowed Locke's ideas when he wrote the Declaration of Independence. The opening lines of that famous document assert,

> We hold these truths to be self-evident, that all men are created equal, that they are endowed by their Creator with certain unalienable Rights, that among these are Life, Liberty and the pursuit of Happiness. That to secure these rights, Governments are instituted among Men, deriving their just powers from the consent of the governed.

Jefferson explained that our new American government existed solely to protect our rights. Each individual should expect their government to develop laws that help protect our personal safety (life and liberty) and also protect our personal property (the pursuit of happiness).

Just eleven years later, during the Constitutional Convention in 1787, Gouverneur Morris from Pennsylvania wrote the Preamble to the United States Constitution, which adds a list of specific objectives that our laws should try to achieve:

> We the People of the United States, in Order to form a more perfect Union, establish Justice, insure domestic Tranquility, provide for the common defense, promote the general Welfare, and secure the Blessings of Liberty to ourselves and our Posterity, do ordain and establish this Constitution for the United States of America.

The United States Constitution is the basis for every law in America, upon which all other laws receive their authority. In this document, the framers highlighted five main purposes behind our laws: (1) to help the union of states; (2) to protect people from suffering injustice; (3) to ensure that people can live together peacefully; (4) to protect the nation from invaders; and (5) to provide opportunities for each person and each family to live in the best way that they see fit. The first and fourth purposes deal with laws that create the agencies of government, the legislature, the courts system, and the military. The second, third, and fifth purposes are the ones that explain why we have laws that govern our behaviors—including all drug-related laws.

To summarize, we create laws to regulate drugs because we hope that they will help people to live together peaceably in safe and secure living conditions. If drug laws do not protect individuals from harm, or if they do not protect individual property from harm, they must be changed. Like all criminal laws, the drug laws are intended to limit harm. Almost all of the public debates related to criminalization and decriminalization are rooted in differing opinions on what is harmful, who is harmed, and how to best protect individual safety and property.

How Do We Define Harm?

In simple terms, "harm" means the same thing as "damage" or "hurt." If a drug is harmful, we believe it causes damage or it hurts someone physically, mentally, or emotionally. This is easy to understand but not always easy to identify. Some sorts of harm are obvious—you take a drug, and then you get sick and die. That harm is very easy to identify, and we call those types of drugs poisons. Other sorts of harm are not as obvious. When the drug impacts our potential, or our ability to focus or to learn, or damages our ability to judge between a good idea and a bad idea, these are also harms. In such cases, the hurt is not always easy to see. In some cases (in fact, many cases), the drug user may not see the harm at all, though others do—especially in how the drugs affect the user's behaviors, their relationships, or their job performance.

We usually think first about how drugs affect the user, but we also need to consider how they can affect others who live in close contact with the user. For example, if a drunk driver loses control of their vehicle and hurts a bystander or damages someone else's property, then we would say that the use of alcohol hurt someone other than the user. Or if an intoxicated parent neglects their children or if the drug causes the parent to lose self-control and they physically abuse their children or their spouse. These are obvious signs of harm to others. Other less obvious hurts would be when a drug impacts the users' ability to learn, communicate, or interact with others, in which case the drug damages relationships, job performance, and academic potential. Each of these drug effects could indirectly hurt those who depend upon and love the user.

Lastly, we also consider the harm that drugs may indirectly cause to society at large. If the addicted drug user feels such strong urges to take the drug that they break other laws to obtain the money necessary to support their addiction, then that harms society. Users who burglarize homes, rob strangers for money, steal property to sell, or engage in other criminal actions for money (like prostitution or violence) are harming their communities. Users often commit crimes both when they are intoxicated and when they are completely sober but are looking for a way to be intoxicated. Other social harms include the lost time that accrues when the user is intoxicated and community loses out on their service—the addicted user may not be able to work, pay taxes, or help contribute to the common welfare. This can also happen if drug use makes them physically ill or if it causes them to be put into jail because they stole or became violent.

Shifting Standards behind Definitions of Harm

Because harm to the individual and to society is not always easy to see, there is usually some debate over which laws are most effective in limiting harm to the user and to society at large. The definition of harm reflects general consensus in society about what is right behavior and what is wrong behavior. These standards of morality usually influence and define our legal priorities in some way.

During the first three centuries of American history, from colonial times to the mid-1960s, most of the laws governing behavior (including drug laws) were based on moral principles founded on Judeo-Christian biblical teaching. During Puritan times, the laws required by God and personal morality were often difficult to separate from the state laws used for fellow citizens and community. After the American Revolution, there were laws against violating the Sabbath and against public drunkenness and other immoral behaviors. These laws were justified on the principle that a society's moral health was just as important as its physical health. Crime was seen mostly as the byproduct of moral weakness, and during the 1700s, drug laws relating to the improper use of drugs and alcohol were established to protect people from habits that encouraged moral weaknesses.

Later, during the nineteenth and early twentieth centuries, our society became more secular and less bound by presumptions of Judeo-Christian values. In the process, the definition of harm also changed. For many reasons, by the mid-1960s American voters became less interested in laws that mostly protected the moral health of society and instead focused more attention on laws protecting physical health and rights of personal property.

Some critics argued that biblical-based laws related to sexuality and drug use unfairly limited the rights of individuals who do not share the same religious standards of moral behavior. Changing priorities prompted national debates that affect many different laws, including whether the government should be able to criminalize birth control or marital infidelity, whether divorces should be more easily obtained, and whether laws against drug and alcohol use should be reconsidered. Behaviors that caused obvious physical harms to others were usually unquestioned—there were no movements to decriminalize driving under the influence of alcohol, and there were no efforts to encourage drug use among school-aged children who were still developing physically and mentally. However, criminalization of behaviors that appeared only to threaten moral health or that posed other less-visible dangers to moral character were seriously questioned. For drugs, some advocates for decriminalization argued that if drug users wanted to hurt themselves, and if there are no obvious examples of physical harm to others, then why not let them?

These discussions grew out of disagreements over the definition of harm and the purpose behind drug laws. Should drug policies protect society from actual harm to health and personal property, or should they also keep people from making bad choices? Laws that seek only to protect the public's moral health reflect "legal moralism." Critics, especially those who supported decriminalization, argued the government should not be involved in legal moralism. Others argued that the difference between a moral choice and a danger to society was too difficult to determine. Instead, they focused on whether drug use caused crime, and if they did, drug laws should protect nondrug users from actual offenses against the public order (this is called the "offense principle").

Most lawmakers supported penalties for recreational drug use because they were necessary to protect users and to protect society from the unseen effects of drug addiction (such as property crimes and violent crimes). A small minority of lawyers argued for the decriminalization of certain drugs, especially marijuana and other hallucinogens. They believed that most drugs were not harmful to the user and were prohibited only because they offended moral expectations of traditional Judeo-Christian values. A small but growing decriminalization movement argued that existing drug-control laws caused more harm to individual freedom than they helped in protecting moral health and public safety. They also asserted that crime rates would decline when drug use was no longer criminalized and when recreational drugs were no longer illegal to purchase.

These cultural debates arose near the end of the 1960s when the rates of violent crime and public rioting in urban areas were very high. Lawmakers were not convinced by decriminalization arguments, and throughout the 1970s, recreational drug use was controlled through a combination of criminal penalties and some mandatory treatment options. Nevertheless, the idea of decriminalization began in the 1970s, and that marks the first time that legal theorists seriously engaged in debates over the legal justification for drug laws and their effectiveness.

Controlling drugs through criminal penalties and mandatory treatment was most popular during the 1970s–90s. Yet, decriminalization (and legalization) movements continued to grow and became popular in some states like Oregon and Alaska. After many years, decriminalization gained much more support during the 2000s and 2010s. Public opinions about the morality of drug use changed in many regions, and more than half the states adopted more lenient drug policies and enforcement measures. During the 2020s, the morality of drug use and the legal justification for drug-control laws continue to be fiercely debated.

Difference between Criminal and Civil Laws

There is a spectrum of public opinion about recreational drugs. Very few people believe that there should be no drug prohibitions at all. Similarly, on the opposite side, almost no one believes that all drugs should be legalized. Those advocating for stronger criminal penalties also recognize that not all drugs pose the same risks of harm to individual users or to those around them. They reserve the harshest criminal penalties for drugs that are most prone to abuse and which offer the least potential for therapeutic value. At the same time, those advocating for decriminalization usually recognize that some drugs are very dangerous and ought to be regulated in some way. Generally, decriminalization advocates believe drug use should be treated as a health issue and not through criminal penalties. They also support more government investment in addiction treatment programs and increased regulation of drug manufacturers and retailers through quality control measures, taxation, age-based restrictions, and public education programs.

To understand the differences between policies, we must first define some key terms.

1. Legalizing a drug means to make it available without penalty. Legalization does not mean there are no regulations; it just means that the regulations usually involve quality control and age restrictions.
2. Decriminalizing a drug means that the drug is still not permitted for sales, or indiscriminate use, but violations involve civil penalties rather than criminal penalties.

Some states criminalize all recreational drug use; others decriminalize certain drugs but continue to criminalize others. Some states have fully legalized certain drugs. Decisions about criminalization, decriminalization, and legalization are mostly made at the state or local (city) level.

In states where all drugs are criminalized, buying and selling cocaine (e.g.) is illegal, and violators caught doing so will get arrested and face jail time after a court conviction. In states where some medical marijuana use has been decriminalized, someone caught possessing marijuana may not be charged with a crime, though they may be given a ticket with a fine and a recommendation to seek treatment options if they do not have a valid prescription. There is no arrest and no jail time. In states where recreational marijuana use is legalized, there is no enforcement of marijuana at all, except in terms of where it can be sold and to whom.

Criminal laws lead to penalties that include some amount of jail time (and, in the most extreme cases, may involve penalties of death). Civil laws usually involve fines, compulsory training or treatment programs, or prohibitions against participating in certain activities. Legalization does not remove all laws but mostly restricts penalties to civil laws. If a grower in California violates state laws by operating without a valid license, the plants may be confiscated, and the grower will probably be fined and perhaps given some prohibitions against growing, selling, or buying in the future. By contrast, almost all states have criminal penalties for selling drugs in or around school zones. Violations of these laws usually involve jail time to remove the offenders from society in order to protect vulnerable children who attend schools—even when the same drugs might be legally purchased in another district.

Differences between criminal and civil laws also refer to the kinds of enforcement options. Civil laws may be enforced by police officers, but they are often also enforced by agents of regulatory offices. Inspectors checking licensing requirements of marijuana farmers or dispensaries may not be police officers but may work for a state or local agency authorized to enforce regulations. By contrast, anyone arrested for a criminal violation is taken into custody by a law enforcement official. Civil violations may be handled through administrative bodies, while all criminal violations must go through the court system to ensure constitutional protections of due process.

Often, the same violation may involve both civil and criminal penalties. For example, a drug dealer who sells marijuana to underage students on school property may be arrested on criminal charges for selling in a drug-free zone. They may also be fined for selling marijuana without a proper license. In another example, an impaired driver who runs through a fence and crashes into the front porch of their neighbor's house will likely be fined for the destruction of someone else's private property. They will also likely be arrested under criminal charges for driving under the influence (DUI), which would result in arrest and immediate incarceration (jail time).

People who support drug decriminalization policies want to replace criminal drug penalties with civil penalties or with voluntary addiction services. People who support drug criminalization usually want to maintain clear criminal penalties, as well as mandatory addiction treatment requirements. Members in both camps usually recognize the need for both civil and criminal enforcement options.

Federal, State, and Local Jurisdictions

The United States is based on a federal system of government, which means that we have one federal constitution that provides the basis for laws governing the national government; plus we also have fifty different state governments based on their own state constitutions. In addition, each state is divided into smaller local divisions of counties (or boroughs), and within those there are cities, townships, and rural communities.

Few people encounter all levels of law enforcement at once. Most police officers we meet on the street work for the city or township that we live in. The vast majority of criminal cases are handled by these local police officers. If you drive on the highways, you will also likely encounter County Sheriffs who work for the County government or State Patrol Officers who work for the State. It is less common for ordinary citizens to interact with federal officers unless they are attempting to cross an international border. US Border Patrol agents or the Immigration and Customs Enforcement (ICE) agents work alongside Federal Transportation Security Administration (TSA) agents, and we usually see both kinds around airport security checkpoints. Most people do not come in contact with other federal agents, such as the Federal Bureau of Investigation (FBI) or the Drug Enforcement Agency (DEA), and the Alcohol, Tobacco and Firearms (ATF) agencies.

Drug laws may be enforced by any of these officers at many levels of government: local, state, and federal. However, there are limits to each jurisdiction. The Tenth Amendment to the US Constitution states, "The powers not delegated to the United States by the Constitution, nor prohibited by it to the States, are reserved to the States respectively, or to the people." In plain language that means that anything that is not explicitly mentioned in the US Constitution will be handled by state governments. That does not mean that states can pass any laws that they like. The Fourteenth Amendment states, "No state shall make or enforce any law which shall abridge the privileges or immunities of citizens of the United States; nor shall any state deprive any person of life, liberty, or property, without due process of law; nor deny to any person within its jurisdiction the equal protection of the laws." That means that state governments must provide *at least as much* protection of civil rights as the federal government.

When combined these two Amendments to the US Constitution allow for considerable variation in drug laws between the state and the federal jurisdictions. Using the Fourteenth Amendment, the federal government may establish the minimal threshold of protection. If drug use is viewed as a civil right, federal criminalization of recreational drugs means that users have very little protection. Individual states, however, may provide greater protection of drug use than the federal government. That is why some states can decriminalize certain drugs that remain illegal at the federal level.

Some critics argue that drug laws are intended to protect the user and the communities they live in. Therefore, the federal prohibition of recreational drug use is itself viewed as a minimum level of protection, and states that legalize these drugs may be providing less protection than the federal government. That would violate the Fourteenth Amendment. So far, the US Supreme Court and the US Department of Justice (DOJ) have not interpreted drug laws in that way.

The Tenth Amendment declares that any powers not specifically identified in the US Constitution should be handled by the states, and only three crimes are specifically mentioned in the Constitution (counterfeiting, piracy, and treason). All other laws are generally grouped under an Article I clause authorizing the national government to regulate interstate commerce. Since drugs are not mentioned explicitly anywhere in the US Constitution, the Courts (and the DOJ) assume that states retain authority over their own drug laws, and the federal government may not interfere with how a state chooses to deal with drugs within its borders. As a matter of practice, the federal government will not enforce its federal drug laws within states where those same drugs have been legalized. Instead, they focus on the transportation of illegal drugs over state lines (which falls under the "Commerce Clause" of Article I).

Selective Enforcement

Though all drugs are regulated in some way at both the federal and state levels, the enforcement of these laws is left mostly up to local law enforcement at either city, county, or state levels. Unless drugs are transported across state lines, DEA agents are rarely involved. Federal policies ensure federal agents do not enforce federal drug laws in states where those same drugs have been decriminalized or legalized. The Federal DEA proposed reclassifying marijuana from a Schedule I drug to a Schedule III drug in mid-2024. That does not mean marijuana has been legalized. Recreational use of marijuana continues to be illegal everywhere under federal jurisdiction. The reclassification means that the drug is more easily prescribed for medical use in every state that authorizes it. Prior to federal reclassification, only forty-one states permitted the medical use of marijuana.

Any policy that determines when to arrest or when not to arrest is called "selective enforcement," and such decisions commonly impact the enforcement of regional drug laws. Selective enforcement not only exists between federal and state jurisdictions but also between certain native tribal districts and within some cities. For example, in 2024 the Ho-Chunk Nation in Wisconsin decriminalized marijuana, even though (at the time) the rest of Wisconsin continued to prohibit recreational marijuana use. State police officers have authority to make arrests even in the Ho-Chunk Nation districts, but state authorities adopted a policy that allowed Ho-Chunk Nation police to handle such matters exclusively. In another example, a Milwaukee police officer who pulls over a motorist for a traffic violation may encounter marijuana in the car, which is illegal in Wisconsin. However, the city police officer may choose not to enforce the state law because the city of Milwaukee adopted a policy of nonenforcement for minor drug possession.

Selective enforcement may also apply to the court system. Using the example of the Milwaukee police officer above, they could choose to enforce the state marijuana laws and arrest the motorist for possession. However, the local Milwaukee district attorney would likely choose not to prosecute the case. Police may make arrests, but the prosecutor's office decides which cases they take to trial and which cases they dismiss. Such variations in enforcement mean that some federal drug laws will not be enforced by state or local governments, and some state laws will not be enforced by local governments.

Drug Policies versus Drug Laws

Actual enforcement of drug laws depends heavily on the jurisdiction of law enforcement (federal, state, or local) and the policies of selective enforcement at each of these levels. There is, however, another group of drug-related rules that exist outside of the legal system. Public agencies, private companies, and voluntary associations (like athletic clubs) may all develop and enforce their own drug policies that exist in parallel to any local, state, or federal laws.

For example, even though recreational marijuana is legal in Colorado, the Colorado Department of Education requires random drug and alcohol tests for all school bus operators and anyone else in "safety sensitive transportation" operations, including pilots, truck drivers, train engineers, subway operators, and others. Individuals who fail a random drug test are removed from their jobs. If they do not break any other laws, they are not arrested, and they do not face criminal charges. State drug policies require drug-free operators of transportation equipment that could cause harm to passengers. These are drug policies and not drug laws.

Similarly, private companies may also implement drug policies to regulate their employees. If a restaurant has a drug-free policy, that means their chefs, bartenders, and server staff may be asked to take random drug tests to maintain their employment. Employees may choose not to take these tests, but they risk losing their jobs. If employees want to work at that job, they must willingly submit to certain job-related conditions. Workplace drug policies are not enforced by law, and violations of such policies do not involve police, fines, or jail time, but they may result in termination from the job.

Athletic associations also have a long history of drug policies that prevent players from using performance-enhancement drugs. Some steroids are legal for students to take for their own purposes, but they are prohibited by High-School Athletic Associations. Students may be forced to leave the team (and the sport) if they fail a drug test. Professional sports associations, like the National Football League (NFL), Major League Baseball (MLB), and the International Olympic Committee (IOC), all have strict drug policies with established drug-testing schedules and prescribed penalties for violations. Athletes who fail their drug tests are usually not liable to any criminal prosecutions, but they may be fired from the team or prohibited from competing in the sport at any level.

Organizational drug policies are usually more restrictive than local, state, or federal drug laws.

Conclusion: Laws Are Rules Chosen by Society

We regulate and criminalize drug-related activities because we believe that individual safety and the safety of private property are more secure and protected as a result of such rules. However, ultimately, all laws reflect moral priorities of the society that created them. Mostly, these priorities determine the extent of potential harm that the drug-related activity may pose to the user and the surrounding community.

When considering drug laws, lawmakers evaluate potential damage to physical, psychological, and moral health. Though we do not often talk about morality in the twenty-first century, most decisions about potential harm reflect general presumptions about moral priorities. If the nation does not believe that government should get involved in moral decision-making (legal moralism), then the harm from drug use is evaluated only according to its impact on physical or emotional health. If the nation believes that the state should reflect certain moral standards to help ensure the general safety of the community, then the physical and emotional harms are considered as potential risks to moral character. In cases where recreational drug use poses obvious risks of physical or emotional harm to the user or to others, such as with School Bus Drivers, there is much greater agreement among policymakers about drug policy.

If there is a greater consensus that the use of particular types of drugs (such as recreational opioid use) poses more physical and emotional danger to the user and to others, then it is more likely that the drug will be criminalized. Conversely, in regions where the public consensus believes that certain drugs (such as alcohol or tobacco) pose the least harm to the user or to others, then it is more likely that these drugs will be regulated through civil measures (decriminalization or outright legalization). Lastly, if the risk of harm to the user is significantly greater than the potential (less visible) risk of harm to others, traditional protection of civil rights tends to prefer civil regulation rather than criminalization. (This is in recognition of the inherent right to "the pursuit of happiness" even if it leads to limited self-harm.)

The majority of public debates over drug-control laws focus on whether civil remedies are more (or less) effective than criminal laws. Other questions relate to whether the sellers (legal and illegal dealers) of regulated drugs cause more harm to society than the users of these drugs. Decriminalization proposals that only affect users tend to be supported more than proposals that also propose more lenient penalties for sellers and manufacturers.

The American federal system allows each state to establish different drug policies. However, federal laws require broader public consensus to reflect all regions of society—urban, rural, rich, and poor. State levels of government more closely reflect the cultural priorities of the people who live within their unique regions, and these regions often have unique priorities. The cultural standards of heavily urban populations in New York City will not likely be the same as those found in rural populations of Wyoming. Some states tend to be dominated by Republicans, and some by Democrats, and some reveal a mixture of both groups. Similarly, advocates for criminalization and advocates for decriminalization often congregate in certain regions. Even within states, the people who live in dense cities tend to reflect different definitions of personal safety and protection of private property than those who live in the rural farmland areas.

The remaining chapters of this section outline debates over the harms of various drug types and public movements to decriminalize (or maintain criminalization) certain drugs are judged as matters of public safety, health, and civil order. First, we consider the sociopolitical spectrum of definitions of drug addiction (Chapter 2). Then we outline the history of drug-control laws in the United States during the twentieth century, including a more detailed history of drug decriminalization during the twenty-first century (Chapter 3). We also provide a brief discussion of both criminalization and decriminalization in other countries around the world (Chapter 4). Lastly in this part, we tell the stories of specific decriminalization movements in various fields, such as medical marijuana and state-based experiments that involve broad decriminalization of all drugs (Chapter 5). Readers are encouraged to consider both the arguments for and against decriminalization as a reflection of how the public identifies and guards against potential harm to individual health, public safety, and the protection of private property.

2

The Social Politics of Addiction and Policy Priorities

Are drugs addictive? Can users choose not to take drugs?

These are unusual questions because we hear of people who struggle with addiction every day. People take certain drugs like alcohol, tobacco, marijuana, cocaine, and other opioids and find it very difficult to stop taking them—that is a sign of addiction. Other people engage in certain behaviors like gambling, viewing pornography, or even playing certain video games, and they seem unable to stop.

The American Psychological Association defines addiction as a phenomenon that exists when someone engages in a behavior that is harmful to themselves or to others, and wants to stop the behavior, and has tried to stop but is unable to stop. The term "addiction" is used often, and addiction treatment centers exist in every state to help people stop engaging in behaviors that they know are harmful.

Even though we use the term routinely, the question of addiction is still debated. No one can know for sure whether someone is physically compelled not to stop a behavior or if they simply choose not to stop the behavior. In other words, do the chemicals in drugs make people lose the ability to stop taking them? Or do people blame drugs for their own choices?

The question of addiction is important because it opens the debate over whether laws should prevent people from doing what they want to do to themselves, or if they should be prevented from making self-destructive choices that are harmful to themselves and will be very difficult to undo. If drug use is a byproduct of addiction only, then users lose the ability to choose not to consume their drugs, and laws may be more necessary to protect people from falling into habits that they have no control over. However, if drug use is always a choice, then laws that prohibit drug use are interfering with individual preferences. Our understanding of addiction relies heavily on deeper theories about human nature and -our ability to make free choices.

Addiction, Decriminalization and Legalization

Differing opinions about addiction play an important role in whether voters support criminalization, decriminalization, or legalization of certain recreational drugs. Some people believe that drug use is an individual lifestyle choice. Others believe that it is a physical compulsion that is very difficult to resist without medical help. Others believe that it is a habit encouraged by certain social and economic pressures and that the social conditions must be changed if the individuals have a chance of making better life choices.

Part of the debate stems from differences between physical addiction and psychological dependency. Physical addiction means that the body strongly craves a certain drug or behavior and will experience physical symptoms if the drug or behavior is withdrawn. Psychological dependency means that we may feel like we need a drug or to engage in a certain behavior, but we do not show physical signs of withdrawal—only emotional symptoms. It is sometimes hard to distinguish between physical addiction and psychological dependency because our emotional anxiety can produce certain physical symptoms, like increased heart rates, sweating, and an inability to concentrate or focus. Such ambiguous symptoms make it hard for scientists to declare with absolute certainty that some drugs or behaviors are a source of addiction rather than a symptom of some other related cause.

There are also moral elements that determine different viewpoints on the harm of recreational drug use. Some people believe that drugs may be difficult to resist, but why does it matter? If you see drug use as a lifestyle choice that only affects the individual user, you may not see any harm or any need for drug controls. However, if you believe some behavioral choices are inherently harmful to individual character (immoral), you want to protect people from falling into bad habits.

If we recognize different views about addiction, dependency, and morality, we can see there are many possible variations of viewpoints about the potential harm of recreational drug use. However, these variations can all be generally simplified into three main ideological perspectives: (1) libertarian; (2) social welfare; and (3) traditional conservative.

Libertarian View: Libertarians do not believe that addiction is a real medical phenomenon. They argue that people feel psychological dependency, but ultimately, they use drugs because they choose to use them. Drug users claim addiction as an excuse to disguise the fact that they receive social or psychological benefits from the behavior, but because society generally does not approve of their habits (of intoxication), they claim to have no ability to stop. The theory assumes that everyone has free will, and therefore the decision to use or not to use drugs is more a matter of economic preferences. People make choices because one option is easier (or more pleasurable) and more affordable than the alternative option.

Libertarian theories apply economic standards to political and cultural conditions. Jeffrey Schaller, a popular psychologist from the 1990s, wrote many articles and books arguing that the idea of addiction was not supported by medical evidence—he believed that no drug is addictive—even potent substances like cocaine, heroin, and amphetamines. Instead, he argued the idea of addiction was created by religious moralists who believed drug use and intoxication were bad for society and therefore concluded that anyone who fell into drug-using lifestyles did so because they succumbed to the temptations of sin. Schaller argued that the idea of sin is itself a moral judgment and has no place in scientific study of human behavior. He also believed most doctors and psychologists receive economic benefits from promoting the idea of addiction because they developed treatment centers as the primary tool for helping drug users to stop using. He claimed many politicians also receive some benefits because they use the threat of drug addiction as an excuse to spend millions of tax-payer dollars to fund antidrug programs. Schaller repeatedly wrote that there was no scientific evidence to support the idea that addiction was a real medical phenomenon.

Schaller was joined by other psychologists, economists, lawyers, and culture commentators who shared his libertarian views. In the 1970s, the Nobel Prize winning economist, Milton Friedman also claimed drug use was a matter of free will and therefore an issue of individual property rights. The Canadian psychiatrist Thomas Szasz argued that diagnoses of mental illness was a form of social control and that drug use did not pose any significant harm to society except in so far as they challenged the traditional moral order. William F. Buckley, a popular American journalist and political commentator, also argued that drug laws mostly violated individual freedoms. He believed that drug use was a personal choice that each individual must make for themselves.

People who make these arguments call themselves "libertarians" because they believe individual liberty (freedom) is the most important aspect of any civil society. They support legalization of all drugs—marijuana, cocaine, heroin (all opioids), hallucinogens, and any other artificial chemical that can be used for recreational purposes. The libertarian viewpoint generally opposes giving the state power over individual decision-making whenever possible, and they strongly oppose laws that promote moral preferences of one group over another. They believe that the government is prone to abusing its power and that less government oversight over individual choices generally results in greater individual freedom.

Social-Welfare View: The libertarian view represents a small minority of the American public. However, they share some common viewpoints with social-welfare advocates who represent a much larger share of public opinion and who also support decriminalization. Most doctors and behavioral scientists disagree with the libertarian view that drugs are not physically addictive. However, they recognize the difference between physical addiction and psychological dependency. Some drugs directly stimulate the release of endorphins or dopamine, and physical addiction occurs because users will experience harsh physical symptoms of withdrawal when they stop using the drug. Other drugs, though, stimulate the release of dopamine indirectly and therefore do not cause as many physical signs of withdrawal and are therefore not physically addictive. Users may become psychologically dependent on any drug, even if the drug is not physically addictive. Any physical or psychological symptom of withdrawal that is harsh enough to compel the user to continue using, even when they know it is harmful to themselves or others, is a cause of psychological dependency and addiction.

The distinction between physical addiction and psychological dependency is linked to other moral and political priorities. Like the libertarians, social-welfare advocates believe that individuals should have the right to choose the sort of lifestyle that they most prefer, and so they oppose any moral judgments when evaluating the harms of drug use to the user or to society. Considering only the potential negative physical effects of drug use on the human body (in terms of withdrawal symptoms) removes any moral judgements as to whether being intoxicated or being sober is good for the user and for society.

Psychological dependency is often judged in terms of socioeconomic conditions that may encourage individuals to prefer drug use to other lifestyle choices. Social-welfare advocates tend to be highly critical of capitalist free-market societies that allow for great differences between rich and poor, and they argue that drug use is a means of coping with harsh sociopolitical conditions. The Democrat mayor of Baltimore, Kurt Schmoke was one of the first nationally recognized politicians to advocate for decriminalization in the mid-1990s. During the 2000s, billionaire investment manager George Soros wrote numerous articles in favor of drug decriminalization and donated more than $32 billion to support decriminalization and other like-minded political criminal justice efforts around the Western world.

Under the social-welfare standards, drug use is evaluated according to strict threshold of physical addiction, which means the potential harm of each drug is measured according to whether it poses risks of physical harm to the user only. Under this standard, opioids (like heroin and cocaine), alcohol, and nicotine are recognized as highly addictive. Whereas other drugs that only exhibit symptoms of psychological dependency, such as marijuana and other hallucinogens (LSD, psilocybin from certain mushrooms, and mescaline from certain peyote cacti), are not judged to be addictive. Using these distinctions, social-welfare advocates believe that addictive substances should be highly regulated, whereas the nonaddictive substances should be less regulated because they pose the least potential harm to society.

Social-welfare advocates support decriminalization of most drugs but only the full legalization of certain nonaddictive drugs for recreational use. Like libertarians, they also believe moral judgments about the use of drugs (like marijuana and other hallucinogens) should not influence criminal laws. Unlike the libertarians, social-welfare advocates argue free market capitalism creates sociopolitical conditions that are harmful to society and that recreational drug use is only a symptom of that harm. They believe government regulation is necessary to impose strong rules that may improve socioeconomic conditions and provide necessary services to help victims of drug abuse. They oppose using jail terms to punish drug offenses because they believe criminalization only hurts the users and does not address the underlying socioeconomic causes of addiction. Instead, they believe governments should treat drugs as a health problem only and use treatment centers and public education programs as less harmful alternatives to deal with real drug addiction. Libertarians and social-welfare advocates often agree in their support of decriminalization laws, even though they have opposite views of what role government should play in modern society.

Traditional Conservative View: The American public is almost evenly divided between the social-welfare viewpoint and more traditional conservative views. To "conserve" means to keep priorities the same, and traditional conservatives strive to maintain the cultural and moral priorities that were most dominant during the nineteenth and early twentieth centuries. They believe that moral standards have changed because the influx of addiction rates created more demand for recreational drug use and thereby altered the long-standing definitions of harm and of responsible behavior. Traditional conservatives share some ideas with libertarians in as much as they believe individuals are born with the freedom to make choices and that drug abuse is mostly a problem of individual decision-making. They also share some ideas with social-welfare advocates in as much as they believe that addiction is a scientific medical phenomenon that makes it very difficult for users to stop their drug abuse once it begins. The main difference is that traditional conservatives do not place as much blame on the sociopolitical conditions for the onset of drug addiction, but they do believe the government plays a strong role in discouraging drug use by modeling appropriate behaviors and through clear penalties for irresponsible drug use.

Traditional conservatives and social-welfare advocates both recognize that addiction is a genuine medical condition. The main difference between them is that conservatives do not place as much importance on the distinction between physical addiction and psychological addiction. They argue that under both conditions, the drug user loses the ability to make free decisions or to make clear judgments because painful physical and emotional withdrawal symptoms make it very difficult to stop using. Traditional conservatives usually evaluate drug use based on its impact on moral decision-making. They do not separate marijuana and other hallucinogens from other physically addictive opioids because both types of drugs lead to psychological dependency, which is always harmful to the user. Any addiction type (physical or psychological) encourages users to rely on the drug as a coping mechanism for dealing with both physical withdrawal symptoms as well as psychological symptoms such as increased anxiety, emotional stress, and other mental health issues. Recreational drug use generally leads to poor moral choices.

The traditional view argues that any behavior that prevents individuals from achieving their physical, emotional, or learning potential is harmful both to the individual and to society at large. Some famous traditional conservatives who support continued drug criminalization include James Wilson, the Chairman of National Advisory Council for Drug Abuse Prevention under Republican President Richard Nixon; William Bennet, the former Drug Czar under Republican President Ronald Reagan; and the Pulitzer Prize-winning journalist for the *Washington Post*, Charles Krauthammer.

Traditional conservatives are set apart from both the libertarians and the social-welfare advocates by their presumption that self-destructive choices hurt society and are morally wrong—sober lifestyles are better than intoxication because sobriety allows individuals to make free choices and to become productive members of society. Lifestyles of intoxication that remove individuals from social expectations and which hurt individual decision-making are not isolated actions but place unnecessary burdens on other members of society.

By contrast, libertarians and social-welfare advocates argue that moral choices should be left to individuals to decide. Traditional conservatives also do not want governments to impose arbitrary moral standards on society, but they believe that the government models appropriate standards of behavior based on Judeo-Christian definitions of morality. They believe laws should discourage drug use and promote sobriety and productivity to protect both the physical and moral health of society.

Traditional conservatives also oppose policies that remove the moral stigma of intoxication. Libertarians and social-welfare advocates are in agreement that decriminalization should remove moral standards associated with drug prohibitions, and they believe social stigma of drug use is the real cause of social harm because it creates a barrier to treatment. Traditional conservatives believe addiction begins with free choices, and social pressures (stigmas) are necessary to discourage people from experimenting with dangerous behaviors. Once users become addicted, it is very difficult for them to end the addiction.

To Summarize: Instead of decriminalization, traditional conservatives prefer clear penalties that discourage any recreational drug use, with especially harsh criminal penalties for those who manufacture and sell the illegal drugs to vulnerable populations. They support limited incarceration (jail time) for drug users because that guarantees their participation in treatment programs.

Libertarians believe drug use is a personal decision and that addiction is not a scientifically demonstratable medical phenomenon, so they believe legalization would have no impact on addiction rates or drug use. They do not support using laws to impose moral values on individuals, and they also do not support increasing the size and tax burden of government to spend on drug users who willingly choose their behaviors.

Social-welfare advocates believe decriminalization would remove the moral stigma of drug use while also encouraging compassionate healthcare alternatives for users who are addicted. They believe addiction rates may increase temporarily after drug decriminalization but also argue that the increased treatment opportunities would result in reduced levels of incarceration for drug offenses and lower levels of addiction overall. Social-welfare advocates encourage government-funded treatment programs but do not support forced participation because that is too similar to incarceration.

These three viewpoints reflect a broad spectrum of differences in opinions among lawmakers, policy-makers, and academics. Many people do not always know why they hold a particular viewpoint and may find themselves agreeing with ideas from two (or even all three) camps. They may agree with some conclusions without fully realizing the larger ideological viewpoint from which it arose. If you understand the reasoning behind each viewpoint, you will be more likely to hold consistent conclusions.

Twenty-First-Century Risks of Harm from Addiction

General health risks associated with any recreational drug use include increased cardiovascular disease (lung and heart), stroke, cancer, and mental illness. Almost every drug will increase or decrease heart rates, breathing, and blood flow and cause noticeable changes in memory, concentration, mood, and irritability. Specifically, opioids such as heroin, morphine, and their commercially prescribed derivatives, as well as fentanyl and other synthetic versions, pose very high risks of heart attack and stroke. These synthetic drugs are responsible for the highest incidence of drug overdoses and emergency room visits (by a factor of three to one) and are most responsible for drug-related deaths every year.

Drugs that are smoked (such as marijuana and crack cocaine) significantly increase the risk of emphysema, respiratory illnesses, and allergies. Drugs that are injected often lead to increased skin infections, blood-borne diseases, and embolism (blood clots or air bubbles in the blood stream). Hallucinogenic drugs such as psilocybin (mushrooms), LSD, ketamine, and PCP do not often lead to immediate physical threats, but they can induce manic behaviors that result in serious accidents and death. Psychosis is a mental condition that occurs when the drug user no longer distinguishes between reality and imagination, and all hallucinogens (including marijuana) include higher than average risks of psychosis.

According to the Substance Abuse and Mental Health Services Administration (SAMHSA) and the Drug Abuse Warning Network (DAWN), rates of drug-related emergency room visits increased by 300 percent between 1995 and 2022, and the Center for Disease Control (CDC) noted that the number of overdose deaths became so high that they lowered US life-expectancy rates after 2018. In addition to direct physical risks, there are also indirect harms caused by increased incidents of risky behaviors—intoxicated driving, the loss of motor control resulting in physical accidents around the home, and increased risks of sexually transmitted diseases as a result of generally lowered inhibitions. A 2007 study estimated that the medical costs related to drug use were $193 billion, and during the 2020s hospital costs of emergency room visits alone due to drug overdoses were about $5 billion a year (Langabeer et al., 2021). According to the 2023 National Health Statistics Report by the CDC, the number of drug-induced deaths in 2008 surpassed deaths caused by motor vehicles and firearms and by 2024, the number of drug-induced deaths had doubled from where it was in 2008.

Between 2020 and 2024 the National Drug Threat Assessment published by the DEA identified International Drug Cartels as the primary source for illegal drugs flowing into the United States. All types of drugs originate south of the American border, including cocaine, marijuana, and opioids. The most lethal of these three is a synthetic opioid fentanyl, which was first developed as a pain reliever and approved by the Food and Drug Administration (FDA) in 1960. Since the 2010s, very large quantities have been smuggled into the United States in pill form and then sold to buyers illegally through social media. Throughout the 2020s, the DEA identified fentanyl abuse specifically as the greatest threat to users in their annual threat assessments.

Fentanyl is fifty times more potent than heroin and a hundred times more potent than morphine. Around the 2000s, it was synthesized into a variety of forms, including powders, pills, liquids, lozenges, sprays, and patches and that made the drug much more easily accessible to illicit users. It is frequently included with other drugs used in vaping devices in order to increase the psychoactive effects. In 2010, there were a few hundred deaths associated with fentanyl. By the 2020s, the CDC reported that number had surpassed 100,000 deaths per year, outpacing mortality rates for other deadly drugs such as methamphetamines and cocaine by two and three times. It is the single largest cause of accidental death in America, above auto accidents, drowning, and falls.

All three ideological viewpoints recognize the harm of drug use. They differ over whether the drug use is caused by addiction or by some other socioeconomic reason. Libertarian viewpoints continue to argue that addiction is not a medically proven phenomenon. Statistical evidence of drug abuse in the twenty-first century has caused their viewpoint to shrink to a small minority within the scientific community and among lawmakers and policymakers. Social-welfare advocates argue that some drugs are clearly more dangerous than others—fentanyl and opioids especially present obvious dangers. However, they also argue that marijuana is not any more dangerous than alcohol and therefore should be regulated in similar ways with special licenses and age restrictions. For this reason, libertarians generally join with social-welfare advocates when debating drug policies. All three ideological viewpoints can recognize the potential harms of drug abuse—both physically and socially. Ultimately, the main difference between the libertarian or social-welfare views and the traditional conservative viewpoints is over the question of whether encouraging sobriety is a moral issue that should be supported by governmental laws.

Marijuana Use and Changing Public Opinion

Deliberate intoxication is what most distinguishes marijuana use from alcohol use. Most people (70 percent) drink alcohol without becoming intoxicated. They can drink alcohol for the taste. However, marijuana use is only intended for intoxication—no one uses marijuana without feeling its psychoactive influences, which include euphoric feelings, altered perceptions, decreased inhibitions, and impaired motor functions. If we compare alcohol to marijuana, we must use binge drinking as the point of comparison because that is the only situation that involves the same level of intoxication as marijuana use. Binge drinking is defined as taking five to seven drinks in a two-hour period to achieve full intoxication that alters mood, perceptions, inhibitions, and motor functions. The 2024 US National Survey on Drug Use and Health indicated that daily marijuana use was four to ten times more common than daily binge alcohol use. This is a dramatic change from 1992 when alcohol users were ten times more common than marijuana users. The study also showed that daily intoxication from either drug has multiplied fifteen times (1500 percent) during the thirty years between 1992 and 2022.

The main cultural difference between the 1990s and the later 2000s is that the federal war on drugs during the 1980s and 1990s stressed the importance of sobriety (no intoxication), whereas the decriminalization culture of the 2010s emphasized responsible recreational drug use, which presumes frequent intoxication. During this later period, the alliance of libertarians and social-welfare advocates overcame the opposition by traditional conservatives, and the public generally changed its views of marijuana use.

Conclusion: Cultural Tools in Twenty-First-Century Environment

All three ideological viewpoints recognize the potential harm of drug addiction. The question is how should a democratic society best respond to potential dangers that drug abuse and addiction pose to individuals and those who live around them while also respecting the rights of individuals to make their own decisions?

By the 2000s, two main answers to this question competed for public support. On the one side, libertarians and social-welfare advocates stressed the importance of moral diversity in our society, and so they believed that individuals have a right to intoxication, even if that means consuming drugs for recreational use. Both groups supported decriminalization and legalization of certain drugs (mostly marijuana). On the other side, traditional conservatives continued to stress the general dangers of intoxication and especially the risks posed by recreational drug use. They argue that drugs used primarily for the purpose of intoxication are most likely to lead to dependency and addiction and therefore cause collateral damage to society and should be highly regulated with criminal sanctions. Any drug that is least likely to be useful for medical therapies should be outlawed entirely, and those that have medical purposes should be rigidly safeguarded against recreational use (and abuse) through strong punishments for illegal drug dealers and milder punishments that emphasize mandatory treatment options for users. There is no widespread national consensus on issues of criminalization, decriminalization, and legalization of recreational drug use.

3

The Story of American Drug Controls and Alternatives to Punishment and Criminalization

It is very popular to claim that drugs and alcohol have been used for thousands of years, and therefore ancient tradition proves that drug use is a universal part of human society. Advocates for the decriminalization of recreational drug use believe intoxication is a natural human activity.

There may be many reasons for decriminalization, but the claim of historical precedent is not a legitimate justification. In terms of recreational drug and alcohol use, historical records do not show thousands of years of legalization. In almost every ancient account, excessive alcohol use (or drug use resulting in obvious intoxication) is highly regulated in one manner or another. In some cases, the regulation involves very strict laws that include harsh punishments for the user but especially harsh for the provider (dealer) of these drugs—including the death penalty. It is only recently, in the twenty-first century, that we have seen examples of large-scale civilizations decriminalizing recreational drug use. Recent trends seem to go against historical precedents, and that is why drug decriminalization and legalization are so controversial.

Earliest History of Alcohol and Drugs

Alcohol is the earliest psychoactive drug developed by humans. ("Psychoactive" means that it affects the emotional and cognitive abilities of the user.) The earliest beer was developed more than 4,000 years before the first civilization, sometime between 8000 BC (before the Christian era) and 7000 BC, but that ancient beer would not have looked anything like the clear liquid that we consume today.

Archeologists have discovered certain grains and other traces of alcohol in various ancient containers to identify the presence of beer. Based on other research into the kinds of grains and sugars available at the time from these traces, "beer" was actually a form of porridge that our neolithic ancestors ate rather than drank. This mixture contained fermented grains, which included small amounts of alcohol, but at levels that would have been so low that the user would not have experienced any noticeable impairment in their motor skills. They would have just felt a greater sense of satisfaction than they would have felt after eating other foods.

There is some debate among archaeologists whether the earliest example of beer was consciously associated with alcohol or intoxication by the people who consumed it. It is suggested by some researchers that people ate the beer porridge because it was nutritious and made them feel better, but it did not noticeably impair their abilities. The highest likely blood alcohol levels reached from these early forms of beer would have been less than 0.05 percent. If cars had existed around 7000 BC, our neolithic drivers would have been able to eat their beer porridge and legally drive without any impairment. As late as the mid-2000s BC, some written fragments from ancient Sumer recommended mothers send their children off to school with at least two containers of beer in their lunches, which suggests that the concoction was viewed as a food supplement. These and other examples support the argument that the earliest forms of beer were not viewed as sources of intoxication but as sources of nutrition.

Over the span of about 4,000 years, as human societies refined their ability to process grains needed to make bread, they also refined their ability to make beer in a more decidedly liquid form—not to be eaten like porridge but to be drunk like a beverage. Bread yeast was also useful for fermenting alcohol, which means that we see the development of intoxicating beverages right around the same time that we see the development of complex bread forms and the systematic domestication of cereal grains, such as wheat and barley. Beer is usually made from fermented barley.

Wine was always a beverage, but it was developed a little later—perhaps 2,000 years later than beer. The earliest reliable evidence of wine production comes from a tiny village in southeast Europe (modern Georgia) and is dated around 5800 BC, though the first evidence of systematic wine production does not appear for another 1,000 years in the mountains south of the Caspian Sea. The first wine press found in modern Turkey, south of the Black Sea, dates from around 2800 BC, which was about 700 years after the first cities and civilization arose in Mesopotamia. It was also around the same time that beer assumed its more liquid form. References to wine and drunkenness can be found in the Old Testament (Gen. 9:20-27), but they are mentioned in connection with a curse that followed a bout of drunkenness. At this time wine, more than beer, was associated with intoxication.

Almost every culture around the world developed a form of beer at some point near the time that they developed their regional form of bread. In Japan, there was no barley or wheat-based grain, so they brewed a rice-based liquor from fermented rice (called sake) around 500 BC. Wine and other distilled liquors developed later and were limited to regions in which they developed. Distilled liquors appear to have been invented in India around 500 BC and did not reach Europe for another 1,200 years, during the Middle Ages. Ancient Americans developed a beer a few centuries before the arrival of the Spanish, but wine and distilled liquors did not come to the Americas until after European contact in the 1500s.

Psychoactive drugs other than alcohol were discovered much later and were also limited to particular regions. There is some evidence that the intoxicating effects of cannabis (marijuana) were known as early as 750 BC in China, where the tomb of a medicine man (a shaman) was found with three-quarters of a kilo of marijuana buds bound in a package next to his body. Later, around the mid-400s BC, the Greek historian Herodotus wrote about Scythian villagers throwing cannabis seeds into the fire to produce an intoxicating smell.

Mostly, though, the earliest references to cannabis and opium describe them as medicinal drugs used for therapeutic purposes and are mostly referenced only in early Roman herb manuals between the first and third centuries. The first explicit evidence of cannabis use as a recreational drug came from a thirteenth century-Arab sheik who was condemning the practice. He referred to the local practice of eating hashish (a wax-like substance derived from concentrated forms of cannabis) as a crime punishable by the removal of one's teeth. There is very little evidence of recreational use of opium until after the 1200s.

Archaeologists uncovered evidence of very early drug use (alcohol first and then cannabis 5,000 years later), but the most direct evidence from written records suggests that recreational use of these drugs was not socially acceptable even during these ancient times. One of the earliest examples of written laws, Hammurabi's Code from Sumer (*c.* 1720 BC), refers to the responsibilities of tavern-keepers and sets forth harsh punishments for those who take advantage of alcoholics—inflating prices to meet the demand of the addicted drinker was punishable by drowning, and serving beer to criminals (or known drunkards) was punishable by death from burning.

As an archeologist from the 1960s, David G. Mandelbaum, explained, "Though alcoholic drink in [ancient] Sumer was used in worship and served as a means of consolidating society, in certain contexts its use was potentially antisocial and immoral, so the state tried to eliminate the disruptive side effects of alcohol." (Mandelbaum, 1965) Alcohol was used, but as soon as civilization developed to the point that more potent alcoholic beverages were easier to make and more accessible to the general public, and therefore as soon as intoxication became more common, it was almost immediately subject to some form of social control.

The First Social Control: Fear of Poison

Drugs and alcohol impair the user's motor skills and their ability to make responsible decisions. In a modern society with locked doors and roaming police officers, the momentary lapse of judgment may not always result in great harm to the user or to those around them. However, in ancient times, if someone was rendered incapable of contributing their fair share of work toward gathering food and protecting the village, they became a burden to the community, and the associated behaviors were condemned. Alcohol and recreational drug use was strongly limited by custom.

In some cases, these customs began from simple fear. Any sort of drug use can be lethal, and that was true during ancient times. The Greek example of cannabis seeds burned on an open fire would have produced very little intoxicating effect beyond the mild sense of euphoria (happiness). However, other herbs can be poisonous and result in great sickness or death almost immediately. There is some evidence that as early as 3000 BC, American Indians of southwest Texas ate potent herbs, such as peyote extract from a particular variety of cactus plant, which induces hallucinations. This was long before there were any sustained villages or agriculture in the area. These Mesoamericans must have successfully identified these plants for their psychotropic properties, but this was a dangerous process. Ingesting other cactus varieties found in the same region could lead to paralysis and serious skin and abdominal sickness. Choosing the right variety required some skill and experience.

Several thousands of years later, the Aztecs also used psilocybin mushrooms in their rituals—though it is not clear for what purposes. These mushrooms are not deadly, but they can induce extreme hallucinations. To use these, the Aztecs would have had to distinguish between psilocybin and the more common cone cap mushroom, which is quite deadly and looks very similar to psilocybin. An untrained eye might pick the cone cap expecting to experience hallucinations and would instead poison themselves to death. At least a half dozen deadly types of mushrooms in the Americas could easily confuse native gatherers, leading to their deaths.

For this reason, most herb collection was limited to a highly select group of people—usually the local shaman or medicine priest, who learned the tricks of distinguishing the potentially useful herbs from the potentially deadly plants. The Chinese shaman who was buried with the large package of cannabis was probably one of the very few people in his region who knew the psychoactive properties of the drug. Whatever he used it for, it was likely limited to his own control, which is why the drug was buried with him rather than distributed to someone else after his death. These drugs were not widely used, and they were mostly limited to the small collection of people who were trained (according to their own standards) in medicine. Other untrained people would fear sickness or death if they ate the wrong types of plants.

Most of the drugs that we know from ancient history are listed in books that were intended for the doctors of their era, who were charged with the responsibility of using drugs as safely as possible to help their patients. There is very little evidence that any drugs were commonly used recreationally by the general population. Among the native Americans, the use of peyote was limited to specific religious ceremonies, and most natives only very rarely experienced these effects. There is no evidence that these ancient cultures used psychoactive drugs for recreational use without strong social prescriptions.

The Origin of Drug Abuse

The drugs that are abused most frequently in the twenty-first century were first invented during the 1800s as medical treatments. Opium was known to Portuguese and Dutch sailors as early as the 1600s, but that knowledge was relegated to a tiny group of people who traveled to Asia (mostly sailors), though the number of international traders and travelers increased significantly throughout the 1700s.

In 1804, a German doctor Friedrich Serturner isolated the psychoactive ingredient of opium to create morphine for the first time. The German pharmaceutical company E. Merck & Company later began marketing morphine to doctors commercially as a general pain reliever in 1827. Within a generation, morphine addiction became a noticeable problem among patients. English chemist C. R. Wright synthesized heroin in 1874, but it was not sold commercially until another German company, Bayer, began marketing it as a cure for opium dependency in 1897. Five years later, medical journals in the United States promoted the use of heroin as a "step down" cure for morphine dependency in 1902. Heroin was more powerful than morphine, but at the time, it appeared to have fewer side effects.

Cocaine was derived from coca leaves that were originally found in the Andes Mountains of South America. Ancient Peruvians used to chew the leaves for mild pain relief, though only the upper classes were allowed to do so—the lower classes did not have access to the medical priests who were in charge of the mild drug. Chewing coca leaves produces no other noticeable psychoactive effects. After the European discovery of the Incan practice, coca leaves remained a minor pain relief option in a medical doctor's kit during the 1600s and 1700s.

A German scientist Friedrich Gaedcke isolated the active ingredient of coca in 1855, and Albert Niemann later purified the substances in 1860, which he then named "cocaine." The substance was ignored for more than twenty-five years until the drug became used in several popular "elixirs," which drew the attention of more serious medical doctors. Sigmund Freud started prescribing cocaine as a mild analgesic, and his colleague Karl Koller began systematically experimenting with its properties as another potential anesthesia. He published his findings at the Viennese Medical society in 1884.

Within ten years, cocaine was promoted as a safer analgesic alternative to the chloroform for minor operations. Chloroform had been used to render patients unconscious during operations since the 1830s, but it was unpredictable and often resulted in accidental deaths on the operating table. Cocaine was viewed as a safer alternative for minor procedures. The addictive properties of cocaine were not fully understood until the 1890s when cocaine overdoses became more publicized. The discovery of Novocain in 1905 by Alfred Einhorn largely ended cocaine's use as general anesthetic within the medical community because Novocain was judged to be much safer than both chloroform and cocaine.

German researcher Lazar Edeleano synthesized the first amphetamine in the late 1880s, and it was reformatted into a crystal form in 1920 by a Japanese pharmacologist, Nagayoshi Nagai. That later version was called methamphetamine and was marketed as a quick stimulant for asthma patients. By the 1930s, doctors began prescribing these "pep pills" to treat depression, weight gain, morning sickness, and narcolepsy. It was not until much later, after the Second World War, that the medical community fully realized the strong addictive nature of methamphetamines, at which point they began more closely regulating their use.

Though marijuana (the cannabis plant) was known in central Asia for hundreds of years and was used periodically as a recreational drug during the late 1800s in Central America, it was largely unknown in the United States until the twentieth century. Hemp is a variant of the cannabis plant with very long stems and was grown throughout Europe and in the United States during the eighteenth and nineteenth centuries as a useful fiber for making ropes aboard ships. Almost none of the hemp farmers who grew the plant for fiber had any idea of its psychoactive properties—there are no references to hemp (or marijuana) being used as a recreational drug in the United States prior to the twentieth century.

However, after the 1910 Revolution in Mexico, thousands of new immigrants passed from Mexico through the southern border and brought with them the habit of recreational marijuana use. By the 1920s, illegal bars in New York City (called speakeasies) offered illegal alcohol, illegal gambling, prostitution, heroin, and cocaine, and, for the first time among the urban underworld, marijuana. Its use remained largely confined to ethnic neighborhoods and did not become popularly recognized as a recreational drug among mainstream American society until the mid-1960s.

As Western medicine began to develop more potent forms of therapeutic drugs used to relieve pain, the potential for these drugs to be used for recreational purposes also increased. Prior to the 1800s, none of these drugs (morphine, heroin, cocaine, amphetamines) were criminalized because none of them were invented yet. Marijuana existed, but it was largely unknown for its psychoactive properties until the twentieth century. For that reason, the misuse (and abuse) of therapeutic drugs for recreational purposes did not become widespread in American society until the twentieth century.

Temperance and National Movements to Criminalize Alcohol

Until the 1900s, there were no legal prohibitions against heroin, morphine, cocaine, amphetamines, and marijuana because, for the most part, they simply did not exist as a social problem. Alcohol, however, was quite common, and alcohol abuse was recognized as a social problem, which was controlled through both criminal penalties and other nonlegal social pressures. The types and purposes of alcohol consumption changed significantly between the earliest colonial period of the 1600s up to the early 1900s.

The 1600s: Alcohol played a prominent role in early colonial life during the 1600s—both in the more secular southern Virginia colonies and the more religious northern Massachusetts colonies. Colonists might drink with every meal, and yet the Puritans of the north were also known for being very religious and sober. Part of the reason is that the alcohol they drank was mostly in the form of beer, wine, brandies, and some cider. Since small amounts of alcohol (one or two glasses per hour) may be consumed without raising the blood alcohol level high enough to impact motor skills or judgment, these drinks were not viewed as major sources of intoxication. Instead, they were viewed as nutritional supplements to the diet and usually served as a substitute for water as a beverage during meals. Puritans drank, but they believed it was a heavy sin to become drunk.

Intoxication was certainly possible from these drinks, but it was rigidly controlled through social and legal penalties. During the 1600s, tavern owners were usually respectable members of any community because they served beer and food and provided a place for social interaction. Tavern owners were expected to patrol who they served and limit sales to anyone who might be drinking so much that their behaviors were affected. Penalties for public intoxication included fines, whippings, and time in the public stocks, where they would be humiliated before the community (called shaming).

Repeated intoxication could result in banishment from the church and the community. In the same way that food was not viewed as harmful, but gluttony (eating too much) was viewed as a sin. So too, beer, wine, brandy, and cider were not viewed as harmful in themselves, but individual overconsumption leading to intoxication was universally recognized as harmful to the drinker and to the community. Drunkenness was a sin, and the criminalization of intoxication through community laws began with the first colonization in the Americas.

The 1700s: Several developments occurred during the 1700s that changed the way colonists viewed alcohol. Most noticeable was the rapid increase in immigration and population, resulting in millions of new citizens joining the communities. Most of these newcomers were not as religious or as committed to the community standards as those New England settlers who earlier risked life and limb to settle in the untamed wildernesses of the Americas in the 1600s.

Also, the nature of alcohol itself changed from beer, wine, brandy, and cider into more concentrated distilled liquors of rum and whiskey. Partly, this was an economic side effect of the new triangular trade between Europe, Africa, and the Caribbean. Since grain could spoil over long distance travel, farmers found it easier to convert the grain into alcohol and trade the alcohol over long distances to make their profits. The quantity of distilled liquors increased so much during the 1700s that the price of whiskey and rum dropped by half and were often less expensive than beer.

As the type of alcohol changed, so, too, did the taverns that sold it. New "grogshops" or bars that sold only alcohol appeared around the early 1800s, and bar owners were no longer viewed as respected citizens of the community. People drank significantly more, with some estimates of annual consumption of rum or whiskey ranging from five to ten gallons per person per year (i.e., up to twenty-five shots a week, on average). Public pressure against intoxication remained strong, and the same old penalties remained, but they were not easily enforced.

Some new penalties were added, such as forcing frequent drunks to wear a large "D" (for drunkard) on their clothes—partially to shame them and thereby encourage more sober behaviors but partly to inform bar owners not to serve these people alcohol. These measures had some effect, but the increasingly mobile society meant that many drinkers passed from town to town and were not under the force of any consistent social controls. This was especially true for sailors.

The 1800s: By the end of the 1700s, public perception of alcohol changed from serving as a nutritional supplement to becoming a source of addiction and vice. In 1785 (just a few years after the American Revolution ended), one of the signers of the Declaration of Independence, Benjamin Rush, wrote a book titled *An Inquiry into the Effects of Ardent Spirits upon the Human Body and Mind*. In this book, Rush made the argument that "ardent spirits" such as rum and whiskey were sources of addiction, and they could transform honest men into drunkards if consumed frequently.

Rush feared that men addicted to alcohol often made poor judgments, performed poorly in their work, and neglected their families. His was one of the first books that warned about the dangers of alcoholism, and it coincided with the widespread use of alcohol and increasing rates of public intoxication. The book sold 200,000 copies before 1810 and was widely read.

Rush's friend Thomas Jefferson agreed with the diagnosis of alcohol addiction and complained that too many politicians had fallen under the spell of whiskey and rum. Benjamin Franklin also warned of the dangers of hard liquor in his *Autobiography*, which appeared in 1791. Neither Franklin, nor Rush, nor Jefferson had as many concerns about beer, or wine, or cider because those forms of alcohol were usually drunk with meals as a beverage and not drunk for the purposes of achieving intoxication. However, whiskey and rum were almost always drunk with the goal of feeling the effects of intoxication. Like most of the leaders of their time, these framers of the US Constitution condemned the condition of being drunk.

The Second Great Awakening (Early 1800s)

The generation from 1800 to 1830 witnessed great cultural changes. The specter of atheistic radicalism during the French Revolution resulted in the deaths of 30,000 to 50,000 civilians and also led to the Napoleonic wars that swept across Europe from 1789 to 1815. Around the same time, the rising prevalence of public intoxication at home combined with the deep burden of implementing a never-before-attempted democratic republic in the United States. These three elements (radicalism, intoxication, and republican idealism) together triggered a national movement among Americans to rekindle their religious faith and recommit themselves to more moral lifestyles. This period is usually referred to as the Second Great Awakening, and it swept across the country from north to south, helping to bring about a renewed sense of American unity through a common Christian faith.

During this awakening, a new movement promoting clean and moral living arose called "temperance." Temperance has been recognized since ancient times as a virtue of moderation and moral self-restraint. Instead of living excessively for the sake of personal pleasures (like gluttony, drunkenness, and greediness), the temperate person restrains their preferences to ensure they are not enslaved by their passions and are thus better able to care for their personal needs. Individual self-restraint allows people to better serve their family, their community, and God.

Restraint from hard liquors was a major part of the Temperance Movement. A famous minister of the time, Lyman Beecher, started the Connecticut Society for the Promotion of Good Morals in 1812. This was just one of dozens of similar societies that formed during this period. Western Farmers started the Union Temperance Society of Moreau and Northumberland, New York, and the national American Society of Temperance began a few years after that, in 1826.

A necessary part of any Temperance Society was when members were asked to formally sign a "pledge" to abstain from hard liquors, tobacco, and other immoral behaviors (such as sex outside of marriage). By 1829, 100,000 people had taken the pledge, and two years later in 1831, there were 200,000. In 1835, there were 1.5 million people who signed the pledge—just about 12 percent of the entire population (or one out of every eight people). More than 30 percent of the residents of New York City signed the pledge in 1837.

The Temperance Movement of the 1830s shifted into a political movement by the end of the decade. These societies petitioned their state governments to criminalize many aspects of alcohol consumption, ranging from limits on the amount that could be consumed to imposing high taxes on hard liquors to outright prohibition of alcohol altogether. More than half the states passed such laws between 1838 and 1855, and thirteen states prohibited alcohol altogether.

Most state-based temperance laws of the 1850s that criminalized aspects of liquor consumption were overturned before the Civil War, but their impact remained significant throughout the 1800s. Trends of alcohol consumption also shifted. There was much less drinking of "ardent spirits" (whiskey and rum), which were most likely to lead to intoxication, and more consumption of beer and wine (which was less likely to lead to intoxication). The public generally opposed intoxication as a moral failing throughout the 1800s.

The Rise of Drug Regulations and Criminalization (Late 1800s)

During and after the Second Great Awakening, the American public began calling for more controls and criminalization of certain aspects of the alcohol trade, especially those that seemed most likely to enable public intoxication and the breakdown of family responsibilities. In a similar way, during the late 1890s, the American public also reacted with more laws criminalizing areas of medical drug sales that would be most likely to lead to public harm. Criminalization through legal penalties usually followed public awareness of public dangers. New laws followed new medical breakthroughs that revealed greater potential for abuse and addiction.

There was never a time during the 1800s when recreational drug use was legal—it was simply not yet recognized as a public danger. Pharmaceuticals were dispensed to doctors, who were expected to maintain control over their dispensation. If doctors discovered that one of their patients was becoming dependent on morphine or heroin and developing signs of addiction, they were duty bound to take efforts to restrict the patient's access to the drug.

Unfortunately, most drugs during the 1800s were poorly understood. As mentioned earlier, cocaine was developed initially as a drug to help patients who already had addictions to opium and morphine. It was not seen as a recreational drug, so it was not viewed as a source of addiction in its own right. Cocaine was not easily accessible outside the hands of a doctor, and it was assumed that anyone who purchased it would be using it primarily for some therapeutic purpose.

Pure Food and Drugs: Industrialization changed the way that these potent drugs were marketed and sold. Medicine intended for therapeutic use could be obtained by the general public through new and unanticipated ways. During the 1880s, traveling salesmen often hawked "invigorating elixirs" intended to improve health and overcome sickness and other physical ailments (like rheumatism, baldness, and obesity). These elixirs rarely worked and usually contained mostly alcohol but also included potent drugs such as cocaine, opium, amphetamines, and sometimes even minor doses of poisons such as arsenic and strychnine. Customers bought these drugs directly from the salesmen, even if they had no real medical problems. These salesmen often called themselves "doctors" and took advantage of the general health movement of prior generations, and because they traveled from town to town, these salesmen were usually gone before they had to confront the obvious side effects of addiction.

The late 1890s also saw new industrial marketing strategies that used mail-order catalogs to sell almost any product across states and internationally. Customers could mail away for medical elixirs after the traveling salesmen left town. These concoctions also often included dangerous compounds. Most legitimate doctors condemned these products and called the salesmen "quacks," but there were few national laws to regulate the trade of such items. The first national laws to criminalize certain drugs arose in direct response to the prevalence of quack doctors who sold ineffective (or dangerous) elixirs, as well as the corrupt doctors who willingly sold addictive drugs to their patients for the money that these illicit sales produced.

Around 1900, urban mothers were especially afraid of the quality of food and drugs coming into their homes. Upton Sinclair wrote a book in 1906 called *The Jungle*, which exposed filthy conditions of the meatpacking industry. In the same year, Congress passed the Pure Food and Drugs Act as well as the Meat Inspection Act. These laws were intended to protect consumers from fraud and other dangers entering into the home. The drug-related portion of the law forbade interstate transportation of drugs that were misbranded or dangerous.

The law also specifically required doctors to register all their opium and heroin sales in order to track who was using the drug (and to identify illicit users).

Opium and Narcotics: The global sensitivity to opium addiction increased significantly from the 1870s to the 1900s. Just forty years earlier England used military troops to force China to buy their opium that was being shipped in from India. Some opium arrived back to Europe and England, but it was usually limited to the Chinese neighborhoods. However, by 1910 opium addiction became much more noticeable in other areas in mainstream communities, so China and England agreed to permanently end the India–Chinese opium trade.

The United States also outlawed the importation of opium in 1909, and by 1914 Congress supplemented the Pure Food and Drug Act by passing the Harrison Narcotics Act. This new law required both registration and a special tax for all patients who were prescribed heroin or opium for legitimate medical treatment. More importantly, though, the law also included criminal penalties for doctors who permitted these drugs to go to patients without therapeutic need (the first bill to target drug dealers).

Marijuana was not listed among prohibited drugs under the Harrison Narcotics Act because, at the time, cannabis was almost unknown to the American public. The earliest accounts of recreational marijuana use do not become noticeable until the late 1910s (around the First World War) and then mostly only in the southern states along the Mexican border.

The First World War brought further advances in medical technologies, including the first widespread use of aspirin as a safer form of pain reliever (instead of opium). Nevertheless, the sheer number of wartime patients exposed far more Americans to both the positive and negative effects of therapeutic drug use than ever before. After the war, rates of illegal heroin and opium use increased. In 1923, the Federal Government responded to this social problem by creating the Narcotics Division within the US Treasury Department. Federal authority to enforce drug laws stems mostly from its ability to tax interstate commerce, and that is why the Narcotics Division was created under the US Treasury Department.

Marijuana: Marijuana use did not become noticeable as a source of abuse until the mid-1930s. One famous case in 1933 of a schizophrenic murderer in Tampa, Florida, who killed five members of his family with an ax, made the newspaper headlines. He was high on marijuana at the time of the crime, and the case drew public attention. It later served as the source for the film *Reefer Madness* (1936). Even at that late date, marijuana was still largely unknown to the American public, and the film was intended to create public awareness through a highly sensationalized story. The movie was not widely released, and it did little to increase public awareness of the drug.

Nevertheless, Harry Anslinger, who was head of the Narcotics Division, submitted a bill in 1935 to include marijuana under the Harrison Tax Act. In 1937 the Marijuana Tax Act was passed by Congress, and the drug fell under federal jurisdiction for the first time. Despite this new law, marijuana continued to be a relatively unknown drug until the late 1950s and 1960s. A Gallup Poll taken in 1969 indicated that only 4 percent of adults had ever tried marijuana, and more than a third (34 percent) had no idea what the effects of marijuana were.

Prohibition: From Mostly Alcohol Criminalization to Mostly Drug Criminalization

The Temperance movement of the late 1800s changed its focus during the early 1900s. Instead of promoting general moral restraint and purity in all aspects of life, the movement of the 1900s focused mostly on ending sales of all forms of alcohol. The Women's Christian Temperance Union (WCTU) was largely replaced by the Anti-Saloon League (ASL) as the nation's most dominant political force, and the new campaign concentrated its efforts against dangers of urban bars as a source of corruption for families and in local politics. Bars that served only alcohol were portrayed as the cause of family breakdown, poverty, and crime.

Passing Prohibition Laws: The new ASL campaign was moderately successful during the 1900s–1910s, but the onset of the First World War increased its momentum considerably. Germans were known for beer making, and by the mid-1910s, the opposition to the German military also translated into an opposition to beer culturally. For this and other reasons, the ASL categorized beer and wine together with distilled liquors and then pushed lawmakers to legally prohibit the manufacture and sales of all alcohol, though they did not necessarily focus on criminalizing drinking. This was different from earlier prohibition movements of the 1850s because this focused more on prohibiting alcohol sales rather than on ending intoxication.

Just months after the end of the First World War, the nation passed and ratified the Eighteenth Amendment to the US Constitution, which read, "The manufacture, sale, or transportation of intoxicating liquors within, the importation thereof into, or the exportation thereof from the United States and all territory subject to the jurisdiction thereof for beverage purposes is hereby prohibited." This Amendment was implemented by the Volstead Act, which began the national social experiment known as "Prohibition."

Ironically, the country made more distilled alcohol during the 1920s Prohibition era than it did before—not because there were more violations of the law but because alcohol produced during the 1920s was used primarily for industrial purposes (cleaning supplies, lubricants, paints, etc.) and for medical purposes, as a mixture medium for certain drug types.

Prohibition did not criminalize drinking or intoxication (which was much different from the earlier laws from 1600 to 1800). The Volstead Act only prohibited the manufacture and sales of alcohol for recreational use. On the federal level, it was not illegal to drink alcohol—it was only illegal to import it, make it, or sell it for others to drink. This was the focus of the ASL, and it was different from the earlier Temperance movement which focused mostly on individual moral restraint.

There are many cultural myths about the Prohibition years. For example, it is not true that people drank more during these years, nor is it true that Prohibition created organized crime. Per capita rates of alcohol consumption declined by more than half during the 1920s, and homicide rates from organized crime were at their highest levels twenty years *before* Prohibition (between 1900 and 1910).

Prohibition was effective on many levels. It limited rates of binge drinking and the effects of intoxication. Public welfare agencies reported significant declines in the number of family problems related to alcohol, while doctors reported that the rates of cirrhosis of the liver and alcoholic psychosis also declined substantially during the 1920s. In terms of reducing harm to the health of the users and to the community, Prohibition's criminalization of recreational alcohol sales and manufacturing clearly worked.

The main problem of Prohibition was enforcement. The federal government outlawed the importation, manufacturing, and sales of recreational alcohol, but the new law only provided 1,500 federal agents to enforce these prohibitions over the entire country. To put that number into perspective, the City of New York employed over 40,000 police officers for their single city. The Volstead Act expected 1,500 agents to patrol all American coasts as well as all interstate transfers, hidden manufacturing stills, and illegal sales operations (called speakeasies). As a practical matter, the federal government hoped that local police would do most of the law enforcement—but local police in ethnic neighborhoods found in large urban areas did not always share the same cultural priorities as the ASL.

Rural areas of the United States mostly obeyed the new prohibition laws, and alcohol consumption decreased significantly. However, in more urban populations where the highest concentrations of European immigrants lived, there was less consensus over the moral and physical harms of alcohol. Catholics especially did not view alcohol as the prime source of evil (the Blessed Sacrament of the Eucharist was made up of bread and wine). For immigrants who did not grow up under the Temperance movement of the late 1800s, their cultural experiences still viewed intoxication, and not alcohol, as the primary harm to society. Also, for most European immigrants, beer and wine were still viewed mostly as beverages to be taken at mealtimes, which is similar to how early American colonists viewed alcohol in the 1600s and 1700s.

Overturning Prohibition Laws: There were many reasons why Prohibition was overturned in 1933. One large reason was due to the growing imbalance between urban and rural populations. In 1900, more Americans lived in rural communities than lived in cities. By 1930, that ratio had reversed itself. Since the large urban populations were generally less supportive of prohibiting all alcohol, the public willingness to overturn the law increased. Rural communities remained very supportive of Prohibition.

Another major reason was the Great Depression. President Franklin Roosevelt and others in the Democrat Party saw the liquor industry as a large untapped tax base as well as a potential source for increased jobs in the private sector. Roosevelt was a successful politician, and his views became more popular as the economic recession worsened. When the states eventually voted on ratifying the Twenty-First Amendment, which repealed Prohibition and the Eighteenth Amendment, the votes passed with a three-to-one margin.

Federal Prohibition was overturned in 1933, but that did not mean that all states repealed their own Prohibition laws. Seven states continued to criminalize alcohol, though five of the states legalized beer or "near-bear" with low alcohol levels and which were least likely to lead to intoxication. Twelve states legalized alcohol consumption only for the home, and twenty-nine states permitted sales of liquor by the glass (but not by the bottle). Almost every state passed Alcohol Beverage Control (ABC) laws that continued to regulate and criminalize certain aspects of alcohol consumption, including prohibition of sales on Sunday and other restrictions to certain hours of the day. In some states, alcohol could only be purchased from state-approved facilities. Using modern-day terms, we could say that these twenty-nine states decriminalized alcohol during the 1930s but did not completely legalize it. Many of these restrictions continue in the twenty-first century. In Alaska, many native villages in rural communities prohibit the importation or sales of alcohol even in the 2020s. Then, as now, the primary concern is the harm from public intoxication and the effect of drunkenness on the family and poverty.

Drug Criminalization: While alcohol was experiencing waves of criminalization and decriminalization, laws governing potential drug abuse became more rigid from 1900 forward. The primary difference between alcohol use and the misuse of potent drugs intended for medical use was that alcohol could be consumed without any intoxication at all. If consumed with meals, in social situations, at rates of less than one or two drinks per hour, alcohol does not lead to intoxication, and the risk of addiction remains very low. The threat of harm to the family and to the community could also be very low.

Certainly, not every consumer of alcohol follows those suggested guidelines, and that is why health officials warn against "binge drinking" (drinking three–four or more drinks per hour, depending on the size and weight of the drinker). High rates of drinking will always lead to impairment. The main distinction between alcohol and recreational drug use is that every single time a drug that was originally intended for medical use is taken for recreational purposes, it always leads to intoxication and impairment of both cognitive and motor functions at some level. Moderate drinking of alcohol (less than two drinks per hour) will not lead to intoxication or impairment. Even after Prohibition of alcohol was overturned, there were no efforts to decriminalize recreational drug use—especially between the 1930s and 1960s. In most cases, existing drug laws became more strict (not less).

The 1950s Pharmaceutical Revolution

The Second World War triggered a massive demand for new therapeutic drugs to deal with battlefield injuries, especially for drugs and techniques that could offer pain relief and halt the spread of infections. Many biochemical compounds were isolated during the 1930s, but it was not until the Second World War that scientists had the proper tools available for mass-producing these biochemical formulas. For example, penicillin was discovered and isolated by Alexander Fleming in 1928, but the process to produce it was very long and cumbersome. During the war, Ernst Chain and Howard Florey figured out a new technique to mass-produce the drug, making it ready for delivery to battlefield hospitals. Chain and Florey each shared a Nobel Prize for their efforts after the war.

At the same time as medical technologies were improving, the system for funding research in all fields also changed significantly. Borrowing the model used by weapon and vehicle manufacturers during the war, pharmaceutical companies used government grant money to subsidize university professors to conduct experiments on promising biochemical therapies. If these research projects were commercially viable, the company would begin marketing the drugs as soon as possible.

The federal government was involved through its oversight with the Food and Drug Administration (FDA), which tested the drugs to ensure they passed public safety expectations before they were permitted to reach the public. At all stages, the goal of this private-public partnership during the 1950s was to encourage innovation as much as possible for a potential high economic return while also monitoring public safety to ensure that no harm would come to an unsuspecting public consumer.

Thalidomide Scare: The diligence of the FDA was proven worthwhile on several occasions. Parke-Davis pharmaceutical company developed chloramphenicol as an antibiotic treatment for infections, similar to penicillin. It was originally advertised as being "completely non-toxic." However, during its initial trial run with the public, several children died after using the product because their unique physiological profiles triggered aplastic anemia. The drug company was sued, and the drug was immediately pulled from the marketplace. This served as a warning for other pharmaceutical companies that they could suffer major penalties for failing to protect against unintended harm to the consumer.

A few years later, the German pharmaceutical company Grünental developed a new sedative that was not supposed to be habit-forming (like opium was). It was called thalidomide and was prescribed throughout Europe and Australia as a wonder drug. After the chloramphenicol incident, the American FDA was hesitant to grant approval and subjected the drug to a series of new testing procedures, even though many European nations approved its use.

In early 1960–1, an Australian doctor noticed a marked increase in the number of rare birth defects in which the baby's arms were shortened or missing, and the hands were elongated and unusable. Working with a German pediatrician, both doctors discovered the link between thalidomide and birth defects, and they published their findings. As a result, the drug was quickly banned in forty-six countries by 1962. At least 10,000 babies were born with deformities prior to the drug ban.

The FDA had not approved the drug for use in the United States, and later, after these discoveries were publicized, President John Kennedy awarded the head of the FDA, Frances Kelsey, with the President's Award for Distinguished Federal Service for her caution with respect to thalidomide. Afterward, Congress passed the Food, Drug, and Cosmetic Act of 1962 to ensure extra diligence with regard to consumer safety and drug use. The American public was strongly supportive of such forceful government oversight over potentially dangerous drugs that could create grave public harm.

Mood-Altering Drugs: Despite the increased regulations, Americans were taking more therapeutic drugs during the 1950s and 1960s than ever before. In 1955, Frank Berger and Bernard Ludwig isolated a new synthesis called meprobamate, which Wallace Laboratories eventually marketed under the name "Miltown." It was a tranquilizer that shared many of the same effects as other opium derivatives but was less potent and easily taken in a pill form. By 1957, the Carter Medicine Company was selling a billion tablets a year, mostly to ordinary adults who were diagnosed with mild anxiety disorders, and used the tranquilizers for its calming effects. Miltown was the bestselling drug ever sold in the United States and accounted for a third of all prescriptions sold during the 1950s (one out of every seven adults used it regularly). It was viewed by the general public as a gentle medicinal tool and was not deemed to be harmful in any way.

Doctors began turning to pharmaceuticals to treat psychological disorders that would have previously been treated with surgery or other physical therapies. Albert Hofman developed a compound called lysergic acid diethylamide (LSD) before the Second World War, but he did not understand its properties for nearly five years. After the war, Hofman realized that his drug was a hallucinogen and started preparing it as a possible treatment for schizophrenia. If the drug altered sensory perceptions in healthy patients, Hofman (and his colleagues) theorized that an additional altering of the sensory perceptions might stabilize schizophrenic patients. A similar drug named phencyclidine (later known as PCP) had previously been isolated and developed during the 1920s and 1930s to treat psychosis.

None of these drugs worked to cure schizophrenia, and in many cases the drugs triggered new schizophrenic symptoms in patients who had not previously shown such symptoms (called psychosis). Still during the 1950s, the search for a cure for mental illness was in high demand for most drug companies. Research was conducted on psilocybin mushrooms in 1958 because it was a known hallucinogen. The psychoactive substance, mescaline, was isolated, but it also never achieved any positive results in curing mental illness—though, like LSD and PCP, it could trigger psychosis if taken by healthy users.

Research into mood-altering drugs during the 1950s was partly responsible for the outbreak of recreational drug use among college students during the 1960s. A small group of writers known as "Beat Poets" of the late 1950s (such as Jack Kerouac, Allen Ginsberg, and William Burroughs) began experimenting with hallucinogens to see if the drugs produced more artistic poetry. They often listed the drug they used in the introductions to their poetry collections. These poets were really read only by a small group of other artists, and the mainstream culture did not pay much attention to them at the time. They became much more influential among college students in the late 1960s.

The Late 1960s Drug Culture

The popularity of recreational drug use changed in the mid-1960s. A part-time lecturer at Harvard University named Timothy Leary was connected with a research study on the effects of LSD on the potential rehabilitation of released prisoners, which later became known as the "Concorn Prison Experiment." The results of the experiment showed no positive effects, but Leary was taking LSD as a personal experiment on himself. He skewed the research results to make it appear as if the drug was successful, and he then began promoting LSD publicly as a pathway to greater spiritual enlightenment. The Beat Poets at the time were drawn to Leary, and together during the early 1960s they became a sort of cultural magnet for the youthful Baby Boomers who were entering college at that time.

Leary's results were quickly refuted by other more reputable scientists, and he was prohibited from ever teaching at Harvard University again. Nevertheless, Leary's prior rank as an adjunct professor granted him some academic credibility that the Beat Poets did not have. He and others began touring the country and stopping at college campuses to encourage students to take LSD and use recreational drugs as a new method for gaining wisdom and insight into their lives. He drew support not only from young students but also from other celebrities who drew upon Leary's alternative identity to increase their own popularity among young students. Aldous Huxley, who wrote *Brave New World* (1932), and Ken Kesey, who wrote *One Flew over the Cuckoo's Nest* (1962), both championed LSD as an elixir of life and a source of enlightenment. They and others helped build the drug-based counterculture movement among college-aged kids who were easily manipulated by their literary fame. The motto of the new recreational drug movement was "tune in, turn on, and drop out."

During the early 1960s, hallucinogens were not illegal to make, buy, or sell because the public had never seen any sizable group of people taking the drug, and so the potential harm was unknown to drug regulators. However, the rise of the new drug-based counterculture triggered noticeable public responses after hundreds of teens and young adults began appearing in hospital rooms or were found dangerously exposed in public parks or highways and who seemed to have lost connection with reality. Mostly, these effects were temporary, but in some cases, the drug use led to dangerous activities resulting in death—trying to race a train or jumping off tall structures because the user believed they could fly.

More importantly, the use of LSD was almost always accompanied by the use of other drugs, including alcohol, opioids (cocaine and heroin), and the relatively new drug, marijuana. Users did not appear to become immediately ill from the hallucinogens, but they frequently died from drug overdoses. Some famous rock stars, such as Janis Joplin, Jimmy Hendrix, and Jim Morrison, died of drug overdoses in 1970 and 1971, during the height of their careers while still in the mid-twenties. Many more celebrities preceded them and followed in their wake. Recreational drug use led users to neglect themselves and others, and heavy users often formed lifelong habits that left them continually going into and out of mental hospitals and other public institutions. By the late 1960s, almost every state passed laws criminalizing hallucinogens as dangerous both to the user and to the general public.

The drug culture was always only a minor segment of the college-aged population. Recreational drug use of hallucinogens among adults during the 1960s was very low (at 1.3 percent), and among college-aged youth a Gallup poll in 1967 reported that only 6 percent of students had tried marijuana. However, those numbers increased rapidly over the next five years, and by 1970 the National Institute of Health estimated that use-rate among young adults aged eighteen–twenty-five was over 16 percent. Marijuana was hardly recognized among adults during the late 1960s, but among college-aged students it was increasingly more common. Students who left their homes in rural towns or middle-income suburban areas came from communities where recreational drug use was almost unknown. However, while in college, many of these students (probably about a quarter) experimented with some drug use—mostly marijuana—and the experiences were then taken back with them to their previously drug-free communities. In this way, recreational drug use emerged as a national problem in the late 1960s, and national politicians began to react to it with more comprehensive drug laws.

Drugs and Crime

More than six hundred riots occurred on college campuses and in urban centers between 1967 and 1969. Millions of dollars in damages were inflicted on cars, businesses, and homes through riots that mostly involved youth who, from the perspective of outside observers, appeared to be intoxicated with drugs, or alcohol or both. The Republican Presidential Candidate Richard Nixon campaigned on the promise of restoring "law and order" to these areas, and he focused much of his attention on crime control and on the consolidation of drug-control laws.

Nixon did not blame the students as much as he blamed the drug dealers and other adults who influenced students to engage in disordered lifestyles and other forms of public disruption. He was elected with strong support in 1968, and Congress passed many of his drug-control bills in 1969 and 1970. Among these was the Organized Crime Control Act of 1970, which accompanied the Comprehensive Drug Abuse Prevention and Control Act of 1970. These laws were crafted to target drug dealers and organized crime syndicates that facilitated the illegal importation and distribution of drugs and to provide guidelines for the responsible therapeutic use of medical drugs for doctors and patients.

The Controlled Substance Act (CSA) was a subset of these laws, which established a single set of federal guidelines for evaluating the potential danger of all drug types. It was written to reflect model anti-drug laws drafted by the United Nations for use by individual countries a decade earlier. In US law, the most dangerous drugs were listed under Schedule I because they were highly prone to abuse and addiction, and the medical community had not developed any protocols for their safe therapeutic use. Some of these drugs included marijuana, LSD, and methylenedioxymethamphetamine (MDMA, also known as ecstasy). Schedule II drugs were also highly addictive, but they were used within the medical community for their potential as therapeutic treatments. These drugs included opioids and methamphetamines. The least dangerous drugs, like prescription-strength cough syrups, were listed under Schedule V.

The move to consolidate all existing drug laws within a single national schedule was prompted primarily by the excesses of the 1960s drug culture among the baby boom-aged youth. Parents were worried about their children being exposed to these drugs without fully understanding their potential dangers—both in physical and mental health terms. Other community partners worried about the impact of drug-induced crimes (especially property crimes) that the increased drug use imposed on local police.

Still others worried about the risk of increased drug abuse on the moral health of the community, which would be harmed by poor judgment, lower inhibitions, and fewer habits of individual self-restraint. The rising drug culture also coincided with the sexual revolution that was becoming more obvious in books and movies by the late 1960s. There was, however, a small minority of Americans who disapproved of all these new laws and who worried about the potential limitations on individual freedom.

The "War on Drugs"

President Nixon announced a "War on Drugs" in June 1971 as part of his speech announcing a new Special Action Office for Drug Abuse Prevention (SAODAP). During his 1971 speech, Nixon claimed that drug abuse was "public enemy number one" and that he was devoting resources to both enforcement and treatment programs. A year later, Nixon announced the creation of the Drug Enforcement Administration (DEA), which would be responsible for coordinating nationwide enforcement of the new drug laws.

Nixon used words that seemed to emphasize criminal prosecution in his approach to drug control, and the new drug laws certainly placed harsher penalties for drug dealers and for organized criminal gangs. As a practical matter, though, he actually devoted most new resources to providing treatment options for users and offenders, both during and after incarceration. The number of arrests for drug offenses between 1968 and 1974 was essentially the same as it had been during the previous five years before Nixon's term in office. What distinguished Nixon from previous administrations is that he promoted interagency cooperation through "Joint Task Forces" that bridged several different law enforcement units, including local police and local social-service agencies. He used the existing Law Enforcement Assistance Administration (LEAA) to coordinate programs and focus on both enforcement and deterrence.

President Lyndon Johnson began the LEAA program as part of his Great Society initiative in 1965, which provided federal funds for local police for education and other outreach programs. Johnson's law enforcement initiatives emphasize noncriminal social-welfare funding models. Under Nixon, the LEAA funding increased significantly, from $50 million in 1968 to $268 million in 1970, $480 million in 1971, and $700 million in 1972. These federal funding programs were aimed at both increasing drug-enforcement laws and increasing alternative interdiction options through youth drug education programs and rehabilitation counseling programs for those already addicted to drugs.

Nixon's War on Drugs was not a new phrase. It was originally coined three years earlier by President Lyndon Johnson in a 1968 speech, just before he left office to support additional funding for the LEAA program. Johnson's "War on Poverty" helped launch his Great Society program in 1965, and he planned to use the War on Drugs as another front in the battle. Nixon kept the same language, and he also made the problem of drug abuse and crime control his administration's top priorities after winning the election in 1968.

Today, the War on Drugs is mostly associated with strong criminal penalties, but in fact it always involves a combination of both enforcement and deterrence through education and addiction treatment. Nixon was the first president ever to put crime control as a prime agenda item for his incoming White House organization plan, so he is most associated with crime control. Since Nixon's speech in 1971, the phrase 'War on Drugs' has become synonymous with criminalization and was used frequently by Presidents Ronald Reagan and George H. W. Bush during the 1980s and early 1990s.

One of Nixon's new programs most often used by later researchers was the National Survey on Drug Use and Health (NSDUH) that was started in 1971. This federal program selected thousands of households in all fifty states to participate in a survey of actual tobacco, alcohol, and drug use of every member of the house aged twelve and above. This survey is still taken every year, and 70,000 people were interviewed in 2023.

Since the best tactic in the war on drugs was to prevent youth from falling into addiction, many new resources were dedicated to drug education programs that targeted schools. In 1975, another national survey titled "Monitoring the Future" (MTF) began surveying students in public schools about their use of tobacco, alcohol, and other drugs in the past week, past month, and at any time over their lifetime. Most of the statistics related to youth drug use come from one or both of these surveys (NSDUH or MTF).

Decriminalization Movements

President Nixon's Controlled Substance Act (CSA) led to the creation of the new DEA, whose primary task was tracking and intercepting illicit drug use. This involves monitoring the use of prescription drugs as well as patrolling drugs smuggled over international borders and arresting criminal organizations responsible for drug trafficking inside the country. These crime-based efforts take up the bulk of news coverage about the Drug War.

To a large extent, the focus on law enforcement, arrests, and numbers of prisoners associated with drug crimes is misleading. The vast majority of offenders who serve long prison sentences for drug offenses were arrested on major trafficking charges as part of a criminal organization, or they were arrested for some other related property offense or act of violence, such as robbery, assault, theft, and murder. It was very rare, even during the 1970s, for drug offenders to be given jail time for personal drug use alone. Since the 2000s began, the number of arrests for drug use alone is almost negligible. Since the Nixon's era of the 1970s, the bulk of the "drug war" has focused on those who are responsible for manufacturing, smuggling, distributing, and selling drugs. Individual victims of the illegal drug market are usually sentenced to mandatory treatment programs unless they are also convicted of other more serious crimes against property or of violence.

In part, the negative association of the "drug war" as an attack on drug users began almost as soon as the CSA passed Congress. Modern opponents of drug criminalization focus most of their energy on two arguments: (1) drug use is a personal right and should not be criminalized and (2) drug users are unfairly punished for exercising their right to intoxication. During the 1970s, the general public was not receptive to the first argument that drug use and legal access to intoxication was a personal right. The skyrocketing rates of drug abuse among youth and the significant increase in property crimes as reported by the Federal Bureau of Investigation's (FBI) Uniform Crime Report between 1967 and 1972 was difficult to ignore (increasing more than 10 percent per year for five years straight). It was much easier for the mainstream public to link recreational drug use and crime together.

However, the second goal of arguing that the drug laws were too harsh, and ought to be softened or that they should be replaced altogether with noncriminal treatment programs was more popular. Mostly, this was because the DEA was already incorporating more treatment programs through their LEAA partnerships, and this alternative was already publicized by the government itself.

Another tactic in support of decriminalization was a movement to make marijuana more socially acceptable as a therapeutic (medical) drug. The National Organization for the Reform of Marijuana Laws (NORML) was founded in 1970, the same year that the CSA was passed by Congress. Since marijuana was listed as a Schedule I drug that was highly addictive and had no known medical value, the first priority for NORML was to find some medical value in marijuana. Throughout the 1970s and 1980s, like-minded academics struggled to find some therapeutic uses for marijuana. The goal for NORML was to legalize marijuana for medical use, and then as it became more socially acceptable as a therapeutic drug, it could be moved from a Schedule I drug into some other lesser category. The tactic proved to be successful because fifty years later President Joe Biden issued a directive to reclassify marijuana from a Schedule I to a Schedule II drug in 2024.

For most of the 1970s and 1980s, though, the War on Drugs was strongly supported by every president from Nixon to Bush and by the general public. President James Carter was less vocal in his commitment to the war on drugs, preferring instead to promote more treatment alternatives. However, presidents Reagan and Bush launched strong public education programs opposing drug use among youth especially. The "Just Say No" campaign was very effective and in the early 1990s, marijuana use among high-school students dropped to its lowest rates since before the emergence of the baby boomer drug culture of the 1970s.

Nevertheless, the critics of criminalization also slowly gained popular support among college professors, who had originally helped to support the rise of the drug culture as college students during the late 1960s and 1970s. By the late 1980s and 1990s, many of these 1970s-era students were now college professors, and they wrote hundreds of books targeting the War on Drugs as an unfair and unjust attack on minorities and the poor.

Baby Boomers and Recreational Drug Use

The baby boomer generation refers to those people who were born during the last years of the Second World War and includes their siblings. This means that anyone born between 1943 and 1957 is generally considered a "boomer." By the 2020s, the boomers were aged anywhere between their late sixties and late seventies. The boomers are often associated with the drug culture of the 1960s because recreational drug use became most prevalent during the time period that most boomers were entering college (roughly from the mid-1960s to the mid-1970s).

Despite their association with recreational drug use, the boomers cannot be categorized by strict moral or religious designations. Modern movements that support libertarian, social-welfare, and traditional conservative ideologies all come out of the same baby boomer generation. All three of these ideological priority sets were then later passed on to successive generations in stronger or milder variations. Most traditional conservatives oppose recreational drug use as adults, but that does not mean that they never experimented with certain drugs—especially marijuana—when they were in college. While many social-welfare advocates experimented with recreational drug use in their youth, that does not mean that they continued to do so as adults.

Growing up in the 1950s, baby boomers always lived in an era when pharmaceuticals were the most popular tool for medical treatments. If you felt sick, depressed, or had an unusual disease, most people assumed that there was a pill that can help make you better. Therapeutic drugs became much more of a routine element in everyone's lives from the 1960s forward.

During the 1980s, most boomers were very supportive of the "Just Say No" educational anti-drug programs because their children were all school-aged, and parents did not want their kids to become addicted to drugs out of ignorance or poor decision-making. However, the 1980s parents were also much more likely than previous generations to give their children therapeutic drugs to deal with emotional and behavioral issues such as hyperactivity, mild depression, and an inability to concentrate.

Recreational drug use among school-aged youth was at a low point during the early 1990s when the "Just Say No" campaign had been in effect for almost a decade. This trend changed toward the end of the 1990s, when the federal war on drugs slowly faded in popularity. In 1992, Bill Clinton was the first president from the baby boomer generation. He was also the first president to admit to smoking marijuana (though he pretended that he did not inhale the drug). Since then, every president has admitted to marijuana use at some point in their youth. President Barack Obama wrote a book about how he frequently used both marijuana and cocaine during his youth in Hawaii.

Experimental drug use in youth does not mean that the same people will continue to use recreational drugs as they grow into adults. However, there is a statistical correlation between higher rates of drug experimentation during youth and the higher likelihood of lifelong habits of recreational drug use as adults. This is especially true of marijuana use. People who use marijuana more than a few times in their youth generally continue to use the drug (off and on) throughout the rest of their lives. The rates of marijuana use among fifteen to twenty-five-year-olds during the 1970s remained more or less consistent as those rates among twenty-five to thirty-five-year-olds during the 1980s, thirty-five to forty-five-year-olds during the 1990s and every decade until the 2020s, when seventy-five to eighty-five-year-olds have comparable marijuana use rates as when they were youth during the 1970s.

In part, marijuana is unique because it is a mild hallucinogen, and it plays a strong role in changing moral attitudes. People who take marijuana are much more likely to have neutral or positive views on recreational drug use than those people who have never taken marijuana. As the boomer generation aged from the 1970s to the 2020s, every subsequent generation (except for the late 1980s) followed similar patterns of marijuana use, which means that by the 2010s, the majority of all age groups had at some point achieved intoxication through recreational drug use.

Boomers first began to attain positions of leadership in politics and in businesses toward the end of the 1990s, which is also when federal priorities of drug control began to change. In 1993, President Clinton's surgeon general Jocelyn Elders recommended a federal study of the potential impact of drug legalization. At the time of her comments, the full impact of the War on Drugs and the Reagan–Bush "Just Say No" campaigns held strong influence on public attitudes. Elders was later forced to resign because her comments related to drugs and sexuality were too controversial. Nevertheless, the state of California relied on Elders's comments leading to a slow campaign to reverse the War on Drugs in their own state and to decriminalize marijuana for medical purposes.

The long-held tradition of public opposition to intoxication as a moral vice changed rapidly between 2000 and 2010. President George W. Bush and other Republicans continued to support the federal War on Drugs, but the Democrat Party and libertarians began promoting alternative options to criminalization. Many Republicans also joined Democrats in supporting medical use of marijuana (though usually not for recreational use). George Soros and other billionaires in the technology industry spent billions of dollars during the 2010s through social media campaigns that helped to rewrite the narrative of the War on Drugs. Most content found in social media is organized through algorithms that present the viewer with content not only based on user preference but also based on marketing concerns and the ideological preferences of the social media platform. These campaigns were very effective, and public opinions on recreational drug use changed dramatically during the early 2000s.

Public Attitudes and Social Media

Social media had a major impact on changing public attitudes between 2008 and 2020, but much of the money in support of the efforts to decriminalize recreational drug use was also given to nongovernment organizations (NGOs) and individual academics who were given large grants to write books on the social costs of the drug war. Journalists and other public influencers were also encouraged (and paid) to write articles on the public harm caused by drug criminalization (not drug use or intoxication).

The results of these marketing efforts can be seen through a simple internet search for War on Drugs. During the 2020s, almost every result in an internet search linked to articles that repeated the same message of a "failed drug war" that caused much more harm than it helped. These articles would not have appeared during the 1980s and 1990s, but after significant influence on social media prioritization of internet content, the new "anti-drug war" and decriminalization movement became very popular—especially among youth and young adults who spend the most time on smartphones and online gaming and social media platforms.

By 2016, the federal War on Drugs was largely abandoned. By the 2020s most of the public rhetoric posted on the internet viewed drug criminalization negatively. The political trends between 2012 and 2020 indicated more public support for decriminalization of marijuana, which was legalized for medical use in thirty-eight states and completely legalized for recreational use in twenty-four states. For a brief period between 2020 and 2024, the state of Oregon decriminalized all drugs (stimulants, narcotics, and hallucinogens).

These trends may not reflect the actual views of the general public. One of the reactions to the strong political and moral messaging on social media during the 2020s is the rise of a small but growing trend of users who reject social media, smartphones, and other forms of digital addiction. More than half of those surveyed no longer trust information found in social media and other online sources. The attempt to normalize recreational drug use played some role in that skepticism.

Nevertheless, changing public attitudes toward recreational drug use has an impact on actual drug use. As the National Center for Health Statistics (within the CDC) reported in 2024, for the first time in American history, more people achieved a state of intoxication from recreational drug use than from alcohol. Sales of alcohol are still higher than sales of marijuana, but that is because the majority of alcohol drinkers (over 70 per cent) do not become intoxicated when they drink. They drink alcohol as a beverage, usually taken with a meal or a light snack, and do not drink to the point of becoming drunk. However, every purchase of marijuana leads to intoxication. In 2024, the rates of marijuana use were higher than the rates of binge drinking, which means that the majority of people who reach the condition of intoxication did so from recreational drug use.

These statistics are a little misleading because a large percentage of people who set out to become intoxicated use multiple drugs (called polydrug use)—alcohol, marijuana, narcotics, amphetamines, and opioids are taken together in some form. This is the most dangerous way to consume drugs, and death rates for accidental overdoses also reached the highest levels in history by the 2020s. Mental illness, depression, suicide ideation (and completion) and crime rates related to theft, property, and violence also increased to unprecedented levels in urban centers. It is still unclear whether rates of recreational drug use lead to these higher rates of mental illness and crime or whether the increased crime culture and mental illness lead to higher recreational drug use. The specific cause of public harm is the primary source of debate in every drug policy issue.

Conclusion: The Long Record of Drug Controls

Since the earliest historical records, drugs and alcohol have played some part in human civilization. However, with very few exceptions, recreational drug use was extremely rare as an acceptable part of any society until very recently. Alcohol abuse was more common, but public intoxication from alcohol was usually condemned by most societies.

The form of cultural control over alcohol and recreational drug use differs from society to society. However, there are some general patterns which appear to be consistent. During times when intoxication is rare, limited to special occasions, or limited to certain groups at the margins of society, there are no explicit laws forbidding alcohol or recreational drug use. If intoxication from alcohol or recreational drug use becomes so common that mainstream society takes notice of the harm to family responsibilities, job potential, and the defense of private property, these issues are almost always dealt with through new laws that criminalize the behaviors that lead to intoxication.

Criminalization became the most common method of controlling alcohol abuse and recreational drug use for most of the period from the 1700s to 2000. Only recently has the public supported any movement to decriminalize recreational drug use or to view intoxication as a matter of personal preference rather than as a potential social harm. However, decriminalization of recreational drug use and the popularity of intoxication as a valid form of recreation is still only a recent social experiment. Public opinion after the mid-2020s appeared to be changing again.

4

Historical Overview of Criminalization and Decriminalization around the World

President Richard Nixon popularized the "War on Drugs" in the United States during the early 1970s, but the global war on drugs began much earlier during the 1800s. The United States played an important role in starting international discussions over the problem of narcotics, but it was not the first nation to push for such agreements. Since the early 1900s, the global war on drugs was encouraged by an international consensus that arose in response to the grave harms caused by the misuse of medical drugs, particularly opium-based narcotics (heroin and morphine). For 100 years, the same international meetings that discussed the rules of war, treatment of noncombatants, and trade policies also discussed the problems of drug trafficking and addiction.

At the turn of the twenty-first century, the international community faced strong marketing pressures from academics (professors) and nongovernment organizations to change priorities in the global war on drugs to favor a new approach of drug decriminalization called "harm reduction." The World Health Organization (WHO) was heavily influenced by this theory at the same time that drug decriminalization movements became more popular in the United States, Canada, and a few other European nations. Some nations responded with entirely new drug policies, which included the legalization of marijuana and decriminalization of other drugs. However, on a global level, the majority of nations in Europe and in the world opposed decriminalization—especially those who suffer most from high rates of addiction or from illegal drug trafficking by large criminal organizations.

As late as the 2020s, most countries continue to criminalize recreational drug use, production, and sales. There is also public pressure to overturn the early decriminalization laws in some European states. Most nations outside of Europe are vocally opposed to decriminalization efforts because they fear that any attempt to remove the stigma of drug use will invariably encourage more drug use, more addiction, and therefore more organized crime. Peru in South America, Kenya in Africa, Singapore in East Asia, Turkey in the Middle East, and the Russian Federation in Eastern Europe are just a few of the more vocal opponents of drug decriminalization.

The First Drug-Trafficking Laws

From the beginning of the early Middle Ages, Islamic nations in Spain, North Africa, and the Near East prohibited alcohol and recreational drug use. Drug trafficking (the transport and sales of illegal substances) was forbidden among Muslim traders, but that did not prevent illegal drugs from passing overland between China, India, and the Near East during the 1300s. Hashish and opium were the first to be abused, and after European sailors came in direct contact with India and the Far East in the 1500s, the misuse of these drugs spread overseas to the Americas and back home to European states by the 1600s. Nontherapeutic drug use among Europeans was fairly limited until the 1700s, and by that time hashish use was mostly confined to sailors in Arab ports of the Mediterranean region, and opium-use was usually only found in Chinese immigrant neighborhoods.

Islam's holy book, the Qu'ran, explicitly forbids intoxication and other addictions among its followers. In Surah Al-Ma'idah 5:90-91, Muhammad warns his followers, "You who believe, intoxicants (*khamr*) and gambling, idolatrous practices, and (divining with) arrows are repugnant acts—Satan's doing—shun them so that you may prosper." There is no explicit mention of drug use in the Qu'ran because recreational drug use was unknown in the seventh century. However, the general prohibition against intoxicants was interpreted by most Muslim scholars in the late 1200s to apply to any recreational drug use. After the problem of opium and hashish addiction began to disrupt certain urban areas, the most common conclusion among Muslim leaders was that drug abuse was a sin and that it was also criminal behavior and should be prohibited with strong punishments—most often, whipping, but occasionally with more severe corporal (bodily) punishments.

Despite these clear prohibitions, local cultural traditions from India influenced Islamic practices during the height of the Mughal and Ottoman Empires (1600s–1700s). The "hookah" is a form of pipe that uses water to filter smoke, which was used for tobacco after trade exchanges with the Americas in the late 1500s. It was also used for hashish by a minority of people. The use of the water pipe is tolerated under Islam, but its use for hashish and other drugs is generally forbidden. Modern marijuana pipes (called "bongs" when used with water) are adaptations of the hookah. A bong includes a mouthpiece attached directly to the pipe, while a hookah uses a hose between the pipe and the mouthpiece. In China, the hookah was further adapted for opium smoking. Chinese pipes do not use water to filter the smoke. The Islamic Middle East is often associated with marijuana and hashish use because of these historic connections. Nevertheless, almost all Islamic countries are opposed to decriminalization of recreational drug use.

Around 1700, the Dutch introduced pipe smoking to the Chinese, who used it for opium. This new method of consumption encouraged recreational opium smoking, which in turn led to stronger demand for the drug. Chinese Emperor Yung Cheng noticed this trend and issued an edict requiring special licenses for opium smoking to ensure that it was used only for medicinal purposes. However, these edicts were not often followed, and the demand for recreational opium did not decline at all.

In fact, illegal drug use increased after the British introduced a new mercantilist trading system between England, India, and China. British traders encouraged local cultivation of opium in India and then shipped the drug around the Indonesian peninsula to the Chinese ports in Canton. There, opium was exchanged for tea, silk, and porcelain, which would be shipped back to England. The value of this network was that the British could reap profits in two stages: one from the sales of homeland products shipped out to India and then another from the sales of Chinese goods back home. The Indian opium was used as a sort of currency to purchase the Chinese products, and since Chinese demand for opium was so high, this system was very profitable during the 1800s. The Dutch followed a similar system in their Asia ports.

The main problem with this drug-trading scheme was that the influx of opium had devastating effects on Chinese society. Within a few decades, the level of crime and corruption in and around the southern Chinese Canton port region became so widespread that it reached the notice of the Ch'ing Dynasty emperor, who lived in the capital city nearly 1,200 miles away to the north. In response, the Chinese emperor Kia King banned opium trade entirely in 1799 and also forbade its cultivation and processing. However, like the edict of his predecessor a century earlier, this new law did not stop the British from importing opium directly from India into China. By 1833, English trading vessels were moving more than 22,000 pounds of opium (1.67 million daily doses) per year.

Opium addiction destroyed the local culture as people lost interest in work, and Chinese officials were easily bribed to support their own habits. In 1839, one local Chinese official committed himself to cleaning the corruption by enforcing the long-standing prohibition against the opium trade. He tried to stop British ships from bringing opium to port. The British merchant vessels responded by calling on local military ships to force their shipments through, and that action triggered the first Opium War between the British and the local Chinese. It lasted nearly three years and resulted in the Treaty of Nanking, which gave control of the island of Hong Kong over to the British as their main trading port, where they resumed their opium trade without any noticeable interruption.

In the years that followed, the opium trade between India and Chinese increased substantially, and the impact on the economy and political corruption of local government officials continued to grow out of control, which again drew imperial attention. Soon after gaining the throne, the Tong Zhi Emperor tried to halt the opium trade, resulting in the Second Opium War from 1856 to 1860. Again, the superior British navy won the conflict, and the Treaty of Tientsin formally legalized the British opium trade within China. Many other factors contributed, but the widespread opium corruption resulted in the complete collapse of the Ch'ing Dynasty in 1908. China reverted to a loose confederation of regional warlords for nearly fifty years.

The 1912 Hague International Opium Convention

By 1900, opium had been synthesized into morphine and heroin, both of which had legitimate therapeutic purposes at that time. In addition, the coca leaves from Central America had been synthesized into cocaine. The English, Dutch, and Germans developed large pharmaceutical industries, which relied heavily on opium and coca imports.

As these legal imports of drug ingredients increased, so too did the illegal recreational use. The social problems that wracked China were beginning to be noticeable in many European port cities. By 1910, most Western nations recognized the great harm to individuals and to the medical profession caused by the improper use of therapeutic drugs. Medical associations joined forces with local law enforcement groups to develop new controls over medical drugs. Though the British, the Dutch, and the Germans gained much wealth from the medical drug trade, the side effects of drug addiction in their own countries led to the first international drug conventions in 1912.

An international convention is an agreement in which multiple nations promise to cooperate in controlling the trade of certain goods. In 1912, the International Opium Convention was signed in The Hague in the Netherlands by a dozen countries including those most affected by the opium trade: China, England including its Indian colonial government, the Netherlands (Dutch), Persia (modern Iran), Portugal, Russia, and Siam (modern Thailand). In effect, this agreement resolved the problem that triggered the opium wars in favor of the Chinese—opium trade was outlawed for any but medical purposes, requiring new registrations and record keeping, to ensure only medical professionals had access to the drugs. The agreement regulated the international sales of opium and morphine, as well as the two newly developed drugs, heroin and cocaine. Marijuana (or cannabis) was not mentioned in the agreement because it was mostly unknown to Europe at this time. The United States used this international convention as the basis for its own drug-control policies enacted by the Harrison Act of 1913.

After the First World War, all the signers of the Treaty of Versailles also signed onto this 1912 convention, raising the number of parties to this agreement to sixty. Six years later, the new League of Nations convened a second international opium convention at Geneva, Switzerland, in 1925. This time, the new agreement prohibited drug trafficking (which means the transport, sales, and production of illegal substances for recreational use) of opium, coca leaves, and "Indian hemp"—which was the new term used to describe psychoactive cannabis used for nontherapeutic purposes. Marijuana was still only little understood, but it was gaining attention in European ports and in some urban centers in the United States. The 1925 agreement was signed by more than sixty parties from all around the globe, but the United States was not a part of the League of Nations, so it did not sign. The global war on drugs was begun by non-American nations.

The Single Convention on Narcotic Drugs in 1961

From 1925 to the start of the Second World War, the international drug-trafficking agreements were updated and revised a half dozen times to include more dangerous drugs as they were developed and to entail more rigorous enforcement measures. Not all parties adhered to these agreements. The Netherlands signed the conventions and even hosted the meetings in their territories, but they enforced the rules in their own lands very poorly. After the Second World War, though, the problem of recreational drug abuse was felt more acutely in all European nations, and the Dutch began to enforce the rules much more conscientiously.

The United Nations (UN) replaced the League of Nations after the Second World War, and the United States played a more active role in international drug control. However, the main pressure for the war on drugs continued to come from Europe and other non-Western nations. In 1946, the League agreements were re-signed under the new UN Economic and Social Council in the tiny village of Lake Success, New York. After fifteen years, seventy-three states representing all the major nations in the Americas, Europe, the Middle East, and Asia came together to discuss a new agreement that would unify and update all the previous international agreements from 1912 to their present day of 1961. The result was the "Single Convention on Narcotic Drugs," which formally replaced all previous agreements and established a new system of international drug control with updated drug lists and legal recommendations.

The Preamble to the 1961 Convention began by explaining why these drug-control agreements were necessary. The opening line declared, "Concerned with the health and welfare of mankind," and while recognizing that new therapeutic drugs were invaluable in easing pain and suffering through new medical advances, the UN body also recognized "that addiction to narcotic drugs constitutes a serious evil for the individual and is fraught with social and economic danger." As the primary international body created to resolve global issues, the UN recognized that it was "their duty to prevent and combat this evil" because the only effective plans would be plans that involved coordinated international consensus.

The primary drugs targeted by the Single Convention of 1961 were opium-related drugs (those that come from the poppy plant), coca-leaf related drugs (specifically, cocaine), and cannabis-related drugs (both hashish and marijuana, which were only starting to be popular in urban centers in Europe and the United States). To clarify, the UN does not create new laws but rather establishes legal standards that it expects member states to utilize when drafting laws in their own countries. The Convention asked members to criminalize the recreational use, transport, processing, and sales of these drugs for any nontherapeutic purposes. Some drugs were deemed to have no medical value (heroin, cocaine, and cannabis) and therefore should be criminalized entirely. Article 36 explicitly asked each signer of the agreement to create laws to uphold the agreement and declare any violations as "punishable offences when committed intentionally, and that serious offences shall be liable to adequate punishment particularly by imprisonment or other penalties of deprivation of liberty."

In plain language, this meant that all nations should create criminal drug laws that imposed significant punishments for violators, including jail time. Article 38 also recommended that each member nation also provide treatment options for users who became addicted to drugs and who are most often the victims of illegal drug use. Criminalization of drug use does not mean withholding treatment options for users. From the start, the agreements that launched the global war on drugs always included recommendations for helping treat drug addiction and to help those users who fell victim to illegal drug dealers. In all these agreements, punishments for those who supply drugs and those criminal organization that exist to violate international drug-trafficking laws are always much more severe than those laws aimed at penalizing users and addicts.

Between 1961 and 1971, many new drugs were invented as part of the pharmaceutical revolution that swept across American and European industries. New forms of laboratory-synthesized stimulants, depressants, and hallucinogens (such as LSD, PCP, psilocybin, and ecstasy) had become increasingly popular both in the United States and in Europe. In 1971, the UN created a new international agreement to deal with these mood and perception-altering drugs, called the "Convention on Psychotropic Substances." Like its sister agreement from 1961, this new agreement began with the explanation that the UN was "concerned with the health and welfare of mankind" and especially recognizing the "public health and social problems resulting from the abuse of certain psychotropic substances." The 1961 and 1971 agreements covered almost all drugs that were most likely to be abused for recreational use by the general public.

Richard Nixon's Comprehensive Drug Abuse Prevention and Control Act of 1970 was largely based on the requirements of the United Nations 1961 Single Convention on Narcotic Drugs. It combined elements of both the 1961 agreement on narcotics and the upcoming 1971 agreement on psychotropics. Nixon did not originate the "War on Drugs" but was implementing a global commitment that the United States had been following since 1912. Nixon was unique because he made drug control a larger part of his election campaign promoting law and order, and that priority brought the issue of consolidated drug control laws more explicitly before the American public. Nevertheless, Nixon was also following the strong global consensus that reflected priorities of the international community. These priorities held that drug addiction causes major harm to individuals and to society and encourages crime and violence.

The baby boomer generation is identified most with the United States, but every Western nation experienced similar population increases following the Second World War. The same sorts of cultural phenomena felt by the United

States were also experienced in democratic nations of central and western Europe. Similar rates of drug experimentation among college-aged youth during the late 1960s were followed by similar renewal of anti-drug commitment during the 1980s. The "Just Say No" was an American campaign during the Reagan administration, but other nations of Europe implemented similar campaigns to protect their school-aged children from drugs.

It is difficult to assess whether the international drug-control laws were successful or not. During the 1970s and 1980s, rates of recreational drug use increased around the world. However, as with the case of modern decriminalization experiments, there is always a question of what levels those rates would have been had the international consensus against recreational drug use not been so clearly defined.

"Tolerance" and the Amsterdam Experiment

The Single Convention on Narcotic Drugs was updated in 1972 to include additional substances to its four schedules (lists) of regulated drugs. It also included more recommendations for treatment options and rehabilitation programs for drug users making it easier to give up their addiction and reenter society as useful members. There was no contradiction between criminalization of drug laws and the goal of rehabilitating users suffering from drug addiction. The laws against drug trafficking—especially illegal manufacturing, transportation, and sales—were always strict, and they sometimes overshadow other laws related to drug use. However, these laws cannot take into account actual enforcement made by the police in the neighborhoods where drug use is most common.

Amsterdam is the capital city of the Netherlands, and it provides the most famous example of a local district where criminal drug laws were not enforced in the same way that the law required. Amsterdam was a port city long before the Netherlands became an independent country. As early as the late 1300s, the district next to where the ships arrived gained a reputation for criminal behavior. Sailors coming off the boats usually headed straight toward local taverns to imbibe in all the activities that they had been missing while at sea. During the 1500s and 1600s, the Dutch were famous for strict moral codes; however, this district known as *De Wallen* was always treated separately. As long as the crimes remained within the small area of a few blocks (about 15 acres), local police would choose not to enforce any but the most flagrant violations. These districts exist in most large port cities and are usually called "red light" districts because prostitutes used to put red lanterns outside their doors to indicate their profession.

There are three red-light districts in Amsterdam. Prostitution was criminalized after the Dutch Protestant revolution in 1578 but was legalized under Napoleon's occupation in the early 1800s. Prostitution was recriminalized again in 1911, but the brothels in red-light districts of Amsterdam were mostly ignored. Wherever prostitution is most concentrated, intoxication and recreational drug use is also most common. Drug laws were mostly unenforced in the district areas of *De Wallen*, *Singelgebied*, and *Ruysdaelkade*. The Netherlands is a very small country, about the size of Maryland, and the people and culture share many common values, so this means that there was general agreement within the population to leave these districts unpatrolled.

During the 1960s, Dutch college students experimented with the same types of protests as students in France, England, and America—like riots elsewhere, these were often fueled by intoxication and drug use. One famous student riot in Amsterdam in 1966 brought strong police reactions, and media images of the conflict surprised many Dutch residents who thought it looked like an excessive use of force. In response, local police met with local politicians and developed an unofficial policy of "tolerance" in certain districts, which meant that as long as the obvious crimes (like marijuana sales and prostitution) were kept indoors, and off the streets, the police would not enforce the laws. Small amounts of marijuana were allowed to be bought and sold in Amsterdam coffee shops, and there was no risk of arrests.

The Amsterdam policy was not decriminalization. Drugs and prostitution remained illegal; however, the 1970s tolerance policy (called *gedoogbeleid*, in Dutch) served as a compromise between rising student drug use and global criminalization of all drugs. The idea argued by local politicians was that students often experiment with intoxication and marijuana use when they are young, but they eventually give up these habits when they get older and assume greater responsibilities in their jobs and for their families. As long as the experimentation was kept separate from really "hard" drugs, like opium, heroin, and cocaine, young people could be allowed to experiment without permanently falling into a lifestyle of crime and drug addiction.

The local tolerance policy was made a national policy in 1975, which officially distinguished between the more potent "hard" drugs like cocaine, heroin, and amphetamines and "soft" drugs, like marijuana. The goal of these policies was to create a safe space for such experimentation without involving criminal penalties. The guiding principle was that drug use should be limited to soft drugs (marijuana), kept to personal use alone (5 grams or less) and should be limited to specific districts (marijuana could only be sold in certain coffee shops).

The program was quite popular among the Dutch, but it did not end up achieving the results they had hoped for. Almost immediately after the introduction of the tolerance policy, other more potent drugs like heroin and cocaine began appearing on the streets. International drug rings from China began importing heroin directly from Hong Kong and Singapore, making the price of heroin cheaper than marijuana and amphetamines. By 1980, there were 10,000 heroin addicts in the small districts of Amsterdam. In 1985, ecstasy appeared on the scene, and one-night club was earning more than $60,000 a month selling it to its clients.

Nevertheless, Amsterdam became famous worldwide as the one place in Europe where marijuana (and prostitution) was tolerated. By the 1990s, Amsterdam became a tourist destination for young people who wanted to experiment with drug use without fear of arrest. The influx of marijuana tourists became a nuisance for the local residents, and Amsterdam began passing a series of laws limiting the extent of public drug use or public intoxication. Prostitution was officially legalized in 1999 and regulated with restrictions on where brothels could be located and who could work in them. However, drug use became more restricted in public areas. The number of coffee shops legally selling marijuana was slowly reduced from 400 in 1993 to 283 in 2000 and 164 in 2024.

Throughout the twentieth century, and even alongside Dutch toleration policies, laws against drug dealers remained harsh—especially for the hard drugs and for criminal organizations. Legally, individuals could buy small amounts of drugs, but in order to supply the coffee shops, certain organizations had to procure large amounts of drugs, which was always illegal. The tolerance policies indirectly encouraged a growing drug culture supported by large criminal organizations. In the 2020s, the Netherlands continues to officially outlaw marijuana use and other drugs, even though the police will not enforce these laws if the amounts of drugs involved are less than 5 grams.

Harm Reduction in Portugal, Spain, and Italy

By the 2020s, the Dutch people continued to have mixed views on their own tolerance policies, especially as the national consensus faced disruption from increasing drug tourism, immigration, and the predominance of criminal drug organizations. However, the Dutch example was long in development before the 2020s, and between the 1990s and 2010s, their tolerance policy acquired a new label with the endorsement of many professors and was experimentally adopted by other European governments. Portugal was the first European state to apply the Amsterdam model of tolerance into a new national model of decriminalization, which became known as "harm reduction."

Portugal followed most of the same trends as other European nations during the twentieth century and adapted itself to each of the international conventions related to drug control. Like Holland, the Portuguese had considerable experience with colonial trade routes in East Asia, which meant that its sailors were also exposed to opium, hashish, and (eventually) cocaine. Around the same time as the United States, Portugal adopted its first comprehensive drug-control law that criminalized the manufacture, sales, and possession of nontherapeutic drugs. Users were potentially subject to jail sentences of up to two years, and drug traffickers could face up to eight years in prison. However, it was not until 1971 that Portugal finally ratified the Single Convention on Narcotics Drugs, which the UN had passed a decade earlier.

Portugal faced a political revolution in 1974, and their youth movement exploded in experimental drug use in a similar way as other nations during that decade. Some of the youth organizations involved with the revolution proposed the idea of drug decriminalization as early as 1976, but it was rejected. In 1973, Portugal passed a new drug law implementing the 1971 UN Convention on Psychotropic Substances, which targeted synthetic stimulants, depressants, hallucinogens, and other mood-altering drugs.

In 1988, the UN adopted its last major international drug convention, which was titled "Convention against Illicit Traffic in Narcotic Drugs and Psychoactive Substances." This agreement specifically targeted international crime organizations that specialized in drug trafficking—drug cartels operating out of Southeast Asia, Central America, and the Middle East were responsible for most of the drug trade moving into and out of Europe and the United States.

Around the same time, heroin addiction became a serious problem in Portugal, largely as a result of the organized crime drug trade. Since heroin involves the use of needles, and needle sharing among addicted users increases the risk of spreading AIDS or HIV, the Portuguese government began viewing drug addiction more as a health problem than as a crime problem.

Spain and Portugal are both located on the same Iberian Peninsula, though they have a long history of cultural separation. In 1992, Spain implemented new drug laws that decriminalized possession of small amounts of any drug, as long as it was not used publicly, and the quantity was small enough to ensure it would not be used for sales. Italy adopted a similar measure in 1993. These were legalized versions of Amsterdam's tolerance policy. When Portugal enacted the new UN Convention, they took the Dutch drug-control model one step further. Concluding that the worst effects of the illegal drug trade were how it brought experimental users into direct contact with experienced criminals, Portugal established policies to help protect these experimental (or occasional) drug users—both marijuana and heroin users—so they would not "be labelled or marginalized" and unintentionally pushed closer into a criminal subculture. What distinguished Portugal from Spain, Italy, or the Netherlands is that they followed this reasoning by shifting its entire drug-control programs from the Ministry of Justice to the Ministry of Health. In effect, doctors in Portugal had as much say over the fate of drug users as the police.

The last step in the decriminalization process came in 1999 when the Portuguese Parliament passed the "National Strategy for the Fight Against Drugs." Unlike Spain and Italy, which continued to criminalize buying and selling of drugs, Portuguese authorities took into account whether the dealers were addicted to their own drugs. Drug manufacturing, possession, use, transport, and sales were still prohibited, but the first agencies to evaluate the offense were administrative bodies—criminal law enforcement was not involved. If the violator possessed only small amounts of drugs for their own use, and if they only used at home (not in public or near children), the police would not be involved. If the violator possessed large amounts (more than ten doses) or manufactured or sold drugs to others for the purpose of earning income, law enforcement would become involved leading to penalties with potential fines and jail time. This was intended to target organized drug dealing.

If the violator suffered from drug addiction and committed any of these crimes to satisfy that dependency, authorities would mandate treatment and other programs to try and rehabilitate the offender so they could return to society. These new laws came into effect in 2001. Neither Spain nor Portugal legalized drugs, but both nations decriminalized most drugs based on the policy of harm reduction. Portuguese cities, such as Lisbon and Porto, have legal marijuana dispensaries for medical use. Their legal models are very closely aligned with Amsterdam's practices of selective enforcement.

Harm Reduction in the Americas: Oregon and British Columbia

Other influential models for European decriminalization efforts came from examples of various states in the United States, which began pushing for marijuana legalization (not decriminalization). Just after Amsterdam's tolerance policy was announced in 1970, several American states also passed laws decriminalizing small amounts of marijuana. Oregon was the first in 1973, followed by Alaska (1975) and then Maine, Minnesota, North Carolina, and Mississippi between 1976 and 1978. At that point, the movement toward decriminalization halted in the United States, and President Reagan's "Just Say No" campaigns gained more traction. No further efforts to decriminalize or legalize marijuana occurred until the late 1990s.

The effort to legalize medical marijuana began in the United States in the 1990s and was mostly used as a first step toward complete legalization. If users could legally buy marijuana for medical purposes, it was much less of a hurdle to legalize the drug for all purposes—including recreational use. European nations did not push medical use of marijuana until much later, beginning after 2021. Their drug-control laws still relied primarily on the criminal model—with Portugal being the only exception (when they transferred drug enforcement from the police to the health ministry). However, in the United States, the movement for medical use was always a movement aiming for eventual legalization—with no criminal penalties at all (either for using or for dealing, manufacturing, storage, or in-state transportation).

President Obama was elected in 2012, and that was also the pivotal year in medical marijuana legalization both in the United States and elsewhere in the world. The massive marketing campaigns on social media, and other large-scale contributions to pro-legalization political campaigns served to shift public opinion on marijuana and the "drug war" very quickly—over the course of only five years. Washington and Colorado were the first states to completely legalize marijuana for recreational use. The next year, Uruguay became the first nation in the world to legalize marijuana in 2013.

Two years later, Oregon and Alaska followed suit during midterm elections. In the meantime, in Europe, the Czech Republic joined Belgium and several other Baltic nations to more fully adopt the Portuguese model of decriminalization. News of marijuana legalization in the United States encouraged other European nations to begin considering legalization for medical use. Between 2016 and 2020, fourteen American states legalized marijuana, plus three American territories. Several European nations began passing laws legalizing medical marijuana in 2021 (Austria, Croatia, Denmark, Estonia, Georgia, Greece, Italy, the Netherlands, Norway, Poland, Romania, Switzerland, and Turkey). The Ukraine legalized medical marijuana in 2024 in part because of the policy change made Ukraine appear more progressive, which could influence American lawmakers' decisions to providing additional funding for its war with Russia. Officially, Ukrainian lawmakers stated that medical marijuana might have potential for assisting thousands of people affected by post-traumatic stress disorder resulting from the country's war with Russia.

The most dramatic changes in European drug laws occurred in the 2020s. The state of Oregon decriminalized all drugs in small amounts in 2020, and the Canadian Province of British Columbia experimented with a similar policy in 2023. Malta became the first European nation to legalize cannabis for recreational use, followed by Luxembourg, and Germany became the largest nation to legalize the drug in 2024 and was later followed by Brazil. Nixon's War on Drugs did not influence European drug controls. Quite the opposite, it was the American legalization of marijuana that appeared to most influence European policies.

International Debate over Cannabis in 2020

In many respects, the trends of marijuana decriminalization and legalization since 2000 seem to suggest that the entire world is giving up on the century-old global war on drugs. However, in this case, appearances are deceiving. In late 2023, there were proposals for decriminalizing and legalizing marijuana in many European nations, including France, Ireland, Czechia, and Belgium. However, as 2024 reached its midpoint, these movements suffered from increasingly negative public reactions.

In the United States, Oregon repealed its 2020 law that decriminalized all drugs in 2024. The increase of crime, rates of drug addiction, and deaths from drug overdoses were mostly responsible. In the Canadian Province of British Columbia, the public pressure to overturn its short-term experiment of legalizing all drugs began to emerge only eighteen months after the experimental law was implemented. There was also renewed pressure within the Netherlands to restrict its once-famous policies of toleration.

Despite many new national laws that promoted harm reduction policies, the majority of countries in the world still strongly oppose any effort to reduce criminal penalties for recreational drug use, drug manufacturing, and drug trafficking. The general consensus among these nations is that harm reduction policies increase drug use and therefore increase addiction rates, and as a result the policy only feeds more drug trafficking and funds international criminal organizations.

Since the 2000s, the World Health Organization (WHO) has been heavily influenced by harm reduction theories. These theories have been promoted by academics and NGOs that are funded by pro-legalization advocates. George Soros and his Open Societies Foundations donated more than $32 billion dollars to promote these research projects. Other technology billionaires like Richard Branson, Bill Gates, and Mark Zuckerberg also contributed many billions of dollars to promote new global agendas. In 2020, based on the dominant theories among professors in support of harm reduction, the WHO recommended six new changes to the 1961 UN Single Convention on Narcotics.

The debate over the WHO recommendations revealed a great divide in the global community over the issue of harm reduction and decriminalization. All of the recommendations were rejected except one, which deleted cannabis from the Schedule IV list of controlled substances. (Schedule IV is used to identify ingredients that could be used to produce other dangerous drugs.) Even this single measure passed by only one vote, and those who opposed the measure voiced their disappointment in very strong terms. The deletion had no impact on global criminalization because cannabis is also listed as a Schedule I drug, which means that it is still listed as a dangerous drug, and all those nations (and states) that passed laws legalizing marijuana continue to stand in violation of the 1961 international agreement. The purpose of the 2020 amendment was to make it easier to conduct more research on marijuana as a medical drug.

Virtually all Muslim nations opposed all WHO recommendations entirely—Afghanistan, Algeria, Egypt, Iran, Libya, Pakistan, and Turkey. They were joined by numerous non-Muslim states in Africa, Central and Eastern Asia, as well as states from Central and South America. The Russian Federation spoke for a cohort of twenty-nine other member states who strongly opposed any changes to existing conventions on narcotics and psychoactive drugs. Echoing the Russian viewpoints, the Asian island nation of Singapore warned that deleting cannabis from Schedule IV "fundamentally goes against our principles of consensus and evidence-based drug policy-making, and threatens to undermine our duty to protect public health and welfare."

Other nations feared that any appearance of weakening international consensus against drug abuse would cause great global harm. Hungary argued that "cannabis has a strong addictive potential which is being continuously proven by the sharp increase of cannabis use itself [and] ... In the light of all these clear facts, the attempt to reschedule cannabis is an extremely irresponsible act in our view." This was joined by the African nation of Kenya, whose representative explained, "The vote negates the letter and spirit of the international drug-control regime." The Egyptian delegate followed by saying, "Egypt is deeply concerned that the outcome of today's voting may be interpreted that these substances are no longer harmful to health which consequently defies the purpose of the scheduling regime. Moreover, it might act as a catalyst for more illicit production and trafficking of cannabis and cannabis related substances."

Other nations that suffer from drug cartels operating inside their borders also voiced similar sorts of strong disapproval. In South America, Peru maintained that "the universal restriction regarding cannabis and its resins" was necessary "in order to prevent the legal basis for the control of the cultivation of the cannabis plant from being eliminated." In Central Asia, Kyrgyzstan began their comments by admitting that more than 25,000 acres of land in their own country are used to grow illegal cannabis, and as a result 80 percent of their population is addicted to hashish. Their government was too weak to fight the drug cartels in their own nation and feared that weakening the international controls would greatly harm their country. The Kyrgyzstan delegate used this 2020 debate as an opportunity to declare that their nation would begin to impose "stricter or more stringent control measures than those provided for by these international contracts." Though many modern Western nations were being influenced by the pro-decriminalization arguments of harm reduction, the rest of the world outside of Europe continues to strongly support the international war on drugs. (All quotes come from the "UN Commission on Drugs Statements on WHO Five Recommendations, After Deleting Cannabis from Schedule IV List," 2020)

Drug Use as a Human Right

Libertarian ideology argues that the rights of the individual should always take preference over the rights of the state over matters of behavior that cause minimal harm to others. Libertarians do not believe that recreational drug use causes any significant harm to others, and so they prefer legalization or decriminalization of drugs. They claim that recreational drug use is a human right.

European nations rarely agree with libertarian views on politics, but they are very sympathetic to respecting human rights. Most European nations generally support social-welfare views of governance, where state agencies have considerable authority over social-welfare issues, including health and drug-related behaviors. As a practical matter, state governments that want to increase their influence over individual behaviors may make use of libertarian human rights arguments to justify harm reduction or decriminalization policies because both of these practices result in greater government oversight.

Generally, in Europe and in Canada, harm reduction policies are justified in terms of scientific theory and other forms of academic support. These nations usually refer to "evidence-based" policies in order to distinguish them from previous "morality-based" policies, in which intentional intoxication was judged to be morally destructive. However, in other non-Western nations where the central government has become corrupted by large criminal organizations that specialize in drug trafficking (called drug cartels), the human rights arguments can be even more useful. Nations in Central and South America share no ideologies with libertarians, and they do not make claims of "evidence-based" arguments to justify drug decriminalization. Nevertheless, nations like Mexico, Uruguay, Columbia, Jamaica, and Brazil still rely on libertarian-based human rights arguments to explain why their nations passed laws that directly violate international drug-control agreements.

Mexico, Columbia, and other Central and South American nations have struggled with the problem of very large drug cartels operating within their countries for nearly fifty years. The US Drug Enforcement Agency (DEA) identified two competing cartels in Mexico that are most responsible for trafficking into the United States (Sinaloa Cartel and Jalisco Cartel). Similar cartels operate in Columbia (Medellin, Cali, Norte der Calle) and in every other Central American nation, as well as in four other South American nations (Bolivia, Ecuador, Peru, and Venezuela). In addition, numerous Asian cartels transport drugs and their ingredients (called precursors) from China and Southeast Asia directly into Mexico, where they are trafficked into the United States using established cartel-smuggling routes.

Drug cartels do not necessarily want legalized drugs because that would mean they would have to compete with other legal drug suppliers. However, they do prefer legalized drugs for medical use because then they can manufacture marijuana openly and then claim that the cannabis (or coca leaves or opium poppy) fields are used for medical purposes only—when, in fact, they are used mostly to supply illegal markets. Every Central American nation legalized medical marijuana in the 2010s or 2020s. In some cases, such as Mexico and Brazil, their national supreme courts used language of human rights justifying marijuana consumption for personal use as a constitutional right. Mexico decriminalized marijuana through a court ruling in 2021, and Brazil decriminalized the same way in 2024 (Table 4.1).

Though European nations generally avoid claims that recreational drug use is a human right, the academic community (professors) frequently use such language. Pro-legalization and decriminalization lobbying efforts of NGOs and libertarian supporters such as George Soros and his Open Society Foundation regularly argue that the war on drugs is a violation of basic human rights. These messages are echoed on American social media platforms.

The massive scope of these public influences means that international bodies like the European Union (EU) Drugs Agency and the European Monitoring Centre for Drugs and Drug Addiction (EMCDDA) often use language that reflects these same social justice concerns. In actual practice, though, very few governments are willing to justify their harm reduction policies by arguing that their citizens have a basic right to use any psychoactive drug for recreational purpose or that they have a right to develop habits of addiction that lead to antisocial and criminal behaviors in their communities. For this reason, though the harm reduction language of the 2010s often reflects human rights sympathies, all European nations continue to criminalize drug trafficking and also prohibit most forms of recreational drug use.

Conclusion: Legal Dilemma of Harm Reduction and Drug Trafficking

Decriminalization of drug laws usually means that individual users who grow, possess, and buy or sell their drugs are allowed to do so only for their own personal use. Drug use and drug possession are not counted as crimes, so individual users do not fear being arrested or labeled as a criminal for their recreational drug use. Most advocates for harm reduction policies argue that drug use and addiction should be treated as a health problem and not as a criminal problem.

At the same time, every nation that decriminalizes drugs for personal use also carries stiff penalties for illegal drug trafficking. In almost every European state that implements harm reduction strategies, if the quantity of drugs is greater than that necessary for personal use (usually about ten times the single dose amount), possession is considered a criminal offense. In every European nation, if there is evidence that the cultivation, storage, or transportation of drugs is

Table 4.1 National Drug Policies by Type as of 2024.

Number of States with Drug Policies by Type (Percentage of Whole)			
	Legalization[i]	**Decriminalization**[ii]	**Criminalization**[iii]
European Union	1 (3) / 7%	15 (16) / 40%	19 / 48%
All drugs	Germany[iv]	Armenia, Austria, Belgium, Bulgaria, Croatia, Czechia, Denmark, Estonia, Georgia, Italy, Malta,[v] Moldova, the Netherlands, Portugal, Spain, Switzerland	Algeria, Cyprus, Finland, Hungary, Ireland, Jordan, Kosovo, Lebanon, Latvia, Lithuania,[vi] Luxembourg,[vii] Montenegro, Norway, Poland,[viii] Romania, Slovakia, Sweden, Turkey, Ukraine
Cannabis only	Malta, Luxembourg		
International trafficking	None	None	All nations
United States	24 (25) / 48% (50%)	7 / 14%	19 / 38%
All drugs	None	OR[ix] (2020–24)	All States (2024)
Cannabis only	AK, AZ, CA, CO, CT, DE, IL, OH, MA, MD, ME, MI, MO, MN, MT, NJ, NM, NV, NY, OR, RI, VT, VA, WA, DC	HI, LA, MS, NC, ND, NE,[x] NH	AL, AR, FL, GA,[xi] ID, IN,[xii] IA, KS, KY, OK, PA,[xiii] SC, SD,[xiv] TN,[xv] TX,[xvi] UT, WV, WI,[xvii] WY
Interstate trafficking	None	None	All states

Source: All facts and figures were compiled by Aharon Zorea, based on the European Union Drugs Agency (EUDA) Report, "Penalties at a Glance" (updated February 16, 2024), and on each state drug-policy histories posted on their respective government websites.

Note: i. Legalization means that small amounts of certain drugs for personal use are legal and will not cause arrest or any administrative citations—similar to decriminalized nonenforcement.

ii. Decriminalization means that small amounts may result in administrative citations but no criminal record. Personal drug use inside residences is not enforced in most EU nations.

iii. Criminalization means any drug amount may result in citation or possible jail time (though criminal charges may still be dismissed, suspended or dropped for first-time offenders who take an approved drug treatment program).

iv. Cannabis legalization and decriminalization of other drugs in 2024.

v. Non-cannabis drugs decriminalized.

(Continued)

Table 4.1 (Continued)

vi. Lithuania re-criminalized all recreational drugs in 2017 (first European nation to recriminalize in twenty-first century).

vii. Non-cannabis recreational drugs (cannabis was legalized in 2023).

viii. Most criminal cases are dismissed for small amounts.

ix. Oregon briefly decriminalized small amounts of all drugs from 2020 to 2024. The legalization was repealed in 2024.

x. First-time offenders only; repeat offenders charged with criminal offense.

xi. Some cities of Georgia have decriminalized marijuana: Atlanta, Clarkston, Forest Park, Savannah, South Fulton, and Statesboro; some counties decriminalized marijuana: Fulton County and Macon-Bibb County.

xii. Decriminalized in Marion County.

xiii. Decriminalized in Philadelphia and Pittsburgh.

xiv. Recreational cannabis use was legalized in 2021 but overturned by State Supreme Court as unconstitutional in 2021.

xv. First-offense possession results in probation (not prison).

xvi. Refusal to prosecute for quantities less than 112gr in cities of Houston, Dallas, San Antonio, Austin, and in Travis County.

xvii. Decriminalized in cities of Milwaukee and Madison.

carried out by criminal organizations, the criminal penalties are significantly increased.

The legalization of personal use and the continued criminalization of drug trafficking creates a logical and legal dilemma. How do legal users obtain their drugs if the large-scale manufacturing and sales that are necessary to satisfy consumer demands continue to be outlawed? This is a problem that Amsterdam's tolerance policies were never able to address. This problem only grew as Holland's drug tourism increased. The result is that criminal drug cartels in the Netherlands grew at faster rates than the rates of individual drug use. This dilemma is also faced by Portugal, Spain, Italy, and any other nation that permits the possession and use of small amounts of illegal drugs but has not legalized drug trafficking. Only Germany, Malta, and Luxembourg have legalized marijuana, and no countries have legalized all drugs.

The harm reduction policy also suffers from the problem of addiction itself. As legal drug use increases (perhaps cannabis only), statistics show that all forms of recreational drug use increase as well. With the partial exception of the temporary decriminalization experiments in Oregon and the Canadian province of British Columbia, no nation has legalized all drugs. Even Oregon and British Columbia continued to criminalize drug trafficking of large quantities. There is no way to resolve the legal contradiction of harm reduction without also legalizing all recreational drug use. Harm reduction policies became popular during the 2010s, but there has been no sustained effort to legalize all recreational drug use. By the 2020s, many nations (and states) have begun to reconsider the extent of their harm-reduction strategies in part because of the legalization dilemma.

5

Specific Decriminalization Movements in the United States

The movement to decriminalize drugs is the most recent form of criminal justice reform in the United States. However, the goal of finding alternatives to incarceration (jail time) is more than 100 years old. It is, ironically, motivated by the same goals that prompted policymakers of the late 1700s originally to build prisons for incarceration instead of inflicting physical punishments. The history of crime and punishment in the United States has traditionally been guided by a desire to treat victims fairly and treat convicted criminals with compassion. With very few exceptions, this has been true for those who commit property crimes, crimes of violence, and drug-related offenses.

During colonial times, judges relied mostly on forms of physical abuse to punish lawbreakers. Convicted criminals could be sentenced to being whipped, shamed, or were sent into exile and in extreme cases were sentenced to death. Almost no one was sentenced to jail except as they awaited their trials. After the American Revolution, the new Republican penal system moved away from physical abuse because it seemed a violation of basic human rights. Incarceration and prison were introduced as models of modern penal reform. The variety of punishment options continued to increase during the 1900s to the extent that modern prisoners face many different forms of correction that do not always involve incarceration. Punishments for drug-related crimes usually consider diagnoses of mental illness, extent of addiction, and other socioeconomic factors of the lawbreaker to determine whether incarceration, treatment, or both will be most effective. In the modern criminal justice system, it is rarely as easy as simply identifying the crime and then punishing the criminal.

Movements to decriminalize drugs in the twenty-first century are just the latest experiments in a long history of penal reform. The goal of decriminalization (and legalization) is to deal more compassionately with addicted users and to encourage more productive lifestyle choices. Treating drug abuse as a health issue means using fewer criminal punishments like jail time. Recent researchers refer to this policy approach as "harm reduction" because it seeks to find the least harm to the user and to society. However, during the early 2000s, the movement to decriminalize certain drugs joined together with separate but related movements. One movement sought to reclassify marijuana as a non-harmful drug (legalization). The legalization movement is not the same as harm reduction, but the combination of legalization and harm reduction movements led to a variety of different policy options that greatly changed the criminal justice system, especially after the 2010s. These movements merged around 2020 to bring about the first statewide decriminalization policy in the United States when Oregon decriminalized all recreational drugs in small amounts.

Both drug decriminalization and legalization movements are experiments in criminal reform. Like their predecessor reform movements that date back to around the start of our country during the late 1780s, the current reforms will only be tested by the passage of time. Every new reform movement is launched with high hopes, but almost always they are faced with unintended consequences that lead to significant changes and alterations (usually after about thirty–fifty years of actual practice). The eventual conclusion of current drug decriminalization and legalization movements may not be fully understood for many decades.

Theory of Criminal Punishment in the United States

The earliest forms of criminal punishment in the American colonies were carried over from the European homelands and were mostly based on English common law. (Common law refers to the traditions developed by previous court decisions made over the span of hundreds of years.) During the colonial period up to 1776, most Americans lived in small rural communities with only hundreds or at most a few thousand people living together. Lawbreakers were easily identified, and most punishments involved some degree of physical abuse. Jails were used only to detain suspects until they could await trial and receive sentencing.

Criminal penalties were based on the severity of the offense and were generally applied immediately, ranging from fines to public shaming to corporal punishments such as whipping or branding. Exile (which means the violator is cast out of the community) and capital punishment (execution) were reserved for the most serious offenses. In cases of crimes involving debts, violators might be sentenced to a form of "house arrest" where they were placed in a jail during the evenings, but they were still able to leave the jailhouse during the day in order to work off their debts.

By the time of the American Revolution, the criminal justice system in the United States held four objectives for their legal punishments:

1. to defend the community from the lawbreaker (defense);
2. to deter others from engaging in the same crimes as the lawbreaker (deterrence);
3. to restore the losses that were created as a result of the crime (restitution); and
4. to reform the lawbreaker so that they would not commit the same crimes again (reformation).

Each type of punishment was intended to meet one or more of these objectives. For example, placing someone in stocks (where the hands and feet are locked in a wooden vice to prevent movement) satisfies the second and fourth objectives. Public shaming was intended to show the rest of the community what happens when you break the law and that shame should prevent others from committing those crimes. At the same time, discomforts of being locked in stocks should teach the lawbreaker not to repeat the same crime. These objectives would also be met through public whipping, branding, or other physical punishments. Punishment of a fine for property crimes could satisfy the third and fourth objectives: the amount of the fine might be used to restore the property to the person who suffered the loss, and an additional amount of money would be charged to teach the violator not to be so careless with other people's property in the future. Lastly, exile and executions were intended mostly to satisfy the first and second objectives. If the lawbreaker is no longer in the community (through exile or death), the community is safe from their future crimes. Also, the severity of the punishments should teach others not to engage in those sorts of crimes. The death penalty was not used to reform the prisoner (it is too late after death) but was used to discourage others from committing similar crimes.

During colonial times, the communities were small, and the lawbreakers were mostly easy to identify, so the punishments were delivered quickly. There was no need for long-term jails.

The Penitentiary as a New Type of Criminal Reform

In English common law, prisons were usually reserved for political prisoners. The king would arrest someone who threatened to undermine his power and hide them away in a prison cell—sometimes for years. The prisoner might be given a trial, but more often they would stay confined until the king died, until they died, or until the king secretly executed them. For this reason, prisons were rarely found in the colonial communities, especially around the time of the American Revolution. Americans did not like any symbols of the king's power.

Americans generally believed that holding political prisoners was a violation of natural rights, and our constitution explicitly forbade "bills of attainer" (i.e., when a group of people are outlawed without a trial), and it also guarantees a host of rights to ensure fair and equal process of law, such as rights of grand jury, indictments, protections against search and seizure, the right to attorney, right to free speech and silence, trial by jury, and many other protections found in Article III of the US Constitution and the Bill of Rights (the first ten Amendments). From its beginning, our new American government planned a criminal justice system that treated each suspected lawbreaker with fairness and equality and prohibited any use of criminal laws as a tool for harming political opponents. Legal practices that seemed like an abuse of governmental power were opposed in the same way that American revolutionaries had opposed the English king.

In addition, the Eighth Amendment guaranteed against "cruel and unusual punishments." This means that if, through the course of fair and equal criminal due process, a person is found guilty of breaking the law, then the punishment must be compassionate to the lawbreaker and also, in some way, be helpful for the rest of society. Corporal punishment was legal in the late 1700s, but only if the physical penalties could protect society or help encourage others to avoid crime and to help reform the criminal. Punishments should not be used as a display of government power to inflict harm. As such, the use of torture and the unnecessary infliction of suffering was prohibited. This also meant that convicted criminals must be treated with respect for their basic human dignity.

The first prisons in the United States were developed shortly after the American Revolution by religious missionaries seeking to find new alternatives to corporal punishments. After a short-lived experiment of housing convicted criminals in an abandoned mine shaft in Connecticut, the first two prisons in America were built in the late 1810s and 1820s in Pennsylvania and New York. The Pennsylvania model began as an experimental wing added onto an old city jail (previously used for short-term durations only), where sixteen prisoners were held in complete isolation in solitary cells. The idea behind the experiment was borrowed from religious monasteries—if inmates were completely excluded from society for a period of years, their lives could be permanently reformed, much like a religious conversion.

These early prison experiments were called "penitentiaries" because the prisoners were encouraged to be penitent (meaning they should feel sorrow for having done wrong and then promise to live a reformed life thereafter). Prisoners were sent to these institutions by the state to be reformed. The "Pennsylvania System" encouraged such extreme isolation that prisoners were required to live in silence twenty-four hours a day and were even given masks whenever they left the cells so that they would not be able to interact with other people. Prisoners were given a Bible when they first arrived, and afterward their only conversations were with prison ministers preaching to them.

Meanwhile, in upstate New York, another prison was developed in the late 1810s by a group of Quaker missionaries. They also began by using isolation techniques but later moved in a different direction and encouraged prisoners to use their time to work together in peaceful quiet and harmony. This "Auburn System" combined fresh air, exercise, and communal labor as necessary ingredients for individual rehabilitation. It still required silence most of the time, but it followed an opposite theory of rehabilitation as the Pennsylvania system because Auburn encouraged a sense of interpersonal community between inmates inside the prison, whereas Pennsylvania encouraged individual repentance and isolation.

Leaders and experts in criminal reform came from all over the world to visit both the Pennsylvania and New York penitentiaries as models for more enlightened prison reforms in their home countries. The French social commentator Alexis de Tocqueville and the English novelist Charles Dickens both visited these prisons in person and wrote about them. Millions of dollars were spent building new prisons in other states and in other countries, all based on the designs of one or the other of these two American experiments. The Pennsylvania prison complex cost more than $780,000 and was one of the most expensive buildings in the country at the time. Americans were committed to more enlightened forms of criminal punishment.

Both of these prisons, and the many prisons that were quickly built during the 1830s as copies of these two models, were publicized as humanitarian reform efforts. Instead of physically abusing lawbreakers with whipping or branding, they were given intensive reeducation to encourage inmates to reenter society as productive members. Instead of relying mostly on exile or execution for major offenses, serious crimes could be dealt with through long prison terms. Incarceration (jail time) was recognized as the latest reform effort during the mid-1800s. An extended stay in prison promised an opportunity for individual redemption and change, which reflected the new republican values of the

American democratic experiment as well as the religious priorities of the Second Great Awakening.

Later Waves of Criminal Justice Reform

Monastery-like prisons were welcomed as the most advanced reform in the 1830s, but that cultural fashion did not last long. As a practical matter, almost every new reform usually leads to new problems, which require another reform effort to resolve them. These new problems are called "unintended consequences."

During the 1860s and 1870s, prison labor gangs were implemented as a reaction to the problems of solitary confinement that had not been expected by earlier reformers. Instead of encouraging spiritual reform, living in complete isolation often caused prisoners to go insane. By the time of the Civil War, after thirty years of experimentation, most experts in criminal punishment viewed long-term solitary confinement as a form of cruelty. Instead, they recommended housing prisoners in large common rooms and then sending them outside of the prison to work every day in work gangs to promote community and productivity. Chain gangs were viewed as a reform alternative to individual confinement only.

Over time, the work gangs produced their own unintended consequences. Large common rooms were soon described as "seminaries of crime" rather than monasteries of reform—with older criminals teaching the younger ones how not to get caught in the future. Also, some prisons were making a lot of money from their prison laborers, and during an era of industrialization and a rising labor movement in the 1880s, these practices were heavily criticized.

The public viewed sentences of forced labor as a form of exploitation, so another reform movement in the 1890s sought to end chain gangs, and state governments responded by building larger and more durable prisons to handle large populations safely. Escape-proof prisons with clean cells, better-quality food, and new recreation yards became the new standard of prison reform during the 1930s and 1940s.

Also beginning in the early 1900s, psychologists were brought in to perform regular checks on inmates, and their mental health was monitored as closely as their physical health. New discoveries of genetics and the importance of family histories led to another criminal reform movement in which repeat offenders were categorized according to their family background and natural disposition to crime. One expression of this movement was to sterilize prisoners (as well as others in psychiatric hospitals who were deemed to be "feebleminded") as a scientific solution to the social problem of crime. Sterilization meant that the inmates would no longer be able to have children, and experts believed that would help protect future society from the corrupted genes that caused criminal behaviors.

A US Supreme Court case, *Buck v. Bell* (1927), upheld the constitutionality of forced sterilization and ruled that it did not violate the Eighth Amendment prohibition against "cruel and unusual punishments." In writing the Court's opinion, Justice Oliver Wendell Holmes explained that "experience has shown that heredity plays an important part in the transmission of insanity, imbecility, &c." and "if incapable of procreating, might be discharged with safety and become self-supporting with benefit to themselves and to society." He concluded, "It is better for all the world if, instead of waiting to execute degenerate offspring for crime or to let them starve for their imbecility, society can prevent those who are manifestly unfit from continuing their kind." In this particular case, he ruled that Carrie Buck should be sterilized because "three generations of imbeciles are enough."

The sterilization reform movement was strong in the 1920s and 1930s, but it also fell out of public favor after the Second World War. When stories of Nazi atrocities in Germany were compared with American stories of perfectly normal inmates being subjected to medical procedures against their will, the public again became horrified by the old "reform" practices. This public awareness led to new reform options for handling prisoners.

During the 1950s, many doctors and psychologists believed that criminal behaviors were the result of various forms of mental illness. One of the solutions (at the time) was a frontal lobotomy—which is a procedure in which some of the brain tissues were deliberately cut in order to limit designated brain operations related to emotions. Thousands of lobotomies were performed in psychiatric wards and in certain prison wards. The goal was to help inmates by making it more difficult for them to grow angry and commit crimes of passion (or to fall into depression). Again, like the sterilization movement before it, all forms of involuntary surgeries such as frontal lobotomies were discouraged by the mid-1960s, and they fell out of practice as new reform efforts emerged to take their place.

These and many other medical solutions to criminal behaviors rose in popularity at some point during the twentieth century, and they were all later condemned as inhumane, harmful, or otherwise disrespectful to the health and dignity of inmates later in the century. Many millions of dollars were spent on these efforts, and each new reform was motivated with a sincere desire to help convicted criminals through rehabilitation, to prevent new generations from becoming criminals, and to protect society from harms caused by crime.

These reforms may be viewed as barbaric in the twenty-first century, but at the time, they were each viewed as scientifically justified (evidence-based) and were always promoted as being the most helpful for inmates and the best way for protecting society at large. This process of reform continues today. Researchers still have not discovered a perfect solution to explain why people commit crimes, violate social rules, or engage in self-destructive behaviors. As a result, they have yet to discover the perfect solution to deal with these problems.

Addiction Treatment and Incarceration

As early as the Civil War, experts in criminal justice noticed an obvious link between addiction and criminal behavior. At the same time that new prisons were being redesigned to satisfy the latest criminal justice reform models, there was also an effort to create different types of institutions to treat addiction, both among criminals and among the general public so that they would not fall into crime.

Addiction treatment centers were available for people before they became criminals or for those who had already been convicted of crimes and wanted to reform their lives after serving their sentences. In some cases, judges began referring convicted criminals who had obvious addiction problems to these treatment centers *instead* of being sent to prison. These reforms began more than a century ago, and they were the precursors to the modern drug decriminalization (harm reduction) movement.

In the late 1800s, drug abuse was not widely recognized as a social problem because there were so few drugs that could be abused: marijuana was largely unknown in the United States, amphetamines were not invented yet. Cocaine, heroin, morphine, and opium were invented but were still largely limited to medical use. By far, the widest and most available drug of abuse was alcohol. As such, the criminal court system mostly targeted alcohol addiction as a potential reform option first.

In 1864, the first alcohol treatment program in the United States opened as the New York State Inebriate Asylum. By the 1870s, there were more than 120 addiction treatment facilities. Many doctors and psychologists became famous for their treatment programs for addiction, including Sigmund Freud and Charles Towns. In the 1890s, police departments of most large cities included "drunk tanks" where people were taken to sober up when they were found grossly intoxicated in public—instead of being sent directly to jail. Wealthier alcoholics avoided police detection by drinking more privately, but they also often enrolled in private sanitoriums to treat their addictions, which were usually very expensive.

Around the same time that the sterilization movement began, some local and state court systems began offering alcohol addiction treatment at state expense for criminals who were already incarcerated for other crimes. By the 1910s and 1920s, many states passed laws forcing inmates to undergo treatment programs as prisoners, and these programs helped popularize addiction support groups within the general society as a post-incarceration rehabilitation program.

Bill Wilson founded Alcoholics Anonymous in 1935, and he catered primarily to people who had been struggling with addiction for most of their lives. Many of these admitted alcoholics were professionals and upstanding leaders of their communities, while others had been convicted of petty crimes and were frequently in and out of prisons. The book *Alcoholics Anonymous* (AA) was published in 1939 and helped create a worldwide mutual aid organization to help recovering addicts from falling back into their addiction. The AA continues to be a popular international support group for recovering alcoholics.

Treatment centers that focused on morphine addiction became popular after the First World War, and in 1929, the Narcotic Farms Act authorized federal money to establish drug treatment programs for criminals. One model drug farm built in 1935 in Lexington, Kentucky, was used to treat both male and female prisoners who were incarcerated for crimes that were in some way related to their drug addictions. It combined the requirements of a prison with the facilities of a hospital. Inmates were encouraged to work on the farm as a form of therapy, but they were not forced to. Doctors and psychologists used the farm as a center for experimental treatments, and it was considered one of the most advanced reform movements of the time.

The Lexington Farm operated for forty years and was renamed as part of the US Public Health Service and later as the National Institute of Mental Health (NIMH) Clinical Research Center. It eventually fell under public criticism as an example of inhumane treatment of prisoners during the 1960s. The inmates did not always undergo treatment with their full knowledge or consent, and they were sometimes subjected to medical procedures that had not yet been proven to be safe and effective, so the potential risks were higher than average. Some of these experiments were later judged to be too controversial, and the Lexington

Narcotics Farm was closed down in 1967 and transferred to the Bureau of Prisons.

Treating prisoners with addictions in ways that are different from those who engage in ordinary violent crimes of greed or passion is a very old idea in American history. With each new generation, new treatment programs are introduced and are usually welcomed as the latest advancement in criminal justice research. Over time, though, almost all of these programs are eventually ended or significantly modified after unintended consequences arise that are judged by later generations to be more harmful than they were helpful. In this way, new proposals are usually introduced to solve the new problems, and the reform cycle continues.

The Great Society and the LEAA Wave of Reforms from 1960s to 1990s

The baby boomer generation was reaching their late teen years during the early 1960s, and the next decade saw them grow into young adults. Since most crimes are committed by youthful offenders, the overall crime rate in the country increased steadily. According to the Uniform Crime Reports by the Federal Bureau of Investigation (FBI), there were 160 violent crime offenses per 100,000 people in 1960, and just five years later, in 1965, that rate increased to 200 per 100,000 people. Public opinion became concerned by growing crime rates associated with youth movements, the new drug culture, and the appearance of increasing urban unrest (like riots, muggings, auto thefts, and assaults). The assassination of President John Kennedy in late 1963 seemed to affirm a sense of civic disorder, as did later assassinations of Dr. Martin Luther King, Jr., and Senator Robert Kennedy in 1968.

Shortly after his inauguration, President Lyndon B. Johnson (LBJ) initiated a broad political agenda, which he called the "Great Society." It included dozens of new federal laws related to civil rights, urban development, youth education, and criminal justice reforms. To combat rising crime rates, he launched a national conference of experts called the "President's Commission on Law Enforcement and the Administration of Justice" in 1965. After two years, their first major report titled "The Challenge of Crime in a Free Society" (1967) introduced dozens of new federal policies and laws that ushered in massive changes in how we apprehend lawbreakers, how we protect their rights during trial and sentencing, and how we punish them. Some of the more important crime reform laws were the Criminal Justice Reform Act, the Prisoner Rehabilitation Act, and the Bail Reform Act.

Criminal Justice Reform Act (1965): This created the Law Enforcement Assistance Administration (LEAA), and well as the National Institute of Justice (NIJ) and the National Institute of Law Enforcement and Criminal Justice (NILECJ), all of which focus on gathering statistics and research related to crime, crime-control, punishment, and recidivism (the rates of repeated crimes). LEAA programs were responsible for most of the new experimental reform ideas related to drug decriminalization and legalization that arose in the 1990s. These agencies served under both Democrat and Republican administrations, and they reflect both the ideas of advocates promoting harsher sentencing guidelines, as well as those advocates proposing new alternatives to jail time. These agencies served as general clearinghouses for all types of reform movements in American criminal justice.

Prisoner Rehabilitation Act (1965): A dozen or more major reform bills from 1965 to 1970 set the foundations for the later decriminalization (harm reduction) movements of the early 2000s. One of the first laws was the Prisoner Rehabilitation Act of 1965, which established federal guidelines for sentencing alternatives other than traditional incarceration.

Alternative sentencing was not new. As early as 1913, the State of Wisconsin had introduced the Huber Law, which allowed criminals convicted of misdemeanor offenses the opportunity for work-release furloughs while serving their sentences. This meant that during the day, they could go out and work to support themselves and their families and then return to their jail cells at night. In some cases, they were allowed to remain at home and simply report their whereabouts at regular intervals.

Other states followed Wisconsin's example. North Carolina copied the Huber Law for their own state in 1957 and applied the same practices for felons. Maryland and Michigan followed the model shortly thereafter, and in 1965, Johnson's programs applied the opportunities nationally for federal inmates. It also established guidelines that all other states could follow. This reform was especially useful for inmates who were suffering from addiction and who needed help improving their home environments, their education, and work training skills to escape the urban drug culture.

Bail Reform Act (1966): Around the same time, the Bail Reform Act became the first major reform of federal bail procedures since the Eighth Amendment was passed in 1789. The new law established as a goal the elimination of bail for routine crimes (noncapital cases), including drug-related offenses. Bail refers to the money that defendants deposit with the courts to assure that they will be present for the trial and for sentencing. The new law meant that attorneys could argue for limited or even no bail for most cases if the defendant can demonstrate family or community ties and employment. Even repeat offenders could be granted substantially reduced bail amounts. This law reduced the number of inmates housed in local jails as they awaited trial.

Spectrum of Criminal Sentencing Options

Policies for drug reform can come from the libertarian, social welfare, and traditional conservative viewpoints along the ideological spectrum. During the 1960s and 1970s, the same people were often found promoting many different reforms that reflected strongly different ideological priorities. One example was the Democrat Senator John L. McClellan from Arkansas.

McClellan helped lead the President's Commission on Law Enforcement and was a strong advocate for many of Democrat President Johnson's Great Society reform efforts, including the Bail Reform Act, the LEAA programs, and the 1968 Safe Streets Crime bill, which provided more diverse alternatives to incarceration for drug users and other lesser offenses. McClellan was also a leading voice behind the key programs of Republican President Richard Nixon's Law and Order reform efforts, including the Organized Crime Control Act of 1970 that established more rigid penalties for serious offenders and the Comprehensive Drug Abuse Prevention and Control Act of the same year, which established the new drug schedule system that continues to exist today.

Opinion polls from the late 1960s indicated that the American public strongly favored more proactive laws to address rising crime problems. However, there was less consensus as to exactly how those laws should be framed—the public mostly wanted action and was willing to experiment. Generally, as new laws were passed enforcing harsher penalties for violent crimes (murder, rape, aggravated assault, and organized crime), there were just as many new laws, programs, and new government funding sources for alternatives to incarceration and jail sentences, especially for less serious offenses.

Some experimental reform efforts from the 1960s and 1970s continue to be fully funded and implemented in the 2020s. A few of these include probation and parole, drug treatment alternatives, halfway houses and work-furlough systems, and community engagement programs.

Probation and Parole: Probation means that an offender is found guilty of a crime, but instead of serving all of their time in jail, the offender is allowed to serve some portion of their sentence outside of jail entirely. Parole means that the inmate is released early but is still under government supervision. Typically, if the defendant has been found guilty, and their sentence is suspended so that they serve no actual jail time, they are on probation. If the defendant is actually sent to jail and then released early, they are on parole.

For most crimes, inmates are allowed to earn up to a third of their sentencing time off for good behavior while in prison. However, in many cases—especially those involving drug-related offenses—convicted lawbreakers may more easily receive probation where most or all of their sentence is converted into regulated time outside of jail. This is most often the case if a defendant agrees to drug treatment or other counseling services, and in exchange, their required jail time is substantially reduced or eliminated altogether.

The American Bar Association reported that both parole and probation were used much more routinely beginning in the late 1960s and 1970s. By 1981, 63 percent of people under correctional supervision were on probation, and 11 percent were on parole. These rates changed very little in the decades that followed. In 2004 and 2019 a little more than half of all convicted criminals were on probation (58 percent in 2004 and 53 percent in 2019), and more than a tenth were on parole (11 percent in 2004 and 13 percent in 2019; see Dervan, 2024). Statistics on the number of American "prisoners" sometimes fail to distinguish between those individuals that are actually in jail and those prisoners who are under correctional supervision but are not physically in jail. Usually, more than half the number of prisoners cited in most statistics do not physically reside in any jail cell.

Drug Treatment Alternatives: As part of the movement to increase probation options, most state and federal programs also increased the number of publicly funded drug-treatment centers for addicted users before, during, and after criminal arrests. By 1998, nearly 73 percent of local jails had access to substance abuse treatment programs, including detoxification, education, and self-help groups. More than 90 percent of large institutions with 1,000 or more inmates included these programs within their facilities. Between 50 percent and 60 percent of inmates took advantage of these programs during the 1990s and early 2000s. However, after the drug legalization movement became more popularized around 2010, the number of inmates voluntarily seeking treatment in these programs declined significantly to less than 20 percent (Belenko, 2013).

Halfway Houses and Work-Furlough Systems: Part of the 1965 Rehabilitation Act provided authority to create halfway houses, which are government-developed facilities where inmates live under minimum security but with some supervision. During the 1990s and 2000s, these options were modified by the invention of electronic ankle monitors that allowed inmates to be tracked wherever they were. That meant inmates could even live in their own homes. The purpose of these programs is to provide offenders with opportunities to develop new skills and new lifestyle habits that keep them away from the drug culture that led to their initial arrest and incarceration. These options are routinely made available for first-time offenders or those addicted to drugs and who could be rehabilitated with proper supervision.

Community Engagement Programs: The vast bulk of the LEAA funding (which amounted to more than a billion dollars per year at its height) was directed toward the development of new law enforcement techniques and community engagement programs. Some of these new reforms were focused on improving law enforcement to more safely apprehend suspected criminals (new technologies, new communication techniques, and new chemical detection tools)—these would form part of the traditional "law enforcement" strategies. Other reforms focused on developing local community cooperative arrangements to prevent youth from falling into habits of crime (neighborhood watch programs, community tribunals, and police engagement programs in local schools)—these measures formed part of what we call today "harm reduction" strategies. Both sorts of strategies were promoted under LEAA. The particular goals and expressions of these programs changed with each new decade between the 1970s, the 1980s, the 1990s, and the 2000s, but the basic frameworks of each reform program have not been dismantled.

Almost all reform proposals that remained popular during the early 2000s grew out of the wave of changes in the criminal justice system that were initiated between 1965 and 1975. Some of the recent decriminalization proposals built off these new experiments, and some grew up in direct reaction to those experiments. Decriminalization arguments in the 2010s mostly focus on harm reduction and trying to find alternative models of discouraging recreational drug use other than incarceration and law enforcement.

It is not correct to describe the War on Drugs of the 1970s and 1980s as if it were only focused on harsh prison sentences for any form of drug crime. In practice, the War on Drugs always included a combination of clear prison terms for certain types of offenses (usually those involving murder, other violent crimes, or crimes that hurt children), as well as a wide variety of other lesser punishment options that included community service, drug treatment, education, and rehabilitation, and sometimes incarceration. Like all other innovations in criminal justice in American history, the War on Drugs was part of a much larger reform movement.

Marijuana Legalization Movement

One movement related to drug use was not immediately tied to criminal justice reform. The early efforts to legalize marijuana have always sought to remove cannabis from the Schedule I list of dangerous drugs of 1970 and to legalize and normalize its use as an ordinary recreational activity. This is not a criminal reform movement because it does not seek to end the use of marijuana, and it does not admit any social or cultural link between marijuana use and local crime.

Beginning in 1970, the National Organization for the Reform of Marijuana Laws (NORML) set out to remove marijuana from the list of Schedule I drugs. The Comprehensive Drug Abuse and Control Act (CDA) had just passed in 1970, and the new law followed United Nations (UN) guidelines by identifying drugs according to their likelihood of causing harm, their risk of abuse, and the medical community's ability to use the drug for therapeutic purposes. Similar drug schedules were used by the UN in its Single Convention on Narcotic Drugs of 1961, which identified dangerous drugs and established protocols between nations to prohibit their use within each nation and their trafficking between nations—most European nations adopted new laws very similar to the American CDA. Marijuana was included in the UN Convention and was also included in the new comprehensive American drug law in 1970.

It is important to recognize that marijuana was much less well known in 1970. According to Gallup's first poll on the subject in 1969, only about 30 percent of adults even knew what the effects of recreational marijuana use were. Marijuana had become a popular drug among college students and was best known within the sixteen to twenty-five-year-old age demographic. Only later, during the 1970s, would it become so widely known as it is today. This is important because marijuana was only ever recognized as a dangerous drug that altered the sense of perception and stimulated mild cognitive delusions (usually of pleasure and of paranoia and grandeur). No one in the United States or in Europe believed there was any potential medical value in the drug—it had never been used in the United States or in Europe for that purpose. There is no historical precedent for using marijuana therapeutically to treat medical problems prior to 1970.

Marijuana was listed as a Schedule I drug because it had no medical value, and the medical community had no therapies that included marijuana. For that reason, after the passage of the Comprehensive Drug Act, NORML set out to find some medical value for marijuana so that it would be removed from Schedule I and relisted in another schedule that would allow for greater public access. The ultimate goal for NORML always was to remove marijuana and cannabis from any list of prohibited drugs and to promote complete legalization. This movement was largely promoted by younger baby boomer college-aged students and graduates who believed that marijuana was not harmful and that marijuana use should be accepted as a normal recreational behavior—that is why the acronym of their organization was NORML.

In 1970, NORML was a very tiny organization that was dismissed by almost all policymakers. It played no role in criminal justice reform efforts. However, as the boomers got older, and marijuana use became more common among the broader population, many former marijuana users entered into large corporations, local and federal politics, and became college professors. The movement to legalize or at least remove marijuana from the Schedule I list of prohibited drugs became much stronger by the 1990s. The first step to legalization was to find medical value in marijuana, and so the first wave of marijuana reform was to lobby for the legalization of marijuana for medical use. The legislatures of several states responded to these lobbying efforts in the 1970s, and marijuana was officially decriminalized in eleven states before 1978.

The marijuana legalization movement stalled during the 1980s because of the impact of drug addiction, organized criminal distribution of illegal drugs, and the rise of drug-related violence and other property crimes, which increased substantially. More importantly, baby boomers had become adults by this time with children of their own, and public opinion strongly favored protecting youth from the dangers of recreational drug use. President Reagan's "Just Say No" programs were harshly criticized during the 2010s (as all reform movements usually are by later generations), but at the time during the 1990s, the program was widely supported by parents and teens and proved very successful in reducing recreational drug use among American school-aged youth.

The 1980s era of strong, comprehensive messaging against recreational drug use led to new laws placing harsh penalties for drug dealers that operated near schools and for criminal organizations that used violence (especially gun violence) as part of their illegal drug dealing. At the same time, the 1980s also saw a surge of alternative drug treatment options, including the development of "drug courts" where those who were convicted of nonviolent drug offenses could be tried outside of the regular criminal court system—a form of decriminalized punishment. Typically, first-time offenders or addicted offenders were sentenced by judges to treatment programs, and these crimes were later expunged from the defendant's records if they rehabilitated and refrained from future drug use. Throughout the 1970s and 1980s, marijuana and other forms of recreational drug use were widely recognized as harmful to the individual and strongly connected to criminal subcultures. Drug legalization was not supported, but the combination of clear law enforcement with other harm-reduction techniques was supported.

NORML and the boomer-based movement to legalize marijuana did not disappear during the 1980s, but it was temporarily paused. However, at the start of the 1990s the new generation of lawmakers were less supportive of the Nixon and Reagan era of "Just Say No" style of drug control. President Clinton admitted using marijuana and was among those boomers who did not view it as dangerous as other drugs. His surgeon general, Jocelyn Elders, publicly proposed the idea of more federally funded research into medical marijuana and also suggested decriminalization as a potential criminal justice reform option. This created a new intersection between the two separate movements—the continuing development of harm reduction techniques combined with NORML's new focus on marijuana legalization as a way to reduce crime and limit prison populations. This combined movement brought many advocates for harm reduction techniques to begin also supporting marijuana legalization as a potential criminal justice reform measure. By 2000, the two movements were sufficiently intertwined with enough strength that many new states began efforts to legalize medical marijuana and to decriminalize various forms of drug possession and drug use at the same time (Table 5.1).

The Problem of Evidence: Policy Effects on Drug Crime Statistics

One of the new phrases used by the decriminalization movement of the 2000s is "evidence-based" policies. In plain language, this means that policies should be based on the evidence of relative harm to individuals and to society rather than on whether they encourage or discourage morally self-destructive behaviors. Evidence-based policies always promote harm reduction because the goal is to find the policy options that limit the greatest risk to both the drug user and the community in which they live. It does not place any moral judgment on whether

Table 5.1 Drug Policies of States or Provinces by Type as of 2024.

	Legalized	Decriminalized	Criminalized
United States	24 (25) / 48% (50%)	7 / 14%	19 / 38%
For all drugs	None	OR[i] (2020–4)	All states (2024)
For cannabis Only	AK, AZ, CA, CO, CT, DE, IL, OH, MA, MD, ME, MI, MO, MN, MT, NJ, NM, NV, NY, OR, RI, VT, VA, WA, DC	HI, LA, MS, NC, ND, NE,[ii] NH	AL, AR, FL, GA,[iii] ID, IN,[iv] IA, KS, KY, OK, PA,[v] SC, SD,[vi] TN,[vii] TX,[viii] UT, WV, WI,[ix] WY
Interstate trafficking	None	None	All states
For medical marijuana	38 (76%)	0	12 (24%)
	AK, AL, AR, AZ, CA, CO, CT, DE, FL, IL, KY, HI, LA, ME, MA, MD, MI, MO, MN, MS, MT, ND, NH, NJ, NM, NV, NY, OH, OK, OR, PA, RI, UT, VT, VA, WA, WV, DC	None	GA, IA, ID, IN, KS, NC, NE, SC, TN, TX, WI, WY
Canada provinces	12 (100%)	0	0
All drugs	BC	None	None
Cannabis only (legalized by national law 2018)	AL, NB, NF, NW, NS, NU, ON, PE, QC, SK, YT	None	None
Inter-province trafficking	All provinces and territories		
For medical marijuana (legalized by national law 2016)	AL, BC, NB, NF, NW, NS, NU, ON, PE, QC, SK, YT	None	None

Source: All facts and figures were compiled by Aharon Zorea, based on the National Conference of State Legislatures Report on "State Medical Cannabis Laws" (updated July 12, 2024) with supplementations gathered from each state's drug-policy histories posted on their respective government websites.

Note: i. Oregon briefly legalized small amounts of all drugs from 2020 to 2024. The legalization was repealed in 2024.

ii. First-time offenders only; repeat offenders charged with criminal offense.

iii. Some cities of Georgia have decriminalized marijuana: Atlanta, Clarkston, Forest Park, Savannah, South Fulton, and Statesboro; some Counties decriminalized marijuana: Fulton County and Macon-Bibb County.

(*Continued*)

Table 5.1 (*Continued*)

iv. Decriminalized in Marion County.

v. Decriminalized in Philadelphia and Pittsburgh.

vi. Recreational cannabis use was legalized in 2021 but was overturned by State Supreme Court as unconstitutional in 2021.

vii. First-offense possession results in probation (not prison).

viii. Refusal to prosecute for quantities less than 112gr in cities of Houston, Dallas, San Antonio, Austin, and in Travis County.

ix. Decriminalized in cities of Milwaukee and Madison.

drug use is harmful to individual character development. It only evaluates policies on whether the resulting drug use hurts the individual in ways that spill over to the community and whether drug laws inflict more costs and harm to the community than benefits.

Since 2000, seven states have decriminalized marijuana, and thirty-eight states have legalized marijuana for medical therapeutic use. Since 2012, twenty-four states have legalized marijuana entirely and decriminalized certain drug offenses related to personal possession and use. One state, Oregon, temporarily experimented with legalizing all drugs for personal use. However, public support for the reform experiment waned as the state saw increases in public drug use, homelessness, and overdoses. The state's legislature overturned the law in 2024. Twelve states have retained all criminal penalties for both medical and recreational use of marijuana, while nineteen states have retained criminal penalties for recreational drug use only.

Most of these reform efforts assume decriminalization will have little effect on existing rates of drug addiction, and removing police from the sphere of drug enforcement will result in an overall decrease in crime rates. The best indicator to prove the success of these legal reform experiments would be statistics that show lower rates of addiction, lower rates of property crimes, violent crimes, and low rates of mental and physical health disorders. Unfortunately, these statistics are not available. There are three main reasons why modern statistics fail to provide the necessary evidence to prove the effectiveness (or ineffectiveness) of decriminalization and other drug-related reform efforts: (1) plea bargaining; (2) nonenforcement of existing laws; and (3) cessation of record-keeping for certain drug-related events.

Plea Bargaining: A plea bargain is an agreement made between the defendant's attorneys and the government's prosecutor office that promises to reduce the charges and penalties for an admission of guilt (or plea of "no-contest," which means the defendant will accept the prosecutor's claims but does not admit guilt). Plea bargaining began during the late 1890s as populations grew in large urban centers. It was a practice of efficiency—so many people were being charged for minor crimes that the court dockets were filling up. To resolve the backlog, prosecutors were encouraged to make deals with the defendants to avoid a costly, and sometimes lengthy, trial.

The Supreme Court and the state's courts of appeal generally discouraged plea bargaining because defendants avoided all the constitutional protections guaranteed through the trial process. However, overcrowded courtrooms forced them to accept the practice. Mostly, plea bargains occurred for local and state crimes because there were so few federal crimes to prosecute. However, when the 1920s federal prohibition laws were in effect, the number of federal court cases increased, so the practice became very common at the local, state, and federal levels. Some estimates suggest that between 50 percent and 90 percent of all convictions were settled without a trial using plea bargaining.

During the 1950s, the Federal Supreme Court wrote opinions in two cases that strongly discouraged the practice of plea bargaining. In *Shelton v. United States* (1958), the court wrote, "Justice and liberty are not the subjects of bargaining and barter." However, as crime rates continued to rise during the 1960s, and courts were once again faced with serious overcrowding issues, and after five new justices were appointed, the Supreme Court changed its view. In 1970, *Brady v. United States* (1970) formally recognized the importance of plea bargaining as an efficient practice that reserves the greatest amount of court resources to the most serious cases.

Why accept a plea bargain? Plea agreements are usually welcomed by both sides. Defense attorneys tell their clients the lesser drug penalty will involve much less time in prison, whereas if they went to trial, the likelihood of much stiffer penalties is high. A study conducted in 2019 and published by the American Bar Association concluded that defendants who reject their plea agreements are between twice and six times as likely to face penalties that are 20 percent to 60 percent longer than those who made plea agreements for the exact same charges (Dervan, 2024). It is almost always in the defendant's best interest to accept these plea deals. For the prosecutor's office, they can avoid the time and expense of a trial and are still able to achieve some amount of penalty for crimes committed.

As of 2024, 97.5 percent of all federal convictions were achieved through a plea agreement. That means only 2.5 percent of federal cases ever go to trial. In some federal jurisdictions, years may pass without any trials. In state cases, 95 percent of all convictions are settled through a plea agreement (Dervan, 2024).

This is relevant because most crime statistics are based on convictions; they are not based on arrests or on the incidents of reported crimes. Generally, during a plea agreement, the defendant may be charged with multiple serious crimes, some of which include very harsh penalties and some of which include minor penalties. Most drug offenses carry minor penalties, while crimes of violence, aggravated assault, and grand larceny (theft) carry long penalties. To encourage the defendant to confess, prosecutors frequently agree to only charge them with lesser crimes (usually drug-related) and will drop the harsher crimes.

The problem with plea agreements is mostly statistical—the resulting conviction rates tend to show a much larger than normal number of drug-related charges, and they also tend to hide the number of original charges tied to violence, rape, or grand theft. Since the 1980s, the number of inmates sent to prison for drug-related offenses has increased every year, while the number of violent crimes (murders and rapes) appeared to be stable. However, the annual reports on crime statistics do not include the number of arrests made that did not lead to conviction, and so they do not reflect the actual number of criminal events. As a practical matter, the vast majority of people who are sent to prison on drug charges were also accused of much more serious crimes of violence or criminal organization at the time of arrest.

Nonenforcement of Existing Laws: Police officers and local prosecutors always have a choice whether to enforce local and state laws or to let them go unprosecuted. As the harm reduction movement grew during the 2000s, several cities and states developed policies that discouraged police from enforcing all laws. For cases of minor drug possession where the drugs were clearly intended for personal use, the officer may confiscate the drugs but let the suspect go free without making an official arrest.

In some cities and states, this policy was also applied to minor shoplifting cases because increasing rates of drug addiction usually results in higher shoplifting rates. If the value of the stolen merchandise was less than $500, $750, or $1000 (or whatever number was less than the felony threshold), local law enforcement would not prosecute. These reforms were promoted as harm reduction policies because addicted users sometimes steal merchandise to pay for their drug habits. Almost all cities include laws that explicitly identify shoplifting as a misdemeanor, with penalties that include fines and some jail time under a year. However, in many cities like San Francisco, Seattle, and Anchorage, the local police will not apprehend suspects if the value of the merchandise is less than felony level. In the mid-2020s, these policies began to change in some cities.

As a practical matter, this means that someone could enter a store to grab electronics or alcohol and leave without paying for them, and the police will probably not attempt to track them down or arrest or charge them. Retail outlets may lock down certain easily moveable items and hire security guards to prevent customers from leaving without paying, but if the customer manages to escape out the door with the product that is worth less than the felony level amount, they will not be arrested. These sorts of petty property crimes are strongly connected to drug use because the items are easily sold or traded for money or drugs. Yet these crimes are rarely reported to the police because the victims know that the offenders will not be arrested, and so these instances of crime are not included in annual crime statistics.

Cessation of Record Keeping: Government agencies collect crime data so that they can know whether their crime prevention strategies are working. However, they only collect data on behaviors that are identified as crimes. If cannabis is legalized in a state like California or Oregon, there is no data collected on the number of people who are found using, buying, or selling marijuana because those actions are no longer considered a crime in that state. This means that statistics that used to be collected on certain types of drug use are no longer collected by law enforcement agencies. This is also true for other sorts of statistics (such as hospital visits, where marijuana use may be implicated). If the substances are not illegal, or if they are difficult to track, the data point is not collected.

From 2000 to the mid-2020s, the amount of data collected related to drug use and addiction declined substantially. This is especially true in states where medical marijuana was legalized and where it was legalized for recreational use. State officials know how many legal sales were made in legal dispensaries, but they have no data on the drug sales conducted through illegal drug deals. In every state where marijuana has been legalized (for medical and for recreational use), the amount of illegal drug sales usually increased by at least three or four times. That is because, though legal, illegal drug dealers do not have to pay licensing fees or taxes, and so their business usually increases when general recreational drug use is permitted through legalization or decriminalization.

During the first quarter of 2024, the Department of Justice Annual Uniform Crime Report indicated sharp declines in all areas of crime: 15 percent decrease in violent crime (including 26 percent decrease in murder and a similar decrease in rape), nearly 18 percent decrease in robbery, and more than 12 percent decrease in aggravated assault. Property crimes appeared to decrease by 15 percent. However, these statistics were almost immediately challenged by critics (such as the Crime Prevention Research Center), who claimed that only 45 percent of violent crime statistics were actually reported to the federal government (less than half) and only 32 percent of property crimes (less than a third). Local police departments and victim advocacy groups reported that the actual instances of crime generally increased substantially over the same time period. The Department of Justice surveys of victims also suggested a 29 percent increase in crimes, even though the annual crime report indicated contradictory trends.

Most incidents that would traditionally be considered crimes are not reported to local police, are not included in court records, and are not collected by national surveys. In 2024, the Department of Justice instituted a new system of statistical estimation to create uniform crime reports, which means the actual numbers are not easily accessible for researchers during the time period near when they actually occurred. Fortunately, there are other anecdotal measures of crime, which include national surveys of public opinion, news articles, or policy actions from large national retail chains. For example, large retail stores like Walmart, Whole Foods, CVS, and others announced store closures in many large urban markets (like Chicago, San Francisco, and Los Angeles) because the rates of shoplifting made their businesses unprofitable.

In later 2024 as the presidential election drew near, the Department of Justice revised its earlier statistics to show that there were indeed increases in property crimes and violent crimes by 4.5 percent during the same period. This caused some observers to conclude that crime statistics were not always consistently reported for other political reasons. Local communities will have access to important data points eventually, but these may not be collected in easily summarized reports. Over time, researchers will sort the data, and the actual rates of crime, addiction, and rehabilitation will be collected. Unfortunately, such data may take many years to collect and analyze accurately.

Conclusion: Decriminalization as the Latest Reform Movement

The twenty-first century began with a strong wave of new experimentation in criminal justice reform, with some substantial changes made in the way local communities dealt with recreational drug use, drug abuse, addiction, and other drug-related crimes. The decriminalization movement, along with its sister movements of marijuana legalization and other harm-reduction policies, are included among a wide variety of reform proposals. These proposals are not new to American society, and they reflect a very long tradition of social experimentation. The original penitentiaries were followed by medical treatments for criminal behaviors, the War on Drugs, and the most recent decriminalization and legalization movements. Drug decriminalization proposals have often accompanied concerns regarding over-policing, mass incarceration, and racial inequities in the criminal justice system. Public support for reform in these areas grew in the 2010s in response to several highly publicized incidents of violence against Black Americans, including the killing of teenager Trayvon Martin by a night watchman who was later acquitted and the police killings of Michael Brown in Ferguson, Missouri, and George Floyd in Minneapolis, Minnesota. Large-scale protests, riots, and social media campaigns (including the Black Lives Matter movement and calls to "defund the police") put pressure on lawmakers and created a political atmosphere that enabled movements related to drug decriminalization and legalization to gain traction.

Every reform movement includes some level of unintended consequences, which means that no single movement is ever perfect, and none of them last as permanent changes. The current drug decriminalization, legalization, and harm reduction policies are (as of the 2020s) still in their experimental stages. It will take several decades to fully learn if they were effective or if their unintended consequences will lead to other future reforms.

Part II

Issues and Controversies

6

Legalization and Physical Health Issues

The legalization or decriminalization of any recreational drug always leads to increased drug use among the general population. Very few researchers would disagree with this, though they may disagree about what that correlation means. Does increased drug use always lead to increased addiction rates? Does increased drug use always lead to more physical health problems for the individual and for the community?

Advocates of decriminalization and legalization recognize that addiction rates will likely increase immediately after new laws are passed, but only temporarily, and then they predict that addiction rates will level off over the long term. Opponents of decriminalization contend that increasing legal access to any drug naturally leads to increased use, which will in turn result in greater rates of addiction both in the short term and the long term. Their fears are that increasing recreational drug use may change the culture of society to the point that it becomes more difficult to resist drug use. Both predictions are difficult to prove with statistics because there are so many other variables involved. Researchers can never know with certainty if it is the drug or other social factors that are encouraging or discouraging increased drug use or addiction.

Specific predictions of long-term effects vary considerably, but there is consensus that legalization and decriminalization lead to increasing recreational drug use overall—especially in the short term. The key question is whether the increased recreational drug use will also increase the physical harm for individual users and whether the medical needs of the community will grow faster than the available resources needed to address them. A closely related question is whether these individual and social harms outweigh the potential advantages of increased liberty for the individual (and within society). In other words, do the possible health costs outweigh the potential advantages of allowing more people to choose their own recreational preferences, which may include recreational drug use?

Prior to the 1960s, when traditional conservative ideologies were more popular, these questions were answered with a strong "yes." According to most Judeo-Christian traditions, recreational drug use is morally wrong because it prevents people from developing their natural gifts and from achieving the potential that God intended for them. As such, these moral considerations combined with threats to physical health justified the minor limitations on individual liberty that drug laws impose. In religious terms, prohibiting recreational drug use encourages individual moral self-restraint.

After the 1970s, popular cultural attitudes began to change. Policymakers and lawmakers were less willing to consider moral health as a deciding factor in determining drug laws. New "evidence-based" policies evaluated the social value of criminalization based on the potential harm that legalized drug use might pose for the individual (and their community), and they then compared that risk against the potential harm caused by increased law enforcement (arrests and jail time) and increased limitations on individual liberty. If the harms of drug enforcement outweighed the harms of recreational drug use, policymakers would seriously consider decriminalizing or legalizing certain drugs. Harm reduction strategies deliberately avoid questions of morality in determining recreational drug policies.

If we do not consider moral implications, the question of physical harm becomes more complex because "harm" is often subjective (which means it depends on individual interpretation). Some people are willing to accept a certain level of physical health risks if it means that they can do what they want to do without other legal penalties. The risk of potential death is generally considered too high of a price to pay. However, other levels of emotional or moral risks depend on individual opinions.

Since the 2000s, policy debates over drug laws have generally been between libertarian and social-welfare interpretations. Libertarians believe that individuals should be able to judge for themselves their acceptable levels of risk rather than the government. Social-welfare viewpoints focus on the long-term costs to society associated with unhealthy lifestyle choices because they try to weigh the needs of the individual against other community priorities that may be competing for limited government resources. Both libertarians and social-welfare advocates oppose policies that reflect moral preferences, and so they both prefer morally neutral, evidence-based, harm-reduction strategies. However, they disagree over the extent to which personal freedoms involving recreational drug use should be tempered by concerns regarding the health of the community.

Short-Term Risks to Physical Health

Obviously, not all drugs are the same, and they do not all pose the same level of health risk to individuals. Drug types may be categorized and evaluated based on their potential for causing overdoses leading to emergency room services. These are considered immediate health risks. These risks are influenced by the manner in which the drug is consumed (eating or drinking, smoking, injecting), as well as the specific drug concentration and the speed at which it is introduced into the human body. In addition, we can assess the long-term risks of the same drug types, if used periodically over the span of a lifetime.

For purposes of risk assessment, we consider five different drug types: (1) alcohol, (2) marijuana, (3) hallucinogens, (4) amphetamines and other stimulants, and (5) opioids and other pain relievers. We only consider nicotine (tobacco) in relation to long-term health effects because nicotine does not pose any immediate health dangers (unless the user already suffers from other serious health issues). The levels of risk are evaluated according to a scale of probability of harm: the likelihood of no negative health risk; the probability of some expected health risks; and the likely risk that high concentrations will reach overdose levels, including the potential of severe trauma or death.

Alcohol: Moderate drinking (one to two drinks per day over a two-hour period) may provide some health benefits. Most research indicates that a blood alcohol concentration (BAC) of 0.01 percent to 0.02 percent may help lower the risk of cardiovascular diseases and type 2 diabetes. More than 70 percent of Americans who drink usually do so in moderate amounts that never result in intoxication (they do not act or feel drunk in any way). Moderate drinking, therefore, poses no immediate health risks.

Nevertheless, alcohol can be deadly under certain circumstances. Risk levels are determined by the concentration of alcohol in the drink and the rate of consumption. A serving of beer averages 4 percent to 6 percent alcohol by volume and generally poses low immediate risks. Drinking extreme amounts (called "high intensity drinking" or "binge drinking") of five–ten drinks per hour will definitely impair physical coordination, increase inhibitions (willingness to take risks), and induce drowsiness. Under typical circumstances, beer will not lead to emergency room visits because the body tends to fall asleep (pass out) before BAC reaches lethal levels.

Drinking hard liquors (whiskey, vodka, gin, etc.) increases the risk because these drinks have much higher concentrations of alcohol per volume. Most hard liquor ranges from 60–100 proof (which is 30 percent to 50 percent alcohol). If the user consumes large amounts of liquor in a very quick period of time, the results can easily lead the victim to the emergency room. Every year one or more college students play drinking games and try to guzzle large tumblers of hard liquor quickly, and in these cases, the BAC may reach lethal doses before the body has time to shut down to prevent further drinking. These cases are rare because the drinker will usually get sick and throw up before completing their drink. Nevertheless, a determined drinker can kill themselves if they force the liquid down.

Acute alcohol poisoning occurs when BAC reaches a level that impairs the central nervous system to the point that the body no longer communicates to the lungs, and the drinker simply stops breathing and dies of asphyxiation (usually within minutes). Lethal doses of alcohol vary depending on genetic disposition and tolerance of the individual, but on average a BAC of around 0.35 percent will usually lead to death. For comparison, general intoxication (noticeable impairment of reflexes and judgment) begins at 0.08 percent, and drinkers begin to stumble and slur their speech at around 0.12 percent. Drunk driving charges are usually triggered at 0.08 percent.

Every year more than 2,000 people die from acute alcohol poisoning, but it is still relatively rare among drinkers. That is because the body usually shuts down before BAC can reach such high percentages (of 0.30 percent or above). The vast majority of acute alcohol poisoning cases involve middle-aged men between forty-five and fifty-five years of age who have long histories of alcohol abuse. Their tolerance levels permit them to continue drinking long after ordinary drinkers have passed out. Many years of abuse have poisoned their internal organs (mostly liver and heart) to such an extent that high BAC is more likely to inhibit the central nervous system and other associated organs such as the heart and lungs.

The criminalization of alcohol during the Prohibition era (1919 to 1933) reduced the rates of alcohol consumption by half as compared to rates prior to 1919. After Prohibition laws were overturned, the gradual decriminalization of most alcohol types slowly caused rates of consumption to return to their previous levels within the span of a generation (about twenty years). By the 1970s and 1980s, alcohol abuse reached its highest level since 1910, which was about 2.5 times that of the Prohibition rates during the 1920s. During the 2020s, abuse rates among the 1970s and 1980s era generation have continued to slowly increase, while the mortality rates from alcohol abuse for all other age groups have declined steadily since 2000.

Marijuana: Like alcohol, the immediate effects of marijuana (or THC, its psychoactive ingredient) depend on concentration levels and the rate of consumption. However, unlike alcohol, moderate consumption of marijuana *always* leads to intoxication. There is no level of THC use that does not reach the threshold of impairment. That is, there is no equivalent between "moderate drinking" and "moderate marijuana use." Routine marijuana use (twice per month) can be more closely compared to "binge drinking" of alcohol, where the drinker becomes drunk twice per month.

Concentrations of THC and rates of consumption also vary considerably depending on the manner in which it is consumed. Smoking marijuana cigarettes involves lower concentrations per volume than other methods of consumption because the smoke vapor is less dense. Generally, THC levels vary widely from 5 percent to 40 percent, at the extreme high end. Like drinking beer, it is almost impossible to reach lethal levels of THC by smoking marijuana alone. The greatest risk of smoking marijuana is the feeling of intoxication and an increased vulnerability to psychotic episodes. Under most circumstances, smoking low-THC marijuana will pose few immediate health risks. Since 2000, the concentration of THC found in average cannabis plants has increased by double, quadruple, or octuple, depending on the strain.

Vapors created from electronic cigarettes (vaping) create much higher THC concentrations. The concentrated dabs used in vaping devices may be as high as 95 percent THC. Consuming THC through vaping or edibles that use highly concentrated forms of THC is more closely comparable to high-intensity drinking of hard liquors. Using modern laboratory methods, THC may be extracted from the cannabis plant and reformed into a butter-like consistency to be inserted into vaping devices or sometimes liquefied into a tincture to be placed under the tongue or turned into a powder that can be added to foods. These extractions have much higher THC levels than the cannabis plant can provide by itself and may reach concentrations as high as 95 percent.

Consuming dabs through tinctures or vaping produces almost immediate effects, and if the THC concentration is too high, overdose symptoms may result within minutes. The user gets sick or may experience panic or other signs of a psychotic episode. Consuming edibles means that THC is metabolized through the intestinal tract, and the effects may not kick in for 20–30 minutes. Edibles pose the greatest risk for emergency room visits because the user does not feel any immediate effect and often continues eating the drug assuming it is a mild dose. When the THC levels kick in, the cumulative effects often trigger immediate overdose symptoms.

Overdosing THC is not the same as acute alcohol poisoning and leads to death only in very rare instances. For many years, scientists did not believe that THC could lead to death because cannabinoid receptors are not found in the cardiovascular system, and therefore no amount of THC will inhibit breathing or heart functions. Prior to 2010, there were no instances of serious THC overdoses resulting in death. Since decriminalization and legalization, the rates of annual emergency room visits caused by THC overdoses number in the thousands, and cases of THC-only mortality rates are no longer zero. Doctors do not know how or why some overdose symptoms lead to death while others do not. In general, overdosing on THC will frequently bring the user to the emergency room, but the likelihood of death is extremely rare.

Other almost equally dangerous immediate effects of THC overdose are cognitive and perceptual. People who have never experienced THC are vulnerable because they may misread the symptoms of intoxication, which often leads to a panic attack and may also lead to physical illness. High levels of THC may trigger psychotic episodes in certain individuals, including experienced users who know what to expect from marijuana. Whether from smoking or vaping or from eating edibles, a psychotic episode means that the user becomes temporarily disconnected from reality and may feel, think, or believe things that are not true. During these episodes the risks of accidental deaths, violent reactions, murders, and suicides are much higher.

During the twentieth century when marijuana was criminalized, the rates of THC addiction were so low that many scientists suggested that it was not physically addictive (and it could not lead to lethal dosing). However, after a wave of states began passing laws decriminalizing and legalizing marijuana, the rates of cannabis addiction increased substantially, and the number of annual emergency room visits grew to thousands and then tens of thousands per year. In comparison to alcohol, marijuana use has increased significantly since 2000, while alcohol use has steadily declined among adults thirty-five and younger. According to the 2023 Center for Disease Control (CDC) National Center for Health Statistics reports, rates of marijuana use among all age groups increased by fifteen times between 1992 and 2022. In the 2020s, rates of intoxication from THC exceeded rates of intoxication from alcohol for the first time. Binge drinkers who reach intoxication one–two times per month accounted for 6 percent of the population, while THC users who reach intoxication one–two times per month accounted for about 11 percent. By 2020, the number of daily THC users (17.2 million) surpasses the number of daily binge drinkers (14.7 million) for the first time in history.

Hallucinogens: Any drug causing alterations in the user's thoughts and perceptions to create false perceptions from their sensory organs is called a hallucinogen. There is a wide range of drugs that fall into this category, including phencyclidine (PCP), lysergic acid diethylamide (LSD), psilocybin (mushrooms), peyote, and marijuana, though marijuana is usually considered in its own category. LSD and psilocybin will not lead to death and only very rarely require an emergency room visit (0.2 percent of cases). That is because these drugs impair the brain functions that interpret perception and do not have immediate connections to the cardiovascular system. PCP is an exception, and it can be deadly in large enough doses, though usually death results from accidents or suicidal acts resulting from psychotic episodes. PCP poses greater health risks because it not only alters perception but also stimulates heart rates.

All hallucinogens carry much higher risks of inducing psychotic episodes, resulting in a range of severity from panic attacks to extreme paranoia. Typical results last for short durations, but occasionally psychosis can linger for longer periods. Moderate use of LSD and psilocybin will result in relatively few emergency room visits. Rates of PCP overdosing leading to death are low but more common.

Hallucinogens are not legal in any state, though some groups (like Native Americans) have religious exceptions for peyote only. Actual enforcement of legal prohibitions varies depending on the city and if the user carries more drugs than are necessary for personal use. Dealing with hallucinogens more often leads to arrests.

Prior to the 2000s, usage rates had been very low—sometimes less than 1 percent of the population. However, legalization and decriminalization of marijuana are suspected of having increased hallucinogen use. In marketing terms, the "halo effect" refers to situations when positive perceptions of one product lead to equally positive perceptions of other related products. By the 2020s, the CDC National Center for Health Statistics reported the use of hallucinogens increased about four times to about 4 percent, and that may be a side effect of shifting public opinion about recreational drug use generally. In either case, rising usage of hallucinogens does not appear to have resulted in immediate public health risks beyond the risk of psychosis and other forms of mental illness.

Amphetamines (and Stimulants): The broad class of amphetamines includes most synthetic drugs (created in labs) that stimulate the central nervous system. These are often legally prescribed for attention-deficit hyperactivity disorder (ADHD), depression, or narcolepsy. They are most often used illegally as a recreational stimulant and are highly addictive. The chemical name for ecstasy is methylenedioxymethamphetamine (MDMA), and though it is usually classed among hallucinogens, the effects of ecstasy most often resemble amphetamines. Cocaine is also usually classed among stimulants, but it is often given a category of its own because the prevalence of cocaine addiction is so high.

Any amphetamine drug, cocaine, or ecstasy tablet can result in overdose symptoms that lead to immediate emergency room visits if taken in large enough doses. One of the defining characteristics of the drug is increased heart rate, blood pressure, and hyperactivity in other systems. These effects all have the potential of creating serious health risks, especially among people who already have preexisting cardiovascular issues.

The probability of overdosing (and death) depends on the potency of the drug, and any drug that is manufactured illegally will have wide variations in its potency when sold by illegal dealers. Methamphetamines are most often made illegally into a crystalized form that can be smoked for an immediate effect (like crack cocaine). It is highly addictive, and increased use leads to drug tolerance over time, which makes accidental overdosing more common. Ecstasy is also usually made illegally in tablet form, which comes in colorful cartoon shapes because ecstasy is frequently taken in a polydrug mixture at dance clubs and is associated with "party" social environments. Illegal vendors who sell these drugs are usually supplied by international drug traffickers, and the local dealer is often unaware of the potency or purity of what they are selling. Users routinely die from even small doses because the drugs were too potent, they were contaminated by other poisons, or because the combined potency of the polydrug mixture was too high.

Due to the unpredictable quality of these drugs, the relative physical dangers of any amphetamine or stimulant use are always very high. Users never know what they are consuming. Also, mixing stimulants with other opioids (depressants) and hallucinogens, called polydrug use, is the most frequent cause of overdosing and death. Users rarely know how each drug will interact with each other, and the untested combinations often result in accidental overdose fatalities.

Most amphetamines are legally manufactured as therapeutic drugs, and if used under doctor supervision, they rarely lead to immediate physical harm. However, recreational use is illegal in every state because it means the user is using without any medical oversight. Cocaine and ecstasy are always illegal because there are no therapeutic uses for those drugs. However, like hallucinogens, actual enforcement of drug possession is not always consistent.

Recreational use of all drugs, including amphetamines, ecstasy, and cocaine, has increased since 2000. It is difficult to determine precisely whether the general increase is a part of the halo effect of marijuana decriminalization and legalization or if it is caused by other social and cultural factors. By the 2020s, methamphetamines resulted in slightly more emergency room visits than cocaine, but both were still less than marijuana and opioids.

Opioids: Drugs derived from opium include morphine and heroin as well as a wide variety of legally prescribed therapeutic drugs intended for pain relief (including a mild sense of euphoria). During the 1960s and 1970s, heroin overdoses were a leading cause of death among drug users. However, by the 2000s, the popularity of heroin was surpassed by synthetic opioids that are much less expensive to manufacture and are often more potent. Most of these are supplied by international drug cartels who flood the American market illegally. Since the 2010s, fentanyl became the leading cause of death from any illegal drug, accounting for more than 90,000 deaths per year by the 2020s, which is many times the rate of all other drug types. Xylazine (known as "tranq") is a non-opioid sedative that has been increasingly used during the 2020s, is usually combined with fentanyl, and is another common cause of overdose deaths.

The Drug Enforcement Administration (DEA) released a public statement in 2024 warning that "the shift from plant-based drugs, like heroin and cocaine, to synthetic, chemical-based drugs, like fentanyl and methamphetamine, has resulted in the most dangerous and deadly drug crisis the United States has ever faced." (*National Drug Threat Assessment*, 2024) The main cause of the danger is the unpredictability of the drug quality. Fentanyl can be deadly with as little as 2 mg, yet the illegal pills seized through DEA raids during the 2020s revealed a wide range of potency, from 0.2 mg to as high as 9 mg (which would result in immediate overdose death).

International drug cartels in Mexico are supplied by Chinese pharmaceutical plants that export raw ingredients for opioid manufacturing by ship. The finished pills are made in Mexico and brought over the southern border into the United States. Since most fentanyl is sold anonymously over social media or directly to the most addicted users in open-air drug markets, there is little opportunity for contaminated batches to harm a dealer's reputation. With almost every dose of methamphetamines and opioids, there is a high risk of a potentially lethal overdose.

Recreational use of opioids is illegal in the same way as amphetamines and hallucinogens. However, inconsistent enforcement often creates a public impression that recreational drug use is usually safe. In the case of fentanyl (and xylazine), that is never true. By the mid-2020s, the DEA and other local law enforcement agencies devoted extensive public information campaigns to warn users that even one dose of illegal opioids may result in death. The practical reality is that a high percentage (estimated at one of three tablets) contains a lethal dose for people who have not developed a drug tolerance. Between 2000 and 2024, the state of Oregon temporarily experimented with decriminalization of all drugs, including amphetamines and opioids. However, the rate of accidental overdose deaths combined with other unexpected social costs forced the experimental laws to be overturned in 2024. Public health is seriously threatened by the recreational use of opioids.

Supply Control and Demand Control

Decriminalization and legalization do not change the dangers of amphetamines and opioids. Both of these classes of drugs are already decriminalized, with the exception of cocaine and heroin, and these drugs are routinely prescribed by qualified doctors to treat recognized health issues and are generally administered safely. These and most other recreational drugs are dangerous precisely because users usually buy and consume them outside the oversight of qualified medical care providers. If they are used recreationally, they are always illegal.

One of the primary arguments used by decriminalization supporters is that removing law enforcement from the problem of drug use will help encourage users to seek out professional guidance and treatment. For prescription drugs that are already decriminalized, existing safeguards set in place to ensure safe consumer use do not influence recreational users. Users who seek out drugs for recreational purposes are always outside this legal safety net. The only way existing policies can further limit criminal restrictions on amphetamines and opioids is to legalize them completely. However, even after legalization, the illegal market for these recreational drugs would still continue to thrive. The example of decriminalized and legalized marijuana shows that legalization usually increases (and not decreases) illegal markets. Advocates of harm reduction drug policies do not focus on legalizing synthetic drugs like amphetamines and opioids but prefer instead policies that emphasize "supply control" goals and policies that emphasize "demand control" goals.

Supply Control: The traditional approach to drug laws is to control the supply of illegal drugs, which means preventing illegal manufacturing, illegal distribution, and illegal sales of the drug. American drug laws include punishments for individual users, but the greatest penalties are always reserved for the suppliers of illegal drugs (producers, dealers, and traffickers). This is also true for most of the international drug-control protocols that have been agreed upon by nations around the world since the early 1900s.

Advocates for harm reduction strategies recognize that illegal manufacturing of harmful drugs fuels drug addiction and other associated social problems. However, they seek to de-emphasize the enforcement of small amounts of production and sales in order to place more emphasis on demand control. Harm reduction strategies usually include no criminal penalties for personal possession or use. They do, however, retain higher penalties for large-scale production operations and international trafficking using large criminal organizations (like cartels).

Demand Control: Traditional drug policies have always included some control over individual demand. These would include treatment and other education programs to discourage youth from falling into recreational drug use and to help those already addicted to escape from their dependency. The difference between harm reduction and traditional drug-control policies is that the older methods included criminal penalties as an added incentive to discourage drug use and to encourage drug-free life choices. Moderate penalties for possession and use usually accompany harsher penalties for illegal manufacturing and trafficking.

Advocates for harm reduction strategies argue that law enforcement is unnecessary for discouraging individual recreational drug use. In fact, they argue that the shame of criminal arrest often causes users to avoid seeking treatment because they fear the possibility of jail time or bad reputations that will harm their employment or educational opportunities. In their most extreme proposals, harm reduction advocates recommend replacing all law enforcement with social services agencies (such as was adopted in Portugal). In theory, money devoted to police would be redirected to treatment and education facilities. In practice, these policies result in more public expenses rather than simply diverting existing expenses.

More commonly, harm reduction policies place greater priorities for using government money to fund treatment programs and for creating safer drug-use environments. These might include providing free needles for users who inject drugs to limit AIDS/HIV or hepatitis and other infections that come from dirty needles or by providing safe rooms with medical personnel in attendance, where users can take the drugs without risk of unattended overdosing (called Overdose Prevention Sites).

As a practical matter, both the traditional drug policies and the modern harm-control policies include some degree of both supply control and demand control. For prescription drugs that are already legal under therapeutic conditions, these terms help to distinguish between decriminalizing drugs that have never been legally available (like heroin and cannabis, in most states and countries prior to 2000) and for encouraging those policies that provide an expanded range of noncriminal options for treating users who abuse therapeutic drugs, which may already be legal under proper medical supervision.

Messaging Dilemma: No law will stop a person from using recreational drugs if they are committed to doing so. If the threat of criminal penalties cannot stop users from abusing therapeutic drugs for recreational purposes, the only other option is to reduce the user demand for abusing those drugs. This creates a policy dilemma.

Discouraging illegal drug use means that state and other educational messages must teach that recreational drug use is dangerous and harmful. However, harm reduction strategies try to reduce the stigma (shame) associated with recreational drug use, in order to encourage users to seek out treatment, which means they avoid negative language associated with drug addiction and do not impose judgment on anyone's decision to use recreational drugs. These two approaches are generally at odds, as the first attempts to dissuade drug use by teaching that illegal drugs hurt us, while the second teaches that illegal drug use is a personal choice. The priority of one message over the other creates considerable public debate among traditional conservatives, libertarians, and social-welfare advocates.

Long-Term Risks to Physical Health

In terms of immediate health risks from recreational drug use, it would appear that (most) illegal drugs are relatively safe. Fentanyl, ecstasy, and xylazine are important exceptions because even a single tablet, vaping a single dab laced with fentanyl or xylazine, or eating a single marijuana edible that has been "enhanced" with such drugs significantly increases the danger of lethal overdosing. Overdosing heroin also carries similar immediate risks of death. Aside from these obvious exceptions, most other recreational drugs carry only moderate to minimal immediate health risks.

Libertarian advocates argue that all (or most) drugs are mostly safe, including cocaine and heroin, and therefore should be legalized so that individuals may decide for themselves whether to accept the potential health risks associated with recreational drug use. During the 1990s, especially, libertarian academics published many books claiming that no drug was physically addictive. Users took drugs because they wanted to; therefore banning drug supplies through criminal prohibitions was useless since a committed user would always find a way to obtain the drug.

Since the wave of decriminalization and legalization laws of the twenty-first century, the potentially addictive nature of most drugs has been demonstrated by numerous clinical studies. The libertarian arguments are less common because the risk from cross-contaminated drugs (especially fentanyl) poses a consumer risk that is too high to justify broad legalization. Nevertheless, social-welfare advocates still argue that for most users, the greatest threat from recreational drug use is from life-long addiction and not from casual or moderate experimentation. Since the greatest risk of potential harm comes from extended use, they believe that government agencies have time to reach addicted users and to treat them before their substance abuse leads to serious medical issues that cause cancer, organ failure, and death.

Long-term risks of recreational drug use appear after many years of consumption. Almost always, these medical conditions only arise in users who have developed strong tolerances brought about by dependency and addiction. If decriminalization and legalization of marijuana increase the likelihood of increased use, dependency, and addiction of any drug (through the halo effect), these long-term health risks may be unavoidable.

Risks of Physical Withdrawal: Many recreational drugs are physically addictive, which means that the body experiences physical pain and sickness when a drug that is routinely consumed is removed from the body. These withdrawal symptoms can be severe and, in some cases, may lead to heart attacks and death if the already weakened internal organs are not compensated with some less dangerous drug analog during the process of curing the addiction. Some drugs, like hallucinogens and marijuana, elicit very mild physical withdrawal symptoms and are therefore described as "non addictive."

As a practical matter, though, every recreational drug can become addictive from a psychological perspective. People who develop dependencies on a drug (or a behavior, like gambling or watching pornography) may train their internal reward systems to become so accustomed to particular forms of stimulation that ending those stimulations will produce very strong emotional and psychological withdrawal symptoms. Some of these reactions can manifest themselves in physical symptoms: high levels of anxiety, increased pulse rates, cold sweats, inability to sleep or to concentrate, and wide variations in emotional volatility (getting angry, sad, or happy in unpredictable ways and in extreme degrees).

Withdrawal symptoms associated with psychological addiction are a long-term physical health risk because they reflect physical changes and deteriorations of the endocrine system and internal organs. Withdrawal symptoms only appear after the user has developed physical tolerance and a dependency on the drug and has tried to stop using the drug but is prevented from doing so because of these harsh physical reactions. Any drug, including alcohol, marijuana, hallucinogens, amphetamines, and opioids, will trigger some degree of withdrawal symptoms in users who have long histories of consumption.

Drugs that are physically addictive (alcohol, amphetamines, and opioids) will have more severe physical reactions as well as psychological reactions. Other drugs like marijuana and hallucinogens may not be physically addictive, but the symptoms of psychological withdrawal can be so strong that the user will repeatedly refuse to stop taking the drug out of fear of the extreme anxiety caused by not using it. If continued drug use is harming the individual's emotional, cognitive, and autoimmune systems, the inability to stop using poses serious long-term health risks. Every drug (and many behaviors) can potentially have these withdrawal symptoms.

Dangers from Smoking: Marijuana, crack cocaine, methamphetamines, certain forms of black tar heroin, PCP and anything in a dab concentration (including fentanyl and xylazine) may be smoked. All smoking is dangerous, but most people associate smoking only with tobacco. There are no immediate side effects of smoking a tobacco cigarette, but there are many long-term health risks associated with smoking including increased risks of almost all cardiovascular diseases and autoimmunity issues (rates of inflammation caused by disorders in the endocrine system). From the 1960s, medical scientists recognized that the increased exposure to nonpsychoactive particles found in smoke (any smoke) is strongly associated with cancer and heart and lung disease because these particles irritate the inner lining of lung tissues and block the body's ability to process oxygen which fuels all living cell tissues.

In 1965, based on the US Surgeon General's report on smoking, all cigarette packages were required to include warning labels declaring that "cigarette smoking may be hazardous to your health." The words have changed, but the general warning has become so successful that by the 2010s, the majority of American students believed tobacco was more dangerous than alcohol and marijuana. Unfortunately, while it is true that smoking is dangerous, it is not true (on any level) that tobacco is more dangerous than marijuana.

In fact, of the possible psychoactive drugs that can be smoked, tobacco is probably the least dangerous. Marijuana smoke is about 700 percent more dangerous than tobacco smoke because the nonpsychoactive particles are much larger and because marijuana smokers do not use any sort of filters, which means smokers get the full exposure to the smoke without any barriers. Crack cocaine, methamphetamines, and heroin also include particles that are toxic to the lungs, in addition to the drugs' other immediate effects that can potentially trigger seizures, respiratory distress (inability to breathe), and death. If the method of taking drugs is smoking, it will always lead to dangerous long-term health effects.

Vaping with electronic cigarettes does not include the same number of particles as tobacco smoke. However, the vapor mist that enters the throat and lungs is almost as deadly. Since there is no combustion, there is a greater variety of chemicals suspended in the liquid mists, including flavor compounds and various oils. Flavor compounds (most often diacetyl) coat the lungs and trigger inflammatory reactions that may lead to internal blistering and tears in the lining. Other liquid oils can produce pneumonia-like symptoms that trigger inflammation of the lung tissue. Vaping technologies were only invented at the turn of the twenty-first century, so most long-term reactions (such as cancer) will require more time to study after the devices have been in existence for 80–100 years.

It is safe to assume that any health risks that are already known to be caused by tobacco smoke are substantially increased by other forms of smoke caused by other recreational drug use. Any drug that can be smoked will increase the likelihood of long-term cardiovascular disease, as well as other physical risks associated with immediate drug use (related to cognition, memory, emotions, and autoimmunity). Vaping avoids certain toxins from combustion, but other un-combusted chemicals suspended in the vapor mists may cause equally harmful physical reactions. The National Institute for Drug Addiction (NIDA) reported that as of 2022, 75 percent of marijuana users smoked the drug, and only 25 percent consumed through vaping, tinctures, or edibles.

Secondary Risks: Lastly, all recreational drugs—regardless of type—will produce intoxication or other characteristics of being "high." Most often, these effects impair physical coordination with slower reaction times. Both alcohol and marijuana impair coordination, though the effects are not noticeable in the same ways. Drink-induced intoxication is noticeable by an inability to walk and by slurred speech. Marijuana intoxication results in slower or disordered speech and slower reaction times. Opium-based drugs also generally result in slower reaction times, while hallucinogens and amphetamines may have little effect on physical coordination. Regardless of whether a drug physically impairs motor functions, they all impair other cognitive functions, like awareness, memory, inhibitions, and judgment (leading to greater risk-taking) and a general vulnerability to abuse (physical and sexual).

The secondary risks that are most deadly are those related to impaired coordination. If you cannot walk straight, there is a much greater likelihood that you will fall down and (potentially) seriously hurt yourself. Similarly, if you drive a vehicle under the influence of alcohol, marijuana, or opioids, slow reaction times increase the likelihood of accidents. Also, decreased inhibitions mean that drivers often take risks (such as running a yellow light) that they may not otherwise take when sober. The vast majority of emergency room visits and deaths caused by drug use (especially alcohol and marijuana) are a result of accidents. Vehicle accidents are the most deadly, but drowning and physical falls are almost as common.

Accidents that do not result in death may still cause serious injuries, such as broken bones, loss of limbs or sight, concussions, and other forms of brain damage. Statistics related to alcohol abuse always include deaths and hospital visits due to secondary accidents, but for a variety of reasons most statistics on the abuse of other drugs do not include the same variety of secondary risks. In this way, the annual statistical reports are not consistently applied across all drug types.

In addition to accidents caused by impairment for the user, there are also serious risks for other people who may be around the user. Obviously, passengers riding alongside impaired users driving in vehicles or innocent bystanders who are hit by impaired drivers face serious physical risks even though they had no contact with the abused drug. In less obvious ways, family members (especially children and spouses) face increased risks of neglect and abuse. If the parents are too incapacitated to take care of themselves, they often fail to take care of basic needs of their children (feeding, clothing, supervision against accidents, and general medical care). For drugs that increase emotional volatility, there is also an increased risk of physical violence (such as from alcohol intoxication, THC-induced psychotic episodes, PCP, and other amphetamines). Children and spouses may be abused by uncontrolled emotional reactions of drug-using family members. Reports of college date rapes indicate that more than half (62 percent) of the males who committed a sexual assault against their date were intoxicated at the time.

Lastly, drug impairment increases the potential for victimization. For drugs like alcohol and many synthetic opioids, the user may become drowsy and generally less responsive. This condition renders them more likely to be physically abused, robbed, or sexually assaulted by those around them. A 2006 Bureau of Justice Statistics Report indicated that nearly three-quarters (about 72 percent) of women who have been raped experienced the assault while they were intoxicated. People who are impaired by any drug are more likely to find themselves in situations where they are victims of abuse.

Other Physical Dangers: Each drug type carries its own physical health risk over long spans of abuse. Abuse of alcohol and most synthetic amphetamines tends to increase the risk of liver and kidney damage (the organs that routinely cleanse the blood are subjected to greater stress when they filter out drugs). Even legal over-the-counter drugs like aspirin, acetaminophen (Tylenol), and birth-control pills can lead to liver damage.

Lung diseases are most associated with drugs that are inhaled—by smoking or vaping. However, any drug that excites or depresses blood pressure may indirectly harm both the lungs and the heart tissues. Drugs that directly affect the central nervous system, such as cocaine, heroin, and various amphetamines, place greater stress on body temperature, heart rate, and blood pressure. Over time, these excessive stimulations may lead to increased heart attacks and stroke risks. Many overdose deaths caused by cocaine, amphetamines, ecstasy, and opioids are due to drug-induced heart attacks. A study from the *Journal of American Medical Association* reported increased death rates from cardiovascular disease (by 1.5 times) among marijuana users over nonusers (Vallee, 2024). These disease rates increased both if the user used marijuana daily and if they only used it less than once a week. A later study that same year reported that marijuana use may corrupt genetic coding at the cellular levels, which increases risks of cancer, birth defects, and accelerated aging, which may impact both the user and their later children and grandchildren (Reece and Hulce, 2024).

When users consume their drugs through injection, there is a much higher risk of contracting infections at the site where the needle pierces the skin. These infections can cause blood diseases, which can also lead to heart attacks and strokes. As a general rule, any drug that artificially stimulates or artificially depresses receptors in the body to achieve euphoria, pain relief, or hallucinations will usually lead to increased risk of diseases because the internal organs, endocrine and nervous systems are excited (or depressed) beyond what the human body is genetically designed to accommodate.

Conclusion: Opportunity Costs of Increased Health Risks for the Community

Any and every drug can pose serious health risks to the individual if used outside of the supervision of qualified medical professionals. Untrained users cannot easily identify contamination across drug types and do not always know appropriate dosage levels. Most harm caused by drugs stems from unintended overdosing from contaminated substances or from the development of long-term tolerance that encourages users to take more than their bodies can handle. Most people do not have access to scientific testing facilities to scan the chemical characteristics of their drugs, and the pressure of physical and psychological addiction encourages users to continue taking their drug more frequently and with increasing potency, even when they know it is harmful.

Libertarians argue that each individual should be allowed to make their own choices regarding their recreational pursuits, especially if those pursuits harm only themselves. This is the argument based on the protection of individual liberty. Social-welfare advocates, however, argue that some forms of drug addiction pose greater risks for the user and for those around them. The choices of people who work as public transportation drivers, who operate large machines, or who are responsible for other dependents including children always impact other people who did not choose to take drugs and did not accept the increased health risks. Traditional conservatives argue that any recreational drug that impairs individual judgment or a person's potential for vocational growth denies society of a potentially productive member.

Drug decriminalization and legalization increase rates of drug use and thereby increases the potential for dependency and addiction. If increased rates of dependency lead to increasing medical health issues for a large percentage of the population, then that could place unnecessary strains on the public health system. Both social-welfare advocates and traditional conservatives agree on that point.

Ultimately, the level of acceptable risk to physical health must be judged by society at large. If voters pass laws that decriminalize or legalize certain drugs, they have chosen to accept the associated risks of increased recreational drug use. They hope that other methods of decreasing the demand for recreational drug use will offset the increased supply. On the other hand, if voters choose to maintain traditional drug laws that focus most on controlling the supply of illegal drugs, they have chosen to accept the associated costs of increased drug enforcement. No law will be perfect, and almost all laws related to drug policy involve some degree of experimentation. Only the passage of time and the unfolding of natural consequences (unintended or not) will reveal which policy is most effective and which priority leads to greater protection of physical health of individuals and society.

7

Legalization and Mental Health Issues

What impact does the decriminalization or legalization of certain recreational drugs have on individual mental health? How does removing the stigma of recreational drug use as an immoral action impact the general mental health of the community? Are evidence-based policies more likely to encourage drug users to seek out treatment for their drug habits? Or will they encourage a new cultural norm that tolerates drug use as a socially acceptable form of recreation? These questions are what stimulate the greatest amount of debate over twenty-first century drug policies.

In terms of obvious signs of harm, tracking influences of drug policies on psychological health is difficult because almost all data collected on the emotional effects of recreational drug use rely on users reporting their own symptoms. Unless the user recognizes the harm that comes from taking the drug, they will not include honest descriptions of harmful effects of drug use. Infrequent drug use may not show the extent of psychological distress, and if used only during times of recreation, drug use may be associated most with the pleasures of the moment. Certain drugs may change user perceptions so that they believe that the drugs help them, even when outside observers would say that the drugs are hurting them.

At the same time, self-reporting also leads to very emotional accounts of harm caused by recreational drug use. Most often, these reports come from users in treatment programs who have struggled with long periods of addiction and who find themselves in very serious difficulties. The fact that they are seeking drug treatment demonstrates that they recognize a strong connection between their drug use and the many mental health, emotional, and relationship problems that they are dealing with. Almost every patient in a drug treatment center, and their family members, has a story to tell about the lure of their first drug use followed by the slow spiral of decline into despair after they fell into addiction. Often, the victims of drug addiction recount their experiences in the hope of warning others not to fall into the same dangers.

Social scientists are often confronted with mixed messages when collecting their data. On the one side are the many stories of occasional users who take drugs to increase the pleasures of their recreational activities and who report that drugs only enhance their lives and their psychological well-being. On the other side, we find a large number of stories from people who suffer directly or indirectly from drug addiction. Symptoms ranging from acute depression to mania or other forms of emotional and financial struggles follow their habitual drug use. More common are stories of spouses and family members or coworkers who have seen their loved ones succumb to drug addiction, often to the point of death by overdose, accident, or suicide. There are wide differences in responses between those who take recreational drugs and enjoy the experience versus those who suffer from the harsh effects of drug addiction. There are ways to account for personal bias when considering these two sets of reactions, and these rely mostly on correlative statistics of drug use, mental health diagnosis, and rates of depression, mania, and suicide ideation and attempts.

Proponents of decriminalization and other harm reduction strategies hope that new policies will make it easier for drug users to better treat their associated mental health problems. Opponents of decriminalization argue that a more lenient drug culture weakens the social tools necessary to help protect experimental users from falling into habits of addiction. In a perfect world, we could point to specific statistics on mental health to establish which side was accurate and which side was inaccurate. Unfortunately, since these statistics rely on subjective self-reporting data points and because statistical correlations cannot eliminate other potential causes for increasing mental health issues, we cannot form any absolute conclusions. By themselves, statistical correlations cannot prove or disprove the effectiveness of drug decriminalization or legalization. Instead, we must consider the intended goals behind drug decriminalization (and legalization) and also recognize existing correlations that seem to follow their implementation.

Physiology of Addiction and Dependency

Libertarians may deny the scientific basis for drug addiction, but the vast majority of scientists believe that physical dependencies on certain drugs are a biochemical process. To begin this discussion, we should clarify our terms:

1. A "drug" is any substance that affects the natural processes of living tissues.
2. "Therapeutic drugs" are used to repair (or sometimes enhance) natural biochemical processes within the human body that have become disordered and may be the source of physical or mental illness.
3. "Recreational drugs" are used for their euphoric or other stimulating effects and are not intended to treat any specific illness.

Recreational drugs are sometimes advertised as having therapeutic characteristics (e.g., some cannabis companies will argue that marijuana use has health benefits), but the most relevant difference between the two types of drugs is the primary purpose for which they are used: recreational drugs are taken for their pleasurable effects, and therapeutic drugs are taken for healing. Both kinds of drugs may be susceptible to addiction. However, drug abuse becomes a social issue when users become dependent on their drugs even when they no longer provide any therapeutic value or when they become harmful to the user's health.

Definition of Addiction: Addiction refers to any behavior (including drug use) that results in harm to the individual or to those around them, and which the person has tried to stop because they know it is harmful but which they are unable to stop. There are three elements to this definition: (1) the behavior (or substance) causes harm; (2) the user knows that it is harmful; and (3) the user is unable to stop the behavior (or stop taking the drug). People who never try to stop the behavior do not know if they are addicted or not. The inability to stop a behavior (or to stop taking some substance) is defined as a dependency, and dependencies are not always addictions. It only becomes an addiction if the behavior (or substance) is harmful. For example, a college student may become *dependent* on coffee, but since coffee does not pose any harm to the student nor threaten harm to those around them, their coffee (caffeine) dependency is not an addiction.

These three variables are part of the reason why addiction is often subject to debate. If someone willingly takes a drug and does not believe it is harmful to themselves or to others and never attempts to stop taking it, then under a strict definition of that scenario, the drug use would not be considered an addiction. However, there is an exception to this definition when the effects of the drug are *objectively* harmful, meaning that outside observers can see the harm, even if the user does not (or chooses not to) admit the harm. For example, a chronic alcoholic may claim that they have no problem with drinking, yet their family and friends can see that the alcohol use is compromising the user's ability to function at work or to maintain peaceful relationships at home. The user does not want to stop drinking and does not appear able to stop. In this case, their alcohol dependency is clearly an addiction because the alcohol is causing harm even when the user denies the harm.

Physiology of Addiction: All addictions involve biochemical processes that include both physical and psychological elements. On the physical side, the body can crave the drug-taking behavior. We discuss that first because it is easiest to explain: every drug causes some effect on the body—that is the defining characteristic of all drugs. Some of these effects are noticeable, like emotional volatility, diminished motor skills, or tiredness. Other changes affect internal processes, like heart rates or insulin production, and may not be immediately obvious. Drugs that produce immediate effects on mood, emotions, and sensory perceptions are called psychoactive drugs, and they are the most likely type of drug to be used for recreational purposes because the user feels the effects immediately, and those effects are pleasurable to them.

Most psychoactive drugs work by stimulating or inhibiting the connections between neurons, which are those cells linking the central nervous system together connecting the brain with other parts of the body. There are an estimated 100 billion nerve cells in the human body, and each nerve cell is connected with thousands of other nerve cells. These cells do not physically touch each other but lay very near each other with extensions that look like fingers that extend outward on each end of the neuron. Cells are turned on when electrically charged ions (positively or negatively) are stimulated, causing one cell to stimulate the next along very long sequences. There are also chemical connections that cause these cells to stimulate in sequence when certain molecules pass physically from one neuron to the next across a space called the synaptic gap. These molecules have special shapes when they leave one neuron, which allows them to fit neatly into receptors in the other neuron. Specific receptors (and combinations of receptors) produce those various effects that influence mood and pleasure sensation, fear and anxiety, excitement, confidence, and many other emotional and cognitive reactions.

Psychoactive drugs work by either inhibiting (or stimulating) chemical connections between neural cells or by serving as a replacement chemical that triggers reactions that would not otherwise be triggered naturally by the body. Alcohol can inhibit (or slow down) the chemical connections. Amphetamines generally stimulate (or speed up) these connections. Marijuana (THC) and other hallucinogens can induce a series of chemical hormone connections that would not otherwise be triggered. Certain drugs stimulate or inhibit the hormones responsible for the sensation of pleasure, relaxation, excitement, or intense emotions. Recreational drug users will directly or indirectly stimulate (or inhibit) certain categories of neural receptors, and this produces the "high" that the user expects.

Since each drug is either over-stimulating or under-stimulating receptors, the body almost always responds by flooding the nervous system with the opposite types of chemicals. This means that if a user takes cocaine to feel excited and energized, then as soon as the drug wears off, the user feels depressed and lethargic. In most cases, users will simply feel sick—upset stomach, headaches, blurry vision, difficulty concentrating, and so on. These are like the effects of a "hangover" that occurs after drinking too much alcohol. These reactions are most responsible for fluctuating levels of tolerance, intensity of withdrawal symptoms, and the probability of dependency or addiction.

Withdrawal Symptoms and Addiction: Dependency occurs in two ways, and it usually follows from repeated use of a drug. Users who first experience a pleasurable effect from the drug will often take the drug again in order to achieve the same pleasurable sensations. However, the body reacts slightly differently with each successive experience, and over time the body will become accustomed to each additional stimulation by preparing extra supplies of the counter-chemicals. Once this happens, the user's body will be expecting to continually receive the drug. If the user does not take the drug, their bodies still feel the effects of the built-up store of counter-chemicals, and these sensations are described as withdrawal symptoms.

Withdrawal symptoms can be very painful and (in some extreme cases) may even disrupt heart rates so much that the user dies. Eventually, withdrawal symptoms fade away, and the user no longer feels these painful aftereffects. This might take days or months depending on the drug. However, in the meantime, most users feel such strong cravings for relief that they cannot wait for the feelings to go away, so they simply take the drug again to avoid the symptoms of withdrawal. Physical dependency occurs when physical signs of withdrawal are so strong that the user feels incapable of not taking the drug. Dependency becomes an addiction when the user continues to take the drug even though they know it is harming their body (or is indirectly harming others).

Another form of dependency that occurs is psychological. For many drugs, the euphoric sensation does not lead to strong physical symptoms of withdrawal. For example, marijuana and other hallucinogens do not leave headaches, upset stomachs, or other physical signs of pain. Nevertheless, the contrast in emotions produced by these drugs, between the "high" and post-high "normal," is often so strong that the user experiences distressing emotional symptoms of withdrawal.

Typically, users become psychologically dependent when they feel depressed, anxious, or otherwise unable to cope with routine experiences after the drug effects wear off, and they retake the drug in order to recover the lost sense of relief. This phenomenon is most common with habitual marijuana users who suffer from "flat affect"—which means they lose the ability to become excited by ordinary activities unless they are under the influence of the drug, so they continually rely on marijuana to experience any stimulating feelings at all.

Any dependency can become an addiction if the user tries to stop taking the drug and then finds it very difficult to stop. They feel a compulsion, either physically or psychologically, to continue taking the drug, even when they no longer want to do so.

Tolerance and Addiction: Risks of dependency and addiction are increased with physical and psychological tolerance. As a physical phenomenon, tolerance occurs when, after repeated use, the body becomes accustomed to a particular drug and therefore requires greater amounts or concentrations in order to achieve the same physical effects. As a psychological phenomenon, tolerance means that people who take the drug repeatedly will "feel" increasingly less of a reaction than what they felt during their first time using it. Tolerance increases the likelihood of dependency and addiction because users tend to increase the frequency, concentration, and amount of drug in order to achieve the same experience that they felt after their first use.

Nonchemical Addictions: The difference between physical addiction and psychological addiction is difficult to determine, and addiction does not always require physical substances to enter the body. For example, an adult may become addicted to the excitement of online gambling (or to the stimulation of pornography or video games). Even though these digital stimulations do not involve the ingestion of any substance, they may still lead to addiction, and they may trigger similar chemical reactions that are caused by outside drugs.

If a gambler recognizes that his habit is ruining him financially and harming his family and other relationships, and if he is still unable to stop, he develops an addiction even though he is not ingesting any outside drug. Similarly, if a computer user becomes so obsessed with watching so much pornography that they lose the ability to become physically stimulated by real-life interactions (becoming impotent), and the behavior harms their relationships, and if the computer user is unable to stop going to the pornography websites, that behavior becomes a digital addiction. Any harmful habitual behavior may be considered an addiction even though it does not involve chemicals entering the body.

That is also why drugs like marijuana that may not trigger physical withdrawal symptoms often lead to intense psychological addiction.

From a psychological standpoint, then, addiction refers to the inability to end the person's dependency on a behavior or on a substance. Researchers discovered that both kinds of addiction involve the same sort of biochemical processes involving dopamine reactions regardless of whether it is triggered by outside drugs or by other instantly stimulating experiences (such as gambling or pornography).

Goals of Decriminalization and Legalization

There is strong consensus that drug addiction increases the probability of mental health problems in the individual. There is also some agreement that these problems increase the burden of social services on the community. The main disagreement is over whether all drugs lead to addiction equally and whether moderate recreational drug use will lead to addiction. The risks of addiction are clear, but the likelihood that any given individual will fall into addiction after engaging in recreational drug use continues to be debated.

Traditional conservatives follow moral standards that recognize patterns of habit: helpful habits are called "virtues," and harmful habits are called "vices." They argue that artificial sensory stimulations will always be more attractive than the sense of satisfaction that comes from hard work, or struggle, and that leads to vice. If recreational drugs can easily stimulate the sense of pleasure, most people will prefer the easy stimulation from taking drugs to their other responsibilities that require more work. This natural preference inevitably leads to addiction, which is why traditional conservatives support laws that discourage easy access to recreational drugs and encourage cultural norms (moral codes) that oppose drug use.

Social-welfare advocates recognize the potential of addiction in any drug and also believe that most people will avoid addiction voluntarily if they are given the resources to do so and if there are fewer obstacles between the user and these resources. They do not agree that any single cultural norm will successfully discourage drug experimentation, so they do not support laws that may shame users for their drug use. Instead, social-welfare advocates prefer a legal culture that does not make any moral judgements on drug use, and in that way, users will feel no shame about seeking treatment if their habits turn into addictions. If the culture imposes moral judgments on recreational drug use, or if there are criminal punishments associated with drug use, the addicted user may avoid treatment option because they do not want to face public embarrassment or because they do not want to risk incarceration. One of the primary goals of harm reduction policies is to remove the stigma (the moral judgment) associated with drug use.

In contrast to both the traditional conservatives and the social-welfare advocates, most libertarians do not believe that recreational drug use is naturally addictive, and so they disagree with any generalized assertion about the risks or dangers of addiction. They believe users will take recreational drugs if the benefit of expected pleasures outweighs the potential costs of intoxication. They do not hold any opinions about the morality of drug use, and they do not want policies to reflect Judeo-Christian priorities over any other moral standard. Therefore, they support decriminalization (and legalization) policies so that each individual can decide for themselves the cost-benefit analysis. They generally do not support government-sponsored treatment programs because they do not believe that the state should be responsible for individual recreational decisions. However, they believe private treatment programs should be available if users believe their habits cause more problems than they are willing to accept. Libertarians recognize a correlation between mental health issues and recreational drug use but reject the idea that drugs may cause mental health problems. Instead, they argue that preexisting mental health problems are what cause users to develop drug dependencies.

Drug Stigma (Shame or Guilt) and Treatment Potential

From the perspective of psychological health, the role of social stigma associated with recreational drug use or with drug dependency and addiction differs significantly between traditional conservatives and the social-welfare advocates. Traditional conservatives believe that human motivation needs both internal and external reinforcements to encourage healthy decision-making. For example, a student may find that smoking marijuana is pleasurable. Although the student might normally recognize potential dangers, it is often hard to worry about future dangers that are not obvious at the moment. Without a genuine risk of immediate consequences, such as getting in trouble with school authorities or with the police, the student may be unable to resist the temptation to seek out the pleasure of marijuana smoking, even though they know that marijuana smoking may hurt them in other ways (such as harming their potential). The potential embarrassment of getting into trouble with authorities may be the added external incentive needed to discourage marijuana use. In this way, the risk of social stigma associated with drug use helps to limit the likelihood of psychological addiction.

By contrast, social-welfare advocates believe that it is impossible to prevent students from experimenting with dangerous behaviors. They sometimes argue that such experimentation is a good practice because it gives each person experience to better recognize what they want and what they do not want. For example, a student may begin smoking marijuana because they encounter the drug in a positive social situation, such as at a party where people who are smoking are laughing and enjoying themselves. That student may find pleasure in the experience, but they also may recognize the risks. If they continue to attend the parties, and if they find they are smoking so much marijuana that their grades are slipping and their other relationships are dissolving, the student will want to seek out some treatment options. As long as they do not feel shame for their brief experimentation, they are more likely to take advantage of available resources. However, if they feel social stigma associated with their drug use, they may hide their addiction and may avoid treatment options, and then their problems may worsen. In this way, social-welfare advocates hope to eliminate any social stigma of drug use so as to keep the addicted user more closely tied to the community where help is most available.

These different perspectives on the role of social stigma lead to considerable debate over public policy proposals related to decriminalization and legalization of certain drugs. Decriminalization policies remove the threat of police involvement in order to reframe drug use as a health issue rather than as a legal issue that threatens existing moral norms. Advocates for harm reduction strategies promote public education programs that teach about different lifestyle options, including potential dangers of addiction. Social-welfare advocates oppose policies that reinforce social stigmas of drug use, because they may lead to more cases of untreated drug addiction.

At the same time, though, if social norms are changed to such an extent that experimentation (and habitual drug use) becomes a routine, normalized form of recreational activity, then young users may be less receptive to social messages warning that drug use can lead to addiction. In their opposite corner, traditional conservatives argue that the lure of drug addiction is too powerful to resist without social stigma and that many drugs impair user perceptions to the extent that they do not recognize the harm. Morally neutral education programs will not sufficiently warn users of the dangers of addiction and decriminalization may (unintentionally) encourage greater drug use because drugs are described without any moral judgement at all and in socially acceptable terms. If recreational drug use is normalized, the ordinary signs of harm may be blunted by a cultural environment that does not provide the necessary cues. In other words, users will not have any objective perspectives to help correct their subjective biases. When the user experiences mood disorders, relationship issues, or problems at work, then without the external stigma associated with drug use, they will likely blame almost any other causes in their lives, except their drug use. If drug use is normalized, why would users see their habits as being responsible for their problems?

From this perspective traditional conservatives oppose removing social stigmas through drug decriminalization (and legalization) because it removes social tools necessary to discourage habits of drug use that cause addiction. In direct contrast to the social-welfare viewpoint, traditional conservatives further argue that once addicted, the lack of social stigma may discourage users from seeking treatment because they do not believe their drug use is the source of any problem.

These are fundamental disagreements, and advocates on both sides see that the preservation or the removal of social stigma associated with recreational drug use as critical to their policy goals. If each side believes that social stigma plays an important role, there is very little room for compromise. This point of contention is one of the reasons why the issue of drug decriminalization and legalization of certain drugs can become so controversial.

Correlations between Drug Addiction and Relationships

Recreational drug use always influences mood and behavior of the user. Sometimes these changes are welcomed by the user, but in other cases, these changes can be unpredictable and can place great stress on relationships and indirectly on the emotional and mental health of the user.

Personal Relationships: Frequent drug use intensifies ordinary relationship stresses. There are strong correlations between drug addiction and rates of emotional volatility, domestic abuse, and child neglect. While under the influence of drugs, behaviors can be unpredictable with moments of laughter and excitement, interspersed with periods of anger and drowsiness. Intoxicated users lose their ability to make sound decisions (judgment) and have less inhibitions, which may lead to abuse (physical and sexual) or child neglect if they forget to feed, wash, or take care of their children's needs.

Whether the relationship is romantic, family-based, or just a friendship, addiction increases the sense of instability between partners in any relationship. Spouses, children, or other partners may feel they can no longer depend on the user because intoxication interferes with normal abilities. Users seem to (and often will) devote more time and attention to their drug than they do to other people in their lives. Addictions often increase habits of deception because users will lie about their habits or try to hide the evidence of their addiction, and these lies also break down the sense of trust.

Communication is usually impaired when users are under the influence of drugs. Also, even when users are not under the influence, their experience of withdrawal symptoms can cause heightened irritability, irrational suspicions, paranoia, and increasing levels of fear, anxiety, and depression. These reactions also interfere with clear communication. More than half of all domestic violence cases involve substance abuse, and the intensity of domestic violence generally increases when one or more partners are under the influence of drugs.

Professional Relationships: There are always opportunity costs associated with intoxication. Users are unable to perform physical tasks as well when they are under the influence of drugs than they could if they were sober. Mental tasks such as decision-making, learning, and tasks that require memory can be more difficult during and after drug use. These effects can have a serious impact on job performance and performance at school. Students living in households where one or more members are addicted to recreational drugs tend to have significantly lower scores on standardized tests. Alcohol and drug abuse is a major contributor to lost workdays and the inability to keep a job. In 2017, the Centers for Disease Control and Prevention set the estimate of lost productivity at about $400 billion per year.

Financial problems are a leading cause of strife in a relationship. When one partner is out of work and the other must provide for their basic needs, there is cause for resentment. Users under the influence often make unwise purchasing decisions or make risky investments. The costs of the drugs themselves are sometimes higher than the amount of disposable income, and addiction usually increases the rate of consumption so that these usage costs continue to rise. Also, since all drugs artificially stimulate the endocrine system, habitual users tend to have more general issues with their immune system, which makes them more susceptible to common illnesses. The costs of medical expenses, even if unrelated to drug use, usually increase as well.

Signs That Drug Use Is Impairing a Relationship: The American Association for Marriage and Family Therapy identified signs that drugs or alcohol use may be interfering with healthy relationships. This list is not unique, and these signs may be found on almost any website that advertises counseling or drug-treatment services:

1. Partners increasingly argue about the use of drugs or alcohol or the activities related to the use of drugs or alcohol (going out, neglect of home and responsibilities, staying up too late, etc.).
2. One partner makes excuses for the other partner's declining performance at work or broken commitments with friends or other family members that arise due to their substance use.
3. One or both partners use the relationship stress as an excuse to increase their drug or alcohol use.
4. Drinking or taking drugs together is one of the few shared activities that both partners enjoy (which means that they have few other interests outside of drugs that draw them together).
5. Arguments become more heated or potentially violent while one or both partners are under the influence of drugs or alcohol.
6. One or both partners require alcohol or drugs before they can engage in romantic or sexual activities.
7. The relationship, or the family itself, gradually becomes isolated from other friends and relatives in order to hide the signs of addiction or as a result of negative encounters that occurred while intoxicated.

If several or all of these signs are present in a relationship, even if the user believes that their substance dependency is not harming themselves or others, these indications should provide some objective evidence that there is harm. If there is harm, and if the user is unable to stop using, then that is an addiction.

Correlations between Drug Addiction and Mental Illness

The causal connections between drug use and mental illness are difficult to determine, but correlations are strong. The range of mental disorders correlated to drug use spans from mild bouts of public anxiety or depression to very serious forms of psychosis and schizophrenia. The National Institute of Mental Health reported in 2022 that nearly 40 percent of chronic drug users have also been diagnosed with serious mental health disorders. One out of three people suffering from mental disorders also struggle with substance-abuse disorders.

Marijuana has been especially tied to high risks of psychosis. A 2024 longitudinal study from the University of Bristol in England known as the Avon Longitudinal Study of Parents and Children (ALSPAC) indicated that teens who smoked marijuana between sixteen and eighteen years of age are twice as likely to experience schizophrenic symptoms of hallucinations and delusions when they reach their twenties. Another longitudinal study published in 2017 by the American Association of Marriage and Family Therapy indicated that mental illness plays a leading cause in the breakup of relationships, as well as the inability to form new relationships. The inability to form stable relationships is a leading cause of depression, anxiety, and other mental disorders. The same study concluded that with more proactive treatments for substance abuse disorders and mental illness, there would be 6.7 million fewer divorces and 3.5 million more marriages over a ten-year period.

Any substances, whether drugs or alcohol, that frequently interfere with normal perceptions and generally increase emotional volatility are more likely to lead to psychological problems. Emotional insecurity and increased anxiety may be addressed simply by removing alcohol or substance use. However, in some cases of psychosis, such as schizophrenia or bipolar disorder, the mental illness may continue even after substance abuse has ended. In this case, treatment options require more than just ending the substance use.

Correlative statistics are a poor source of evidence in judging the effectiveness of drug decriminalization strategies or other legalization policies because they cannot account for other causes of mental illness. However, according to statistical trends compiled by the National Institute of Mental Health, since the waves of marijuana legalization, the rates of serious psychological distress over the past months increased by a third between the 1990s and the late 2010s. In 2011 one in six adults exhibited some form of mental illness with varying degrees of severity, ranging from anxiety disorders to depression, delusions, psychosis, and suicide ideation and attempts. By 2022, that rate increased to nearly one in four adults (from 17 percent to over 23 percent).

The National Center for Health Statistics also reported in 2022 that suicide rates among all age groups, but especially among youth, increased significantly between 1990 and 2022. During the 1990s, when drug use among teens and young adults was at its lowest rate since before the 1970s, the suicide rate was at 6.78 per 100,000 people. By 2000, when the very first states began decriminalizing marijuana, that number had increased to 14.2 per 100,000. In 2022, the rates had nearly doubled to 22.8 per 100,000, which was nearly four times the suicide rate during the late 1980s and early 1990s.

There are many other social changes that also occurred between 2000 and the 2020s, including the rapid increase in smartphone use and continuous access to social media. There are strong correlations between drug use, addiction, and social-media dependency, but it is very difficult to distinguish which social change was most responsible for increasing rates of mental illness. It is possible that all three social changes were contributors.

Conclusion: The Problem of Mixed Messaging

Statistical evidence alone cannot prove with certainty either the effectiveness or the ineffectiveness of drug decriminalization and legalization of certain drugs. However, there are some strong correlations that are difficult to ignore:

1. Since the early 2000s, when marijuana became widely decriminalized at the state level, and since the mid-2010s, when recreational marijuana became more commonly legalized, the overall rate of drug use has increased, and the rate of drug addiction has reached historical levels (surpassing alcohol as the primary source of intoxication for the first time ever).
2. Drug dependency and addiction increases the risk of mental illness, including depression, anxiety disorders, psychosis, and suicide ideation and attempts.
3. Rates of mental illness and other psychological and emotional disorders increased substantially since the 2010s, as more states decriminalized or legalized certain drugs.

Modern society is flooded with mixed messages. Algorithms that determine which posts and messages are more strongly publicized through social media have largely been influenced by marketing campaigns that promote marijuana legalization. Popular entertainment industry (movies and music) generally supports decriminalization strategies and morally neutral messages with regard to recreational drug use. For most teens and young adults who are heavily influenced by their smartphone interactions, marijuana, and other drugs no longer carry the same social stigma that they once carried during the 1980s. Numerous national surveys indicated that most high-school students during the 2010s routinely believed that marijuana was safe and potentially healthy, alcohol was more dangerous than marijuana, and tobacco was more dangerous than both alcohol and marijuana. Based on objective scientific standards, these beliefs are all incorrect. Tobacco is the least dangerous of all three drugs because it carries no psychoactive effect.

In contrast to these morally neutral (or even positive) messages regarding recreational drug use, there are annual statistics that show increasing addiction rates among all age groups, increasing rates of psychological and emotional health problems, and increasing mortality (death) rates from drug overdoses and suicides. The result is that both youth and adults are receiving mixed messages that make widespread consensus among the general public much more difficult to achieve.

Whether intended or not, lawmakers and voters rely on these mixed messages to choose whether to support legal policies that continue to criminalize recreational drug use or to decriminalize (and in some cases legalize) various drug types. The risk of physical death is most obvious, but the more subtle risks of psychological fragility are not as easy to measure and compile. It is always tempting to point to other social changes to explain increasing rates of mental illness. Voters are often informed about potential risks or benefits of certain policy changes, but since the evidence for decriminalization is mixed, voters make decisions based on the hope of change itself and not based on objective evidence. Also, the cultural priorities of the communities (city, state, and federal) are heavily influenced by changing moral attitudes, economic pressures for new business opportunities, and from other influences in popular entertainment (messages from movies and music). Only over the course of time will voters see the results of their election decisions.

During the early 2000s, the cultural tone of voters shifted to support decriminalization and legalization of marijuana as a compassionate and more humane policy decision, which also respected individual freedom of moral preference. During the mid-2020s, many communities began reconsidering those decisions—partially in response to increasing evidence of physical health risks (high mortality rates from drug-overdoses) and partly in response to new evidence of increasing psychological health risks (depression, anxiety, and suicide rates). Since changing attitudes toward recreational drugs and drug policies are still in transition, the ultimate impact of these reform measures may not be fully understood until the 2030s or 2040s.

8

Legalization and Crime

Recreational drug use and crime are so strongly associated together that most drug-related laws and policies focus first on their value in controlling crime and then only secondarily on their value for limiting (or curing) addiction. Using law enforcement to control drug use is so common that the advocates for decriminalization and legalization usually describe the War on Drugs purely in terms of police and punishments. As we have shown in earlier chapters (especially Chapters 3 and 5), American drug laws have always attempted to address both the problem of crime and the problem of addiction simultaneously. Nevertheless, the supporters of decriminalization and legalization of certain drugs would prefer there to be much less emphasis on crime control and more emphasis on curing addiction.

Unfortunately, the symptoms of drug abuse that the public notices most are usually crime. In 1968, President Richard Nixon won his national election largely because he promised to restore law and order, and one of his top priorities was to tackle the misuse and abuse of drugs and to target the criminal organizations that were most often involved with the manufacture, distribution and illegal sales of recreational drugs. The Comprehensive Drug Abuse Prevention and Control Act (CDA) of 1970 created schedules (lists) of all drug types to distinguish between those that were most dangerous (no therapeutic value with highest risk of addiction) and those that were least dangerous (therapeutic value with least likelihood of addiction). The CDA served as the formal federal starting point for comprehensive federal drug laws that would also be enforced by state and local levels of American society. It also implemented international agreements that the United States signed nearly a decade earlier. For Nixon, these laws helped launch his War on Drugs, which he strongly associated with law and order.

Nixon's campaign was mostly successful in so far as the rapid increase in crime rates paused during his administration. Nevertheless, it is difficult to know with certainty whether that pause in crime rates was due to the new comprehensive drug laws or if it was caused by other factors. Between 1970 and 1995, the War on Drugs taught a consistent message that recreational drug use was harmful to the individual and to society. Between 1995 and 2025 the War on Drugs faded, and the public message began to change, so that many states passed laws decriminalizing and legalizing certain drugs (mostly marijuana). Overall, rates of certain kinds of crime declined during the first period and then rates began to increase for other crimes in the second era. However, interpreting these trends is difficult because there is no way to know with certainty whether changing drug laws caused, or were symptoms of, increasing crime rates or whether crime rates were caused by any other social changes that were also occurring during the same years. There is general consensus that overall incidents of crime have increased substantially since the 2010s. However, explaining the precise relationship between crime and decriminalization policies is more controversial and varies largely based on differing ideological presumptions.

What Correlations Can and Cannot Do

A correlation is a relationship between two things; for example, if more people use drugs and if there are also more crimes during the same time, there is a correlation between drug use and crime rates. Correlations can demonstrate relationships, but they do not prove causation between the two things. In other words, A and B may occur together, but we do not know if A caused B, B caused A, or both A and B were caused by other factors. Even though we see increasing drug use and increasing crime rates, that does not mean that the drug use *caused* the crime rates (or the other way around). There may be other reasons why crime rates increased: the economy could be worse, causing people to turn to crime; the threat of global unrest may encourage insecurity; political scandals may inspire a sense of cynicism; rising use of social media and smartphones may erode the basic respect for other people. Also, on the other side of correlation, people may choose to use recreational drugs for many reasons. These reasons may include peer pressure, the quest for excitement, the lure of escapism, the promise of new pleasures, or even the fear of missing out. There may be one reason or many reasons combined. Correlations mostly just recognize patterns between two related phenomena. It is difficult to establish causal connections without isolating one or more variables.

Individual motivation complicates these correlations. Some crimes are obviously connected to drugs: those committed while under the influence of drugs and those cases of people involved in the manufacture, transportation, or distribution of drugs are obviously drug-related. However, other crimes may be committed in order to get the money to buy drugs—or they may be committed for other reasons. There are entire classes of crimes based on passion or greed that may have no connection to drugs at all (even if the person committing the crime is using drugs during commission of the crime). Crime statistics only report on crime types and do not distinguish the motivations for crime because it is very difficult to distinguish between drug-related crimes and nondrug-related crimes.

Since motivations for drug use and for crimes are both complex, it is difficult to make broad generalizations about the success or failure of certain drug policies. It is incorrect to say the "drug war" failed. We may hope that drug policies would lower rates of drug use and other drug-related crimes, but crime rates alone are not enough to declare whether the drug war is a success or failure. In the same way, it is also incorrect to say that decriminalization and legalization of certain drugs (like marijuana) cause crime. This is because, again, by themselves crime rates do not include explanations for why they occurred. Correlations can only indicate that certain categories of crime have increased or decreased following the passage of new drug laws.

Some types of crime clearly decreased after the passage of drug decriminalization laws. For example, there are fewer people arrested for minor possession or use of drugs. In some states, the manufacture, trafficking, and sales of marijuana are legal under certain conditions, and so these crimes have decreased substantially. However, other categories of crime have increased during the same time—for example, property crimes (shoplifting, theft, robbery, vandalism) and crimes of violence and prostitution. These categories may be drug-related. Manufacturing, trafficking, and sales of drugs without proper licensing have also increased because illegal drug markets typically increase after decriminalization and legalization.

We may not be able to prove a causal relationship with correlations, but that does not mean that correlations are unimportant. We cannot know for certain if decriminalization caused crime rates to *increase*, but we can still recognize that it did not cause crime rates to *decrease*. In this way, correlations are informative if they can uncover where particular goals of decriminalization and legalization were, or were not, achieved by the new policies.

Three Approaches and Criticisms of Drug Policy and Crime Control

Social scientists rely on theories of social order based on presumptions about human nature, which also reflect the ideas (ideology) of social interactions. The three ideological perspectives that we use in this book to help explain the connections between drug use and crime rates are libertarian, social welfare, and traditional conservative ideologies. Each perspective reflects unique goals.

Libertarian Drug Policy Goals: Libertarians do not believe in the medical basis for drug addiction, so they believe people are motivated primarily by cost-benefit analysis and that drug use is a personal decision influenced by economic factors reflecting supply and subsequent price points. If drugs are cheap and the demand is high, recreational drug use will be almost impossible to stop. Drug laws that attempt to eliminate the supply by criminalizing drug traffickers and dealers can never be perfectly successful because such social control would require a military police state to patrol all drug markets, and most Americans would not tolerate such intrusions. Therefore, if the drug war only achieves partial reduction in the available drug supply, the result is not reduced drug use but only increased street prices. If you reduce supply, the price increases. Higher street prices create more incentives for drug dealers and traffickers to sell drugs illegally. Furthermore, since law enforcement can never catch all the drug dealers, the risk of drug dealers being caught is relatively low. From this viewpoint, libertarians believe that drug criminalization (the drug war) actually increases the attractiveness of illegal drug dealing. That is why they argue that the drug war causes more harm than it helps because interrupting the supplies without also reducing demand only leads to higher crime rates.

The libertarian solution is to make all drugs legal; then the prices of recreational drugs would reflect actual market forces, causing most drug dealers to find other forms of making money. Since libertarians do not believe that any drug is actually addictive, when the drug dealers no longer feed the recreational drug market, then there will be fewer drug addicts. Libertarians usually argue that recreational drug use remains constant regardless of criminalization, decriminalization, or legal status of recreational drugs.

Critics raise two problems with this libertarian theory. First, almost every medical study affirms that many drugs are highly addictive (both physically and psychologically), which means that addicted users will try to consume drugs regardless of the price or the supply. Increasing access to drugs always leads to increased use and therefore higher addiction rates. Evidence of increasing addiction rates became much more noticeable after the first decriminalization policies of the 2010s, which is one reason why there are fewer people publicly advocating libertarian policies in the 2020s than there were in the 1990s.

The second criticism is that decriminalizing drugs does not eliminate the illegal drug trade. In every state where marijuana has been decriminalized or legalized, the number of illegal dealers increased (not decreased). This is because legalization does not remove government regulation. The price of recreational drugs generally increases after legalization because there are added licensing fees and other taxes that illegal dealers never pay. It is almost always cheaper to buy illegal drugs from illegal vendors because their retail prices will not include markups for taxes, licensing, and other overhead costs. Most states where marijuana and other drugs have been decriminalized report that the illegal markets for the same drugs have increased by three or four times (300 percent to 400 percent).

The last criticism is that libertarians do not recognize the moral harm that comes from drug decriminalization, particularly those involving mental health and sexual behaviors. Statistics cannot tell whether underage girls (and boys) who get involved with sex work did so because they were already on drugs or whether they developed drug habits to cope with their sex work, however there is a strong correlation between drug use and sex work. Most anecdotal research suggests that the majority of girls who enter pornography and prostitution had some prior history of abuse and drug use. However, research studies from the 1990s suggest some girls, and most boys, initially entered the sex industry voluntarily and without any prior drug issues—sometimes because they were looking for new excitement, sometimes because they wanted to prove they were unafraid, and sometimes because they believed the work could be empowering. Once involved, though, rates of drug-use among pornography performers and prostitutes always increase, which suggests that the work increases emotional fragility and encourages more drug-use. Libertarians do not believe sex-work should be criminalized if it is consensual, so they do not view these increasing rates as evidence of social harm.

Social-welfare Drug Policy Goals: The supporters of most harm reduction strategies and other "evidence-based" policies recognize the strong correlation between recreational drug use and increasing crime rates, and they usually admit that a history of personal drug use increases the likelihood of criminal behavior among addicted drug users. Social-welfare advocates argue that criminal drug laws isolate users from the rest of society, which only increases problems of addiction because isolated users have less access to available resources for treatment.

Unlike the libertarian viewpoint, social-welfare advocates do not believe that drug use is always a matter of choice, especially in matters involving street-level buying and selling. Instead, they blame poor socioeconomic conditions that encourage the less empowered members of society to supplement their income through low-level dealing and to also seek relief from their personal struggles by trying to escape reality through intoxication. Rather than pass harsh laws targeting street dealers, social-welfare advocates prefer to focus more attention on changing economic conditions in poor neighborhoods through government-supported retraining programs, housing and redevelopment projects, and by increasing access to treatment plans that target victims of drug abuse.

Instead of a "War on Drugs" that emphasizes law enforcement, the social-welfare advocates support public education campaigns that emphasize responsible drug use, in the same way the liquor industry supports "responsible drinking" campaigns. This approach, they argue, would reduce prison populations who were sentenced for minor drug crimes and would also lower rates of drug addiction in the general public. If addiction rates decline, all the other related crime rates would also decrease.

Critics of this interpretation point out that recreational drug users often fail to take advantage of treatment programs even when they are free and promoted without judgment. When treatment programs are only voluntary, addicted users often do not use their services because they do not want to stop taking the drugs. In the example of the state of Oregon, addicted users were identified and referred to treatment but were not arrested and were not required to use the resources offered. The number of users entering treatment programs actually declined after decriminalization because they were not forced by law to accept treatment. Social-welfare advocates do not support compulsory treatment programs because they fear compulsion is too similar to criminal punishment. This failure of addicts to use available treatment programs can be frustrating for social-welfare advocates who seek to decrease addiction by removing the stigma of recreational drug use. However, if addiction rates do not decrease, even social-welfare advocates admit that crimes associated with addiction invariably increase.

Traditional Conservative Drug Policy Goals: Older policies that rely on law enforcement to punish drug users and drug dealers are based on many of the same goals held by both the libertarians and the social-welfare advocates. Traditional conservatives agree with libertarians that economic incentives often encourage illegal drug markets and that rising crime rates may reflect other causes than mere drug use alone. However, unlike libertarians, conservatives assume that most drugs are highly addictive, which means that any drug habit will likely encourage criminal behavior from users needing to pay for their habit. Pressures of illegal lifestyles will, in turn, increase the drug habit.

In a similar way, traditional conservatives also agree with social-welfare advocates that drug use is a deeper social problem that often reflects poor socioeconomic conditions of urban population centers, and they recognize that users often turn to drugs as a means of emotional escape. Urban poor may become street dealers as an economic opportunity that is easier to pursue than other legal options. However, unlike social-welfare advocates, conservatives do not place blame for these conditions on capitalism or free market societies but rather on the breakdown of family bonds and in the increasing anonymity of densely populated urban communities.

Traditional conservatives argue that the root cause of increased drug use is a decline in character and moral consensus about what is right and what is wrong. The loss of traditional moral standards is as much to blame for drug use as it is for rising crime rates. Supporters of this position oppose decriminalization because it sends the message that recreational drug use is not harmful to individuals or to society. They supported the federal government's War on Drugs campaigns of the 1970s–1990s because those laws sent clear messages that recreational drug use was always harmful to society. Specifically, they endorse rigorous enforcement of existing drug laws, including stiff penalties for dealers and criminal organizations involved in trafficking to create disincentives for people who may consider drug dealing. Conservatives do not believe these laws are perfect, but unlike libertarians, they still believe that the fear of criminal prosecution may be sufficient to reduce the attraction to illegal drug markets.

At the same time, traditional conservatives usually join social-welfare advocates in supporting public education campaigns, drug-treatment options, and alternative punishment options for first-time offenders. The difference is that traditional conservatives do not support morally neutral interpretations. They believe governmental laws against recreational drug use should establish clear social standards emphasizing the harms of intoxication as vices to be avoided. They support clear social stigmas associated with drug abuse and for those who encourage recreational drug use.

Critics of the traditional conservative position argue that they assume people will make (or should make) decisions based on common moral judgments. Both libertarian and social-welfare advocates believe that merely asserting universal moral values is insufficient to stop people from engaging in certain behaviors. They also oppose any moral guidelines that favor one religious (Judeo-Christian) viewpoint over any others. For these reasons, many traditional drug policies are opposed because they are viewed as overly judgmental about behavioral choices. Neither libertarians nor social-welfare advocates support the stigmatization of recreational drug use, intoxication, or related behaviors, including those involving sex.

Summary: Each of these three ideological viewpoints holds policy objectives that rely on unique presumptions about human nature and about the importance of broadly shared moral values related to crime. The same statistics that demonstrate the harm to the individual and to society are usually interpreted in different ways by each group. For the libertarians and the social-welfare advocates, increasing crime rates seem to support the need for more decriminalization laws. Traditional conservatives use the same crime statistics to argue for continued criminalization of recreational drugs and for greater enforcement of existing laws.

Defining Types of Drug Crime

When the public becomes concerned about crime growing out of control because of drug use, they do not always refer to crimes that are only connected to drugs. In 1968, Nixon's law and order campaign reacted to a general cultural tone of lawlessness that included a wide variety of crimes; the fear of mugging or street crimes was most obvious, but other crimes, like rioting, which was unconnected to drug use directly, also triggered strong public reactions. Public perception of these types of crimes is formed mostly by (1) increasing rates of drug addiction and those crimes that are directly associated with drug use; (2) increasing rates of other (indirect) crimes committed in support of the drug use; and (3) crimes that are associated with a subculture that grows in defiance of law enforcement and other social rules.

Addiction and Direct Crime: Crimes committed while the user is intoxicated are an example of a direct drug-related crime. Generally, these crimes are the result of lowered inhibitions or the loss of self-control that follows recreational drug use. Many types of crime fall into this category, but the most common cases involve impaired driving.

Public awareness about the dangers of driving while impaired by alcohol is high, but there is less awareness about the dangers of other drugs (especially marijuana). The National Highway Transportation Safety Administration published many studies indicating that drivers under the influence of THC (the active ingredient in marijuana) are just as likely to crash as those intoxicated by alcohol. In 2020, more than 56 percent of drivers involved in serious or fatal accidents tested positive for at least one drug, resulting in more than $70 billion in damages. Actual drug usage may be higher than these rates suggest because THC metabolizes out of the bloodstream quickly, and most blood tests taken at the accident scene (or later in the hospital) will not record the presence of THC even if the driver was fully under the influence. THC is stored mostly in fat tissues rather than in the blood stream and is not measured in the same way as alcohol. Devices used to test for THC are very expensive and patrol officers in the field do not have access to them.

Other forms of direct drug-related crimes include assaults, thefts, and domestic violence. In 2006 the Bureau of Justice Statistics reported in the National Crime Victimization Survey (NCVS) that nearly half of college students who were victims of violent assaults reported that the offender was on drugs when the crimes occurred, including about 40 percent of incidents of rape and sexual assaults on campuses. The 2004 Survey of Inmates in State Correctional Facilities (SISCF) conducted by the Bureau of Justice Statistics indicated that one of three inmates at state prisons reported they were on drugs when they committed their first offenses. More than half of the inmates convicted for weapons violations, burglaries, and auto thefts were using drugs at the time of their arrest.

Incidents of drug use during cases of domestic violence are much higher than those cases that do not involve any drug use. The American Addiction Centers reported in 2022 that as many as 80 percent of domestic violence incidents involved drug abuse at the time of the violence. Children living in homes with domestic violence are neglected at rates fifteen times the national average, and in 60 percent to 75 percent of those homes, the children are abused as well as the spouses. Children whose parents abuse drugs are three times more likely to be abused and four times more likely to be neglected. Moreover, one in five parents who have adult-aged children with drug abuse problems report that they have experienced physical abuse, and 40 percent reported destruction of private property.

Addiction and Indirect Crime: The relationship between drugs and indirect crime is more complex than those incidents committed while under the influence. Indirect drug crimes occur when perpetrators commit offenses in order to obtain goods or money that are then traded for illegal drugs. Decriminalization does not end indirect drug crime because drugs are never free, and addicted users will find ways (legal or illegal) of supporting their habits. Since drugs often impair job performance, and in some cases render the user incapable of obtaining or keeping a steady job, the problem of paying for drugs becomes more intense. The demand for drugs by users who cannot afford them is a major motivation behind property crimes and armed robbery.

It is difficult to estimate the number of personal robberies or burglaries committed for the purpose of obtaining drug money because the perpetrators do not usually admit to either the crime or their reasoning behind it. However, during the 1990s the University of California in Los Angeles (UCLA) Drug Abuse Research Center compiled a series of studies indicating that drug use was the primary motivation behind most petty crimes such as shoplifting, mugging (stealing purses and wallets from individuals directly), burglary (breaking into homes or cars for valuables to sell or trade for drugs), fraud (check forgeries and credit card theft), panhandling (begging for money on the street), and trespassing crimes that increase with the rates of homelessness among users. A 2020 survey conducted by the US Conference of Mayors indicated that 68 percent of cities cited chronic drug abuse as the primary cause of homelessness among single adults.

Homelessness and Addiction: Not everyone who is homeless is a drug addict. The US Department of Housing and Urban Development (HUD) reports that only about one in three people without a place to stay at night suffer from substance-abuse addiction. However, that HUD statistic refers to any situation where someone needs a place to spend the night—including people who temporarily live with their parents, friends, or other relatives while they await their housing options. The HUD statistic does not refer specifically to the large homeless encampments found in dense urban populations (city centers). These homeless populations have much higher-than-average proportions of individuals struggling with drug addiction. The UCLA Drug Abuse Research Center conducted a study of 64,000 people in urban homeless encampments across fifteen states and reported that three out of four suffered from chronic addiction (75 percent). Other social-welfare outreach groups estimate 80 percent.

Sex Crimes and Addiction: As internet pornography and online dating apps become more popular, the incidents of human trafficking for sexual exploitation (prostitution) increased significantly between 2008 and the 2020s. A prostitute is someone who exchanges sexual favors for money or drugs. The connection between drug use and prostitution has always been high, but in the twenty-first century, the correlation became more complex. According to the Drug Enforcement Administration (DEA), underage runaway boys and girls were often lured into sex trafficking through promises of love, security, and money, and these initial contacts were often established through social media. Once drawn into sex work, these runaways were usually provided drugs to make them more compliant. Frequent drug use leads to addiction, and once addicted to drugs, prostitutes often feel like they must continue sex work in order to pay for their housing and to maintain their drug habits.

The advent of mobile-based internet (smartphones) increased the demand for prostitution significantly and also increased the opportunities for marketing sex work without having to walk the streets. The Mayo Health Clinic conducted a series of studies in the 2020s indicating that increasing access to pornography led to sex-addiction rates of 6 percent to 8 percent among American adults. Sex addiction fuels greater demand for prostitution, which in turn creates increasing demand for more pornography and for younger victims of human trafficking. Many young prostitutes also perform for pornographic film purposes. Drugs are frequently used to encourage girls to more willingly participate in filming sex acts for distribution online, especially marijuana and methylenedioxymethamphetamine (MDMA, also known as "ecstasy"), which are both promoted as stimulating party drugs. Both can be highly addictive.

Prostitution and pornography are legal in some states, but forced sex work is illegal everywhere and is often referred to as human trafficking, which is a form of slavery. Data from the National Human Trafficking Hotline indicates that nearly 20,000 victims are trafficked involuntarily every year, most of whom are female and more than a third who are under eighteen-years-old. The three most common forms of sex work for these victims are travelling prostitutes (10 percent), as participants in pornographic films (8 percent), and as prostitutes housed in smaller private rooms (8 percent). Insider reports suggest whether voluntary or involuntary, more than 90 percent of actors and actresses working in the porn industry use drug abuse as a means of coping with the work, especially marijuana, cocaine, ecstasy, and other opioids.

Role of Addiction in Criminal Supply and Demand

The Centers for Disease Control (CDC), the Drug Enforcement Agency (DEA), the American Medical Association (AMA), and the American Psychological Association (APA) identify three primary socioeconomic conditions that make people most vulnerable to addiction. These are (1) access, (2) affordability, and (3) anonymity. If a user has easy access to recreational drugs, if they can afford to take them, and if the user can take them without letting the important people of their lives know about it, the user is more vulnerable to developing an addiction because there are fewer obstacles in the way of taking their drugs. Decriminalization policies may play a role in increasing the potency of all three conditions.

Access: Traditional law enforcement focuses most on limiting access to illegal drugs. The CDA schedules were specifically designed to limit access to dangerous drugs for those who are most likely to abuse them, and the DEA was created to help enforce those schedules. However, the most commonly abused drugs are not manufactured in illegal drug labs but are made by legal pharmaceutical factories and are often distributed legally to patients through prescriptions.

The National Ambulatory Medical Care Survey (2019) and the National Health and Nutrition Examination Survey conducted by the CDC in 2022 reported more than a billion legally manufactured doses of medicine are prescribed every year to nearly half the American population who take legal drugs at least once per month. In 2003, about 15 percent of the American population misused prescription drugs. By 2021, that percentage had increased to 20 percent, and about 6 percent misused those drugs with some regularity. Increasing the supply of legal pharmaceutical drugs invariably leads to increasing misuse of the same drugs. New drug laws will not change these relationships.

Outside of international drug smuggling, abusers get their prescription drugs from a variety of sources. Patients may take more pills than are prescribed, which is misused. Or patients give away or sell doses that they do not use. In other cases, these drugs are stolen from homes, hospitals, pharmacies, or doctors' offices, and they enter into the illegal drug market. As more drugs become legally available, the number of these drugs that find their way into the hands of drug abusers also increases.

Libertarians are correct when they warn that no laws will be able to perfectly monitor access to recreational drugs. The only way to more effectively limit access to drugs is if members of the general public agree to stop using or diverting legal drugs into illegal vendors. It is public will and individual restraint that ultimately limits access to drugs. However, if the public is not encouraged to view recreational drug use as a social harm, that sort of self-restraint is less likely. Decriminalization and legalization policies generally increase the access to both legal and illegal drugs, and that usually increases the risk of addiction.

Affordability: Affordability is not really within the realm of public policy to influence directly. Libertarians argue that drug-control policies generally increase the price of illegal drugs, making dealing with illegal drugs more attractive. Statistics suggest that decriminalizing drugs makes legal drugs more expensive than illegal drugs, encouraging people to turn to illegal sources. This means that the question of affordability is complex. Unless the state decides to make all recreational drugs free (at taxpayer's expense), increasing addiction rates usually increase crime rates. In this way, affordability is not an obstacle for addicted users. If the user is willing to seek out an illegal market to buy their drugs, they are also often willing to commit crimes to obtain the same drug. Property crimes (theft, burglary, robbery) and sex crimes are often committed to obtain the money necessary for drugs.

The price of a drug is mostly an issue for new users who may be first experimenting with the drug, which is why illegal drug dealers often give the first doses to their customers for free in the hope that they will become addicted and then do whatever it takes to maintain the addiction. Policies may not be able to influence affordability, but increased rates of addiction usually encourage more crime as users seek alternative ways of paying for their drug habits.

Anonymity: Public policy might be able to influence the role of stigma in recreational drug use. Most drug users try to hide the rate of their consumption in order to avoid detection as a drug addict because it is embarrassing to admit that they are unable to control their drug use. If they are able to consume their drugs anonymously in the privacy of their own homes or away from the oversight of other responsible people—like law enforcement, parents, or other loved ones—then the user is more likely to consume more drugs, which is why anonymity increases the likelihood of addiction.

On the other hand, the need for anonymity assumes there is a strong social stigma connected to drug abuse and addiction. Decriminalization could change that. Most harm reduction policies seek to reduce or eliminate the social stigma associated with drug use. This policy goal is based on the compassionate belief that if there is less stigma associated with drug addiction, more people will take advantage of addiction treatment services. However, the flip side of reducing stigma is that the need for anonymity plays less of a factor in controlling addiction. If people are not embarrassed by their drug use, they will be more likely to use them openly because there are no reasons to hide their habits. If anonymity is no longer necessary for increasing drug use, there will be higher addiction rates as a side effect of increased access alone. Removing the social stigma of recreational drug use will likely encourage higher addiction rates.

Conclusion: Interpreting Crime Rates

Policies that decriminalize (and legalize) certain drugs for recreational purposes usually coincide with increasing crime rates—mostly property crimes and also some crimes of violence and sex-related crimes. It is incorrect to say that drugs always cause crime, but it is fair to say that decriminalization policies do not lower crime rates (which used to be the predicted outcome during the 1990s policy debates). There is some general consensus that addiction rates are tied to increasing access to recreational drugs. Affordability and anonymity become less important with the rise of potential crime alternatives and the decline in social stigma of drug use. Therefore, decriminalization policies do seem to be tied to higher addiction rates.

There is some debate as to whether crime rates actually increased as much as is often believed between 2010 and the mid-2020s. (This is discussed in more depth in Chapter 5.) A summary of the central issue is that the accuracy of federally published annual crime reports has been compromised by a combination of three factors: (1) local police increasingly choose not to enforce certain misdemeanors, so they are not reported; (2) many city and state law enforcement agencies fail to report any statistics (less than half by 2024) to federal agencies; and (3) the practice of plea bargaining in criminal trials skews the results of crime statistics by recording rates of lesser charges rather than the more serious charges. If annual crime reports are unreliable, that triggers further debate over whether crime rates have decreased or increased.

Decriminalization policies have certainly led to decreases in the number of people sent to jail for drug offenses. This is because many drug offenses that used to be counted as crimes have been recategorized and are no longer crimes (especially related to marijuana use, production, and trafficking). However, since few people were ever sent to prison on drug possession charges alone, decriminalization (and legalization) policies did not have as serious an impact on conviction rates as might be expected. There is no consensus that decriminalization has led to fewer incidents of crime.

This leads to a controversial question: what is the ultimate goal of drug laws? If the goal of drug policies is to lower arrest rates and conviction rates, then declining crime statistics and reductions in drug convictions indicate that decriminalization policies are probably successful. However, if the goal of drug laws is to lower the number of actual incidents of social harm associated with drug use—whether they are called "crimes" or not—then decriminalization policies are probably less successful. There is a lack of consensus in answering this question.

In part, the lack of consensus is based on the three different ideological presumptions about the role of drug laws in deterring crime. Traditional conservatives argue that the lack of clear moral messaging encourages a culture of lawlessness. If people are not taught that recreational drug use is harmful, they are more likely to disregard other social harms related to respect for personal property, sexual abuse, and civil discourse. Social-welfare advocates argue that hardships caused by socioeconomic insecurities found in capitalist and free market economies create a culture of despair. If people do not think that they will enjoy access to the same privileges as others, they turn to drugs and to crime as means of coping. Lastly, libertarians argue that a culture of hyper-regulation is most responsible for increasing crime because people tend to violate laws that they do not believe are justified by their own interests. People from all socioeconomic levels take drugs because they want to, and drug laws will have little influence if there is no agreement as to their importance.

Each of these three ideological presumptions provides a different explanation for increasing addiction and crime rates that occurred between 2010 and the mid-2020s. Interpreting the success or failure of certain drug decriminalization policies, and other laws that legalized marijuana, depends on one or another of these ideological presumptions. The more aware you become of your own ideological presumptions, the more capable you will be of informing yourself about the potential advantages and disadvantages of each new drug-policy reform.

9
Legalization and the City

Cities pose serious challenges to decriminalization and legalization policies. This is important because about one in seven people in the United States live in just three large urban areas: the larger metropolitan areas of New York City, Los Angeles, and Chicago. Overall, drug use and addiction rates in urban areas are about the same as in rural areas. The main difference is that public displays of drug use and accompanying levels of street crime are more concentrated in high-density drug-trafficking sectors that are most often found in large cities. These areas are usually concentrated into small districts only a few blocks wide and a few blocks long. Yet, the incidents of crime (muggings, car thefts, vandalism, and panhandling) combined with obvious signs of homeless encampments, like outdoor sleeping, tents, makeshift tarps, or boxes, are difficult to ignore, and they can be disturbing for the average passerby.

Recreational drug use occurs in smaller towns of 5,000 people or less and in surrounding agricultural (farming) communities, but the public does not see the harm from drug use in low-population areas as clearly as they see it in urban settings (typically 500,000 people or more). It is rare for a general passerby in a small town to find a person lying spread out along the sidewalk who appears to be sleeping, drunk, or passed out from drug use or who may actually be dead or dying. Yet, in certain districts of large urban centers called "open-air drug markets," these images are common, often a daily, occurrence. Property crimes and vandalism are most visible in these high-density drug-trafficking centers. These areas are also where most social services for drug addiction are located. These neighborhoods draw attention to drug addiction and to decriminalization policies of harm reduction. Such open displays of drug use and abuse are also the first examples that opponents of drug decriminalization point to when they claim the harm-reduction policies are failing.

Scenes of extreme urban drug use do not necessarily reflect the lifestyles of all recreational drug users. Nevertheless, the plight of urban addiction is one of the greatest sources of motivation for both decriminalization and more traditional law-enforcement policy groups. Differing ideological perspectives lead to opposing interpretations as to the meaning of these open-air drug markets in terms of current policy needs and in terms of recommended solutions for addressing those needs. Without public consensus over the relative dangers of recreational drug use, the problems of high-density addiction and crime rates in cities will continue to be a source of controversy.

Open-Air Drug Markets

The Drug Enforcement Agency (DEA) uses the label "High Intensity Drug-Trafficking Areas" (HIDTA) to refer to regions within and between states where the greatest incidents of buying, selling, and transporting illegal drugs occur. This information is helpful for the DEA because they work with local communities and law enforcement agencies to develop strategies to best tackle the higher-than-average illegal drug-trafficking pathways.

Within cities, though, another phrase is used to describe the small districts where drugs are openly bought and sold. These are called "Open-Air Drug Markets," which are well-defined areas where buyers and dealers can easily find each other. Often located at an intersection, a small strip of a few blocks along a particular street, or even in a public park, these districts have few barriers to accessing drugs. Anyone can approach a dealer and buy illegal drugs as long as they look like a potential buyer and do not look like an undercover police officer.

These illegal drug districts operate twenty-four hours a day and sell whichever drugs are in highest demand for the region. During the early 2000s, marijuana, heroin, and crack cocaine were the most popular. By the 2020s, fentanyl, heroin mixtures, and xylazine (known as "tranq") became more popular. In addition, open-air drug markets also provide access to other drug-related crimes, such as prostitution, sales of stolen goods, loan sharking, and other activities associated with organized crime (or "street gangs"). These districts are frequently marked by gun violence because no dealer has a monopoly on crime, and there is always a threat of physical conflict between the many different dealers and criminal organizations who operate in the same general vicinity. Customers are also at risk of violence if they attempt to steal from or interfere with local drug operations.

Most open-air drug markets are located in or around buildings that are easily approached from the outside, but they are also often connected in some way to social media. The homeless drug users who live nearby may appear to be their primary customers, but most of the buyers come from outside of the neighborhood. Highly addicted users may buy from the same dealers up to a dozen times a day. However, homeless addicts form only a fraction of the drug business. One study from the University of Pennsylvania reported that about half of the cars that transported buyers into the Kensington (Philadelphia) neighborhood to buy from drug dealers come from outside of Philadelphia and from surrounding states. Open-air drug markets may appear to represent only a single neighborhood, but they usually become centers of illegal trafficking from users who may live hundreds of miles away. This has always been true for high-intensity crime districts, but social media has greatly expanded the reach of local dealers since the 2010s.

In 2023, a group of sixty families sued the online social media platform Snapchat for its role in providing an anonymous exchange service from which their underage children gained access to fentanyl and other illegal drugs and later died from overdoses. These parents described Snapchat as an online open-air drug market, and the California court system allowed their case to proceed. In most cases, even if the connections are made online, the actual transfer of drugs from seller to buyer occurs in person. Buyers and suppliers often take trips into high-intensity drug-trafficking districts in order to obtain their drugs, which are then passed along in less noticeable settings to ordinary residential neighborhoods. Open-air drug markets provide the most public examples of these drug exchanges, even though heavy recreational drug use may occur in other neighborhoods throughout the city or in smaller rural towns. In this way, the city districts attract most of the negative attention surrounding illegal drug use.

The Kensington neighborhood in Philadelphia was known as the largest open-air drug market along the East Coast. However, almost every large city has its own high-intensity drug district: the Tenderloin District in San Francisco; Boston's "Methadone Mile" located near Melnea Cass Boulevard and Massachusetts Avenue (known as Mass. and Cass); Los Angeles' MacArthur Park; and Chicago's Garfield Park and Rogers Park districts all have histories of public drug use and higher rates of street crime. These districts are overrepresented among national mortality rates. According to the annual drug overdose mortality rates reported by individual City Health Departments, the four largest urban centers (Chicago, Los Angeles, New York City, and Philadelphia) account for 10 percent of all drug overdose deaths in the United States. A combination of smaller cities like Baltimore (MD), Columbus (OH), San Francisco (CA), Seattle (WA), Detroit (MI), Portland (OR), Minneapolis (MN), Milwaukee (WI), and Denver (CO) accounted for another 10 percent of mortality rates nationwide.

Wherever drug trafficking is most intense, so also the rates of drug addiction and overdose fatalities will be highest. Not all cities publish drug overdose mortality rates, but in 2022 most large cities of 750,000 or more self-reported on their health department websites overdose mortality rates of about three deaths per day and these often occur in high-intensity drug-use districts. The CDC National Center for Health Statistics reports that most drug overdoses do not result in death, and the rates of nonlethal overdoses are estimated to be 60–100 per day in large cities.

Actual statistics of drug overdoses in densely populated urban areas are difficult to verify because many users are saved from death by private individuals who supply naloxone doses as an emergency antidote. Naloxone is the generic name for Narcan, and it has been widely distributed to the public since the 2010s. Some cities, like San Francisco, Philadelphia, and Baltimore, fund outreach programs with social workers who go door-to-door to deliver opioid overdose prevention kits in high-risk neighborhoods. These kits include test trips for fentanyl, small 4oz containers of nasal spray naloxone, and various other items that might serve as antidotes to opioid overdose poisoning. The total incidents of people saved from overdose deaths as a result of these privately used naloxone sprays is not fully recorded.

At the same time, the total number of overdose incidents is also compromised by the fact that some of the same users suffer overdose emergencies multiple times. Users who buy drugs on the street many times a day sometimes face more than one overdose threat in their lifetimes—sometimes more than once in the same month. Unfortunately, people with such extreme addictions often die in the street on a day when no one is around to save them. The number of people who die from overdosing is more accurately recorded because dead bodies are always taken to a hospital morgue. Total numbers of drug overdose deaths, however, may not always be collected together at national levels because local hospitals do not consistently report their statistics to federal agencies and because not all cities release such figures to the general public through press reports. There are political risks that come from advertising the number of people who die from recreational drug use, and for this reason, most national statistics of mortality rates caused by drug overdoses in urban districts have been incomplete since the 2020s.

Social Services Dilemma

Decriminalization policies shift the focus of traditional law enforcement drug-control methods, where drug use is treated as a crime that police officers monitor, to new harm reduction policies that treat drug use as a health issue. As explained later in this chapter, most large city governments with open-air drug markets shifted to harm-reduction policies after 2010, and these policies do not involve police or law enforcement as the first tools for reducing drug use. Every large city police department is aware of where the open-air drug markets are. However, they do not intervene in these areas without specific orders from city officials. Instead, police are brought in mostly to participate as first responders in emergency situations only.

Nonenforcement Practices: Periodically, news reports of public drug use, or mortality rates, and of sensational crimes in high-intensity drug-use districts will create public pressure for city governments to address the problems of open-air drug markets. During these times, city agencies will direct police to "sweep" out the most public violations of drug laws, which means sending police out in large numbers to physically remove homeless encampments, send at-risk drug users to treatment facilities (or temporarily to a detox shelter), collect all the trash, and detain dealers who engage in obvious drug operations. At the end of the operation, the streets look physically much cleaner, and the obvious signs of the drug market are shut down for a day or two—or the dealers and users temporarily move to different locations.

In most cases, drug traffickers eventually return to their regular places of business, users return to the streets, and local police officers continue to monitor affairs from a distance. Generally, police only become directly involved in emergency situations where the illegal market is disrupted by gunshots or by other immediate threats to life. These incidents are not uncommon, so it often takes a long time between reporting the incident and when police officers respond due to multiple calls being served simultaneously. Aside from these emergency situations, police usually adopt practices of nonenforcement of low-level drug crimes in high-intensity drug-use districts.

Overdose Prevention Sites (OPS): The most visible forms of public services available in high-intensity drug-use districts are through government-funded, as well as privately funded, social-worker outreach programs. These types of programs often include free health clinics that provide minimal services to help with potential overdose reactions, as well as detox rooms where people can sober up. Drug addiction treatment facilities are usually located away from the open-air drug markets in order to remove users from the conditions that most reinforce their addictions. However, outreach centers usually include phone numbers so that interested users may contact these potential treatment resources.

In some cases, high-use drug districts will include locations with supervised drug use, which are called Supervised Injection Sites (SIS) or Supervised Consumption Sites (SCS). These are only legally recognized in New York City, though many Canadian cities (like Vancouver and Toronto) have dozens of officially recognized OPS sites. Many American cities may have unofficial sites, but they are not legally funded by government money.

The original idea behind SIS rooms was to help reduce the spread of HIV/ AIDS and hepatitis diseases that often spread through sharing of needles. In an SIS room, free sterilized needles are provided for any users who drop in, and there are trained staff available to help users if they struggle with inserting the needles. SIS rooms were initially introduced to deal with the problems of unclean needles, and users would come to receive free needles, and eventually, they often stayed and injected the drugs in the same place. The concept of supervised drug use was expanded for SCS rooms, where users are free to use any drug. These facilities are usually equipped with testing kits for users to better identify the presence of fentanyl, and other clean tools of drug use (pipes, cans to prepare heroin, etc.) that users have access to, for free. In addition, most SIS and SCS rooms are also equipped with supplies of naloxone and reference cards that point users to treatment services if they are asked for.

Legal Issues: In the United States, monitored injection rooms and consumption sites have been operated unofficially (illegally) by nonprofit organizations that see these as an outreach service. Many cities, including Philadelphia, Chicago, and San Francisco, have attempted to create officially recognized OPS locations, but the problem is that they are illegal under federal law and almost all state laws. Cities cannot knowingly violate state and federal laws.

Drug houses are illegal, and any property owner who knowingly permits illegal activities to occur on their premises could be sued or arrested for facilitating a drug house. The risk of arrests may sound harsh at first, but these laws were originally passed and supported by members from both parties who intended to target criminal organizations (drug gangs) that use "drug houses" to attract addicted users and then keep them supplied with drugs in order to evade police detection. Drug houses are also often used to manufacture and prepare illegal drugs. Anti-drug-house laws enable law enforcement to encourage property owners to take greater precautions for their units that may be left vacant. Drug houses are often located in abandoned buildings that are vacated but still owned. These laws place greater responsibilities on property owners to manage their units to prevent them from being exploited for illegal drug use.

If a government provides money to support OPS rooms, they could also be charged with operating a drug house. The goal behind overdose prevention is to save lives by providing trained staff members to be on hand when users take their drugs, but the practical reality is that these locations do in fact enable illegal drug use. Almost all OPS rooms are staffed by former drug users, which is explicitly recommended by the nonprofit groups that run these facilities. The idea is that formerly addicted users have the most experience dealing with problems that arise from injections and consumption. Critics argue, however, that former drug users may not be the best people to discourage current users to stop taking drugs, and these OPS sites encourage more illegal drug use because the immediate risks appear to be greatly reduced.

When the Canadian province of British Columbia announced a three-year experiment in harm reduction by decriminalizing possession, sales and use of small amounts of any recreational drug at 2.5 grams or less, they also officially recognized dozens of OPS rooms around high-intensity drug-use districts. The Canadian decriminalization experiment began at the end of January 2023, but after a year the law had to be revised. The public reacted negatively to OPS rooms and the open-air drug markets that they operated in and especially to the more obvious signs of crime and overdose mortality rates seen on the nearby streets. These negative public reactions forced the Provincial government to place more restrictions on the decriminalization experiment. They did not completely reverse course, but they added more limitations and explicitly prohibited (with legal penalties) any signs of public drug use. The OPS sites were given more funding to continue operating because these rooms shift drug use indoors.

The 501.c.3 and 501.c.4 Non-Profit Organizations: In almost all cases, city-funded outreach programs that provide services for addicted users are handled by nongovernmental organizations called "nonprofits." The Internal Revenue Service (IRS) provides many categories of nonprofit identification because nonprofits are "exempt," which means these groups are free from having to pay income taxes. Two nonprofit types most commonly associated with drug-intervention organizations are 501.c.3 and 501.c.4.

The IRS tax codes defines the first (501.c.3) nonprofit as a charitable organization that includes "relief of the poor, the distressed, or the underprivileged … lessening the burdens of government; lessening neighborhood tensions; eliminating prejudice and discrimination; defending human and civil rights secured by law; and combating community deterioration and juvenile delinquency." In plain language, 501.c.3 nonprofit groups are able to receive public grants and solicit private donations for the purposes of helping public needs. In these cases, "public needs" refers to dealing with social problems related to urban drug addiction. These are popular because people who donate to a 501.c.3 may claim the money in their tax deductions.

The IRS tax codes define the second (501.c.4) organization as a social-welfare organization that is "operated exclusively for the promotion of social-welfare if it is primarily engaged in promoting in some way the common good and general welfare of the community." In plain language, 501.c.4 organizations are very similar to 501.c.3 groups, except that they are allowed to publicly support political candidates. This means that private donations to 501.c.4 groups are not tax deductible. Often, the same public outreach groups will be organized under both categories—one side of their operations collects private and government donations and works only to help drug-related social issues. The other part of the operations focuses on political protesting and lobbying political groups to increase awareness of their causes. In both cases, the actual nonprofit organization may be very small (one director and a few staff members or volunteers), or they may be very large (many directors and hundreds or thousands of employees and volunteers). Almost every group or individual working in high-intensity drug-use districts is part of a nonprofit organization.

The use of nonprofit organizations has increased considerably in the twenty-first century. In 2002, there were a little more than 120,000 nonprofit organizations recognized by the IRS. Twenty years later, in 2022, that number rose to nearly 2 million. Governments at all levels use nonprofit organizations as the primary tools of their public outreach programs. When San Francisco decided to implement a new city-funded program to distribute free needles to high-risk opioid users, they budgeted $30,000 to be given to a single woman who wrote a college essay that promoted the idea. The woman created the Drug Overdose Prevention and Education (DOPE) Project, and four years later, it had a budget of more $100,000. The same nonprofit was transferred to the National Harm Reduction Coalition (NHRC) and was eventually given city funds to distribute naloxone without medical supervision. By 2022, the state of California budgeted $62 million to give to NHRC for their harm reduction programs.

Hundreds of nonprofit organizations follow similar funding paths. Instead of creating new agencies, city and state governments distribute funds directly to nonprofit organizations to handle particular social services. The city of San Francisco spent more than $1 billion on nonprofits organizations in 2023. The Kensington District of Philadelphia contains about 42,000 people in less than a square mile, and it has thirty-six non-profits receiving city funding amounting to nearly a million dollars per year.

Sources of Controversy: The IRS has fraud protection protocols to prevent organizations from claiming to be nonprofit when they are not. However, the number of 501.c organizations (nearly 2 million) makes it impossible to accurately check each one. During the 2020s, many cities faced public scandals when it was publicized in the press that millions of dollars of government money was funneled into nonprofits groups that were using it for personal purposes—and who were often closely linked to the same government officials who authorized the public funding.

Even without public scandal, nonprofits are sometimes criticized because their staff members may earn high salaries. Directors in the NHRC earned anywhere between $94,000 to $141,000 in 2022, and other staff members earned salaries ranging from around $50,000 to $75,000 per year. These ranges may not be unusual for business leaders, but many nonprofits are operated by untrained individuals. Governments do not place any educational or training requirements on nonprofit groups that receive funds. People who direct drug-related nonprofits groups were often themselves formerly addicted. For people who do not work near and around these nonprofits, these situations can be controversial.

To outside observers, using nonprofits to tackle urban drug problems may inspire two different reactions. One positive reaction is that the city governments are giving money directly to help those who are most impacted by drug addiction by enabling those with the most experience to work on the streets and provide aid where it is most needed. One negative reaction is that city governments are spending government money to placate the neighborhood residents who may not be properly experienced to address problems of drug addiction on the streets.

The greatest source of controversy is due to the ambiguous nature of "help." Drug-related problems are complex and often involve human relationships that are not easily measured by drug use or crime statistics. It is very difficult to determine if money given to nonprofit organizations is helping end urban drug problems or if they are enabling these problems to grow worse. Potential conflicts of interest may hide the extent of the public need because it is not in the interest of nonprofit groups to publicly acknowledge that they are no longer needed. At the same time, if drug problems continue to increase even after giving more money to nonprofits, critics may question whether the nonprofits are helping. Nonprofit organizations face a dilemma because their work is not easily measured in terms of "success" or "failure," and their funding relies heavily on public perceptions of need.

This ambiguity leads to four general reactions to the use of 501.c nonprofit groups for implementing city-based drug policies. These reactions range from harsh criticism to strong support.

1. Harshest critics argue that nonprofits are used by politicians to make it look like they are helping to solve a problem without actually fixing anything. They are accused of funneling government money into the hands of their supporters and using nonprofits to appear more virtuous than they are.
2. Moderate critics may accept that politicians are sincere in their commitment to help and also argue that nonprofits do not solve the problem of drug addiction, and the city money is wasted. If drug abuse and related crime shows no evidence of declining, using nonprofits is the wrong solution.
3. Moderate supporters recognize certain economic inefficiencies but still argue that people who operate nonprofits are sincere and provide real human compassion that is a necessary link between cold government bureaucracy and the people on the street who are in most need. In this way, the human contact is worth the money.
4. Strongest supporters argue that nonprofit organizations are essential to modern government because they provide the means by which taxpayers can work with private citizens to share in the responsibility of taking care of the poor and marginalized. Nonprofits do the work that is not practical for city staff bureaucrats.

Summary of Social Services Dilemma: A problem that all large cities face with their social services operations is that they are always located near areas of high-intensity drug use. This is logical because these services should be made available to those who most need them. The problem is that users tend to migrate toward these same districts. Critics argue that OPS facilities may remove some of the risks associated with recreational drug use, including accidental overdose and police arrest, but they do not remove all the dangers, such as increasing addiction dependency, long-term health risks, and associated crime and violence that accompany illegal marketplaces. For these reasons, social services are often criticized because they appear to attract more problems related to drug use than they cure.

When harm reduction operations are established in high-intensity drug-use areas, the rate of drug use and addiction in the district always increases. Rates of property crimes and crimes of violence also increase. For supporters of harm-reduction drug decriminalization programs, these increasing rates do not prove ineffectiveness. Instead, they argue that drug use, addiction, and crime are outside the control of cities and state governments but are related more to poor socioeconomic conditions and to homelessness. Harm-reduction treatment approaches are intended to help victims and are not intended to solve larger social problems. When addiction and crime rates increase in high-intensity drug-use districts these supporters of decriminalization call for more government resources to be directed to the area to help treat the growing demand.

For critics of decriminalization and other harm-reduction strategies, these social-service operations appear to be the cause of higher addiction and associated crime rates. Rather than solving those problems, they enable the problems to grow because there are fewer disincentives for drug use. They recognize larger socioeconomic issues, but critics argue that the public generally expects city programs to actually reduce recreational drug use. Treating users suffering from addiction is helpful, but establishing stronger penalties for drug possession, sales, and use would decrease the rate of addiction and its associated crime. Opponents of decriminalization also argue that removing the stigma and other immediate risks of recreational drug use only encourages more drug use and more addiction, which unintentionally leads to higher overdose fatalities.

Ideological Debates over City-Based Decriminalization Policies

Rates of recreational drug use may be similar within urban centers as in rural communities, but the types of recreational drug use are not the same. Using loose categories, there are two different types of users: (1) the "casual user" who consumes drugs infrequently and believes their habits are not harmful to themselves or to others; and (2) the "extreme user" who consumes drugs daily and recognizes that their habits are causing great harm to themselves and to those around them. People may disagree over which type of user is technically more accurate in their self-identification, but all sides of the decriminalization debate recognize the two extremes in the range of recreational drug use.

Dutch Decriminalization Example: The city of Amsterdam in the Netherlands established its drug policies based on two extremes of drug use. They distinguished between "soft" drugs that are less potent and that people use only periodically and "hard" drugs that are much more potent and that people tend to use frequently due to their heavy addiction. Amsterdam instituted a policy of tolerance for possession, use, and sale of "soft" drugs (such as marijuana) because they believed that if young people are allowed to experiment infrequently with casual drug use, they would be more likely to be kept away from hard drugs that encourage extreme drug use. Amsterdam never legalized recreational drugs, and they continued to categorize heroin, cocaine, amphetamines, and other addictive synthetic substances as "hard" drugs. Instead, they use two separate policies to deal with "casual" drug users and "extreme" addicted drug users. Decriminalization and legalization policies in the United States do not make such distinctions.

The city of Amsterdam also distinguished between people who live in and reflect local Dutch customs and outsiders who are attracted to the city only for the drug experience. Dutch tolerance policies were in place for more than thirty years before Amsterdam gained its reputation for easy access to drugs. Drug tourism became an increasing problem for residents around 2000, and by 2013, the Dutch responded by passing a law mandating coffee shops where marijuana is sold should be small and should only trade with Dutch residents. The law is difficult to enforce. There is no law requiring coffee shops to check residency. However, the intent of the law is clear: only locals who are accustomed to Dutch traditions should be allowed to purchase marijuana. Outsiders tend to create public nuisances and increase the risk of crime, criminal drug-trafficking organizations, and addiction rates. Decriminalization and legalization policies in the United States do not distinguish between large cities and small rural communities. Moreover, high-intensity drug-trafficking districts in the American cities generally provide anonymous access to inexpensive drugs outside of the normal counterpressures of social norms. In this sense, most drug buyers in these districts act as drug tourists.

Difference in Drug-Use Habits: After 2010, fentanyl became one of the most dangerous opioid drugs because it frequently contains very high concentrations, and many users suffer immediate overdose reactions. The most tragic stories of overdose traumas and deaths are told by casual drug users who did not realize that their regular drug supply was tainted by fentanyl. This is especially true for student-aged youth and young adults who took their drugs (often for vaping) as a recreational activity with friends and then found themselves in an emergency room or in the morgue.

For extreme users who live near open-air drug markets, there is no confusion about fentanyl. Dealers sell fentanyl directly, and most buyers in these high-intensity drug-use districts intentionally purchase and use fentanyl daily—sometimes multiple times a day. In the Kensington market, xylazine (known as "tranq") is also increasingly popular. It is a tranquilizer that is mixed with fentanyl to provide users with longer-lasting and deeper effects. Observers sometimes refer to tranq as the "Zombie Drug" because the user becomes completely unaware of their surroundings, lose memory, and appear to be passed out but is still awake. The effects of fentanyl only last a short while, but adding xylazine with the mixture makes the effect last much longer, sometimes many hours or days. Xylazine-laced drugs may be a surprise to casual users, but extreme users are fully aware of what they are buying, and they deliberately choose to consume these potent drugs.

The problem with xylazine, fentanyl, and all other recreational drugs is that the overdose risks are always high. Naloxone has little effect in treating xylazine overdose reactions because it is not an opioid, and so fatality rates are much higher than with fentanyl. Xylazine limits blood flow to certain tissues, which causes open sores to erupt internally and externally. Typical xylazine users have dozens of open wounds all over their body as a result of the drug use. Extreme users know about these side effects, and yet they still use these and other drugs including fentanyl and heroin because the withdrawal symptoms are extremely harsh, and their addictions makes it very difficult to stop using.

Casual users rarely plan to consume such potent drug combinations. They would probably not start a drug habit if they saw the open sores and other publicly perceivable effects of xylazine. No recreational drug user plans to overdose, and yet more than 200,000 people do so every year—with over 100,000 fatalities.

Social Movements and Cities

Some of the more intensely concentrated expressions of the social-welfare position originated in urban centers and in response to events occurring in urban areas. In terms of the story of decriminalization, two movements played a major role in changing drug enforcement policies over the span of six years, from 2014 to 2020: Antifa and Black Lives Matter (BLM).

The name "Antifa" is an abbreviation of "Anti-Fascist Action." (The name was originally used by a German group in the early 1930s and was a shortened version of *Antifaschistische Aktion.*) The first Antifa group to emerge in the United States was in Portland, Oregon, in 2007, called the "Rose City Antifa." It is one of dozens of groups that identify themselves as "American Antiracist Action" groups and became affiliated with another such group, the Torch Network, in 2016. These groups were identified as domestic terrorist organizations by the

FBI because they engaged in violent provocations to achieve their political ends. They were not deemed an immediate threat because members rarely held uniform ideological beliefs or political goals. Instead, they usually targeted their protests issue by issue, without any attempt at consistency.

According to the Congressional Research Service, Antifa groups generally hold four principles: "Antifa groups must (1) track the activity of fascist groups, (2) oppose their public organizing, (3) support antifascist allies attacked by fascists or arrested by police, and (4) not cooperate with law enforcement." (Bjelopera, 2018) The last point means that they must never divulge their association with any Antifa group. As a practical matter, Antifa do not hold any specific ideology, but they generally oppose the police, free market economies, and conservative moral values. They oppose all facets of society that they feel are fascist or racist. They protest for environmental causes, gay rights, indigenous rights, and the rights of the homeless.

The Black Lives Matter Global Network organization began in 2013 with a social media campaign initiated by Alicia Garza, Patrisse Cullors, and Opal Tometi. In response to the widely publicized death of Trayvon Martin, who was killed in a conflict with a Neighborhood Watch volunteer, George Zimmerman, in the city of Stanford, Florida, and subsequently acquitted. The social media phrase "#Black Lives Matter" drew nationwide sympathy. A year later, in Ferguson, Missouri, Michael Brown was killed during an altercation with police. The incident led to massive protests and rioting as well as increasing awareness and support for the Black Lives Matter movement. The Ferguson protests ushered in an era of BLM-supported protests in other urban areas in response to incidents of police violence against black suspects. Between 2015 and 2020, Antifa groups joined at least 50 BLM protests, many of which involved rioting, arson, looting, and altercations with police.

Ideologically, Black Lives Matter as an organization is concerned with more than issues of racial injustice and policing. Cullors described Black Lives Matter as a "feminist framework that grasped the importance of intersectionality." Individually, Cullors explained, "Myself and Alicia [Garza], in particular, are trained organizers; we are trained Marxists. We are super-versed on, sort of, ideological theories." For her part, Alicia Garza described herself as, "queer social justice activist and Marxist" (Horowitz, 2021).

Black Lives Matter is a sponsored organization of Thousand Currents, a 501.c.3 group, which is used as a major distributor of funds for political causes. After the Ferguson incident, BLM was given millions of dollars in donations from George Soros, Bill Gates, the professional basketball player LeBron James, and many large corporations such as Apple, Amazon, Google, Nabisco, Gatorade, and others. According to the Claremont Institute's Center for the American Way of Life, at the height of BLM protest movement during the summer of 2020, the combination of BLM donation groups received $82.9 billion in donations, of which $123 million were given directly to BLM.

The point at which the BLM movement joined with previous drug decriminalization movements came in 2020 after George Floyd died during a police altercation in Minneapolis, Minnesota. By the end of the summer, after 103 days of protests and riots in forty-eight of the largest fifty cities in the United States, most of these large cities adopted new decriminalization policies with noncriminal harm reduction tactics.

George Floyd was arrested and handcuffed after passing a counterfeit $20 bill at a local store. Floyd was disoriented and showed signs of drug intoxication, including delirium and paranoia. He resisted being put into a police vehicle, indicating that he could not breathe. Police officers restrained Floyd after he attempted to flee. One officer placed his knee on Floyd's neck, applying a restraint technique that was part of the Minneapolis Police training and was often used for drug-induced altercations where the suspect is not rational and does not respond to verbal commands. Floyd repeatedly screamed that he could not breathe, but the officer continued to apply the restraint.

The maneuver is not generally considered lethal because there is no pressure applied to the front of the throat, where the windpipe (trachea) is located. During the five years prior to Floyd, the neck restrain maneuver was used on 237 other suspects, and none died. Floyd's autopsy revealed that his system contained a polydrug combination of methamphetamines and enough fentanyl to cause an overdose in most people and that he also had a heart condition. These factors, in combination with the neck restraint, likely contributed to his death. The incident brought police training, procedure, and policy into question.

A video of the police officer restraining Floyd and Floyd yelling, "I can't breathe" several times quickly became viral on social media and elicited protests from around the nation, most of which were directed by BLM operators. Minnesota Attorney General Keith Ellison charged all four police officers involved in the incident, including Derek Chauvin, whose charges were eventually elevated to second-degree murder. Spokesmen from around the country came to Floyd's funeral, and the eulogy was delivered by Rev. Al Sharpton, who claimed that Floyd represented all Black Americans who have always been oppressed in "every area of American life."

Within hours of the incident, riots erupted in cities all across the nation. Minneapolis and St. Paul experienced several weeks of rioting in which 1,500 businesses were looted, destroyed, or burned. The total damage was estimated at $500 million. During the first twelve days after Floyd's death, 500,000 protesters followed BLM events in 550 cities. Three days after that, more than 2,000 protest events occurred in all fifty states.

In a unanimous decision issued one month after Floyd's death, Minneapolis city council members voted to replace the city's police department with an alternative social-welfare agency that relied mostly on outreach workers and emergency responders. This was the first explicit decriminalization policy for a large city. The city of Minneapolis also awarded Floyd's family $27 million in an out-of-court settlement, just prior to the criminal trials of the four charged officers. All four officers were later convicted by a Minneapolis jury after only a very brief deliberation. In an interview after the trial, Attorney General Ellison admitted, "We don't have any evidence that Derek Chauvin factored George Floyd's race as he did what he did." Nevertheless, Floyd's death became a symbol of American racism and police brutality against non-whites (Horowitz, 59).

After the initial riots broke out in cities across the nation following George Floyd's death, the mayor of Seattle, Washington, instructed the police in the East Precinct to withdraw and allow protestors to act without interference. BLM protestors took over the Police Precinct Building and the Seattle City Hall, and then blocked out city streets along a six-block perimeter. They claimed the area as an independent government, which they called CHAZ (Capital Hill Autonomous Zone), and discussed plans for creating a separate flag and their own currency. Leaders issued demands before they would leave the area, including, (1) abolish the police department; (2) retry all people of color who had been sentenced for violent crimes; (3) abolish all prisons; (4) provide free college for people of color; and (5) pay reparation payments to people of color for a history of systemic oppression.

During the time of occupation, all the businesses in the district were looted and destroyed, and two protesters were shot and killed by other protestors along with four other shooting victims, who survived. After three weeks, the protestors attacked the mayor's house and covered it with graffiti. The mayor declared the CHAZ an unlawful assembly and the police cleared away the encampment in a single day.

The city of Portland, Oregon, was considered the center of BLM protests throughout the summer of 2020 because it was also the center of Antifa coordinated involvement. (Rose City Antifa group was the first in the country.)

For nearly four months, rioters formed largely peaceful protests during the day that erupted into violent protests at night. The Portland Police Department declared riot conditions on 18 separate occasions, but violence against city buildings occurred every night, including acts of vandalism, gunshots, arson, burglary, and attacks on police officers and other federal agents.

The riot zone was spread across twenty blocks around the city center and all vehicle traffic was mostly blocked. Unlike the Seattle mayor, the Portland mayor initially opposed the violent protests and ordered his officers to defend the city buildings. However, after four months, the mayor instructed the police to stop using tear gas for crowd control purposes and promised to make substantial changes to crime-control policies for the sake of "justice for black people and all people of color." (Horowitz, p.23) This admission marked the start of Oregon's formal decriminalization of all drugs at the state level.

The riots in New York City coincided with riots in Seattle, Portland, and many other larger cities, which all began on May 29, 2020. More than 500 rioters attacked the 88th and the 79th Police Precincts with bricks and bottles and attempted to take over the buildings. The next day, riots erupted around the city, involving thousands of people and resulting in injured police officers, damaged or destroyed police cars, and the burglary of hundreds of businesses in the SoHo neighborhood district (including Bloomingdales, Chanel, Gucci, Coach, Louis Vuitton).

New York Governor Andrew Cuomo and City Mayor Bill de Blasio signed new laws reforming criminal justice policies that permitted suspects charged with misdemeanor and nonviolent felonies to be released without bail. As a practical matter, this meant that New York Police would no longer investigate or apprehend violations of these misdemeanor crimes—especially when they involve shoplifting or burglary of retail outlets and also for any sort of drug-possession charge. This was a form of city-level decriminalization. The mayor reduced the police department budget by $1 billion dollars, and following the example of the mayor of Washington, DC, the New York City mayor also ordered that "Black Lives Matters" would be painted on the street in large lettering along Fifth Avenue, directly in front of the Trump Tower.

For most of the four years between 2017 and 2021, the BLM organization received strong popular support from celebrities, schools, news media, politicians, and other cultural influencers who supported social-welfare ideologies. It raised $90 million in 2020 and invested its money in $42 million of assets (mostly real estate). BLM stickers and shirts with slogans like "Defund the Police" became fashionable symbols of anti-racism and cultural open-mindedness.

Most supporters had no knowledge of the BLM founders' Marxist ideology, but they shared in a general opposition to racism in America, as did the vast majority of Americans. Many Americans felt that support for BLM was a public announcement of their opposition to racism.

According to a research study by Armed Conflict Location and Event Data (ACLED) and the Bridging the Divides Initiative (BDI) conducted by Princeton University in 2020, there were 633 violent protests during the first 103 days following the George Floyd incident. These were held in 220 locations, and the BLM organization was involved in 95 percent of them. BLM organizers sent out 127 million emails during the summer months, resulting in 1.2 million actions. The presence of Antifa rioters in paramilitary gear was indicated by their common body armor, helmets and face masks, batons, and other military tools that were always present in these conflicts. Alongside the 633 violent protests, there were also 11,400 peaceful protests during the day that did not involve acts of physical violence. In 2023, two years after 2020 summer riots, the Insurance Information Institute reported that nearly $2 billion of insurance claims were filed for property damage caused by the protests. In addition, 14 protesters were killed, all by other protestors. Two police officers were killed, and more than 700 were injured in twenty-five states, as were 100 federal officers (Horowitz, 2021).

Along with concerns regarding institutional racism, public reactions to George Floyd's death came to symbolize the problems associated with interactions between law enforcement and drug users. How should the police, charged with preserving the public peace, deal with drug users who disturb that peace? Does the police mandate need to change, away from law enforcement and toward harm reduction strategies? After breaking down these exchanges in general terms, we can interpret the events of 2020 along our three ideological viewpoints.

Social-Welfare Interpretation: Social-welfare advocates indicate that the increase in drug use throughout urban centers is proof that the War on Drugs is not working. They claim that drug laws and criminal prosecutions do not stop drug use, and harsh police actions fail to address other more significant issues, such as the problems of racism, socioeconomic inequality, the lack of free housing, and the general lack of opportunities available for minority identity groups. The solution to these problems, they believe, requires massive restructuring of how we define crime (often called "reimagining") and how we go about addressing recreational drug-use.

In the specific case of George Floyd, social-welfare proponents say that police should not have attempted to arrest him for passing a small amount of counterfeit money or for taking items by using that money since the value of the items was significantly less than felony levels. As he was obviously suffering from the effects of drug use, they believe that the officers should have taken him to the hospital or administered naloxone immediately, which may have saved his life.

Traditional Conservative Interpretation: The conservative viewpoint sees the increase in drug use throughout urban centers as proof that the legalization of marijuana and nonenforcement of other drug laws has failed to protect both users and the communities in which they live. They believe that drug laws and criminal prosecutions have been declining in their strength due to the "Ferguson Effect" (when police reduce enforcement efforts following any national news event that alleges police brutality). As law enforcement declines, the general welfare of urban communities suffers—both Black and white and both drug users and non-users. Conservatives believe that the solution to these problems requires a massive public commitment to restoring law and order.

In the specific case of George Floyd, conservatives admit that the situation was tragic because a life was lost, but they believe that the police did nothing wrong. They see the officers' later criminal convictions as a result of heavily biased court proceedings. From the conservative viewpoint, the police responded to a criminal violation, dealt with the suspect humanely, and only applied force after repeated acts of violent resistance. Conservatives feel that the restraint technique is safe and that Floyd died from a fentanyl overdose and heart condition that coincided with his restraint. Because officers did not recognize the signs of overdose, the conservative view might recommend more training in detecting these signs and that officers should carry naloxone doses for future situations.

Libertarian Reaction: Between 2020 and 2023, libertarians generally made very few observations because the public emotions were so high that any opposition to BLM protests might be interpreted as supporting racism. Libertarians oppose police brutality, but they also oppose Marxism and the disruption of civil order. As a result, the libertarian ideological base of supporters was significantly reduced. Some joined the social-welfare side more fully to support drug decriminalization, and some joined the traditional conservative side as silent supporters of law enforcement.

Conclusion: The Challenge for Decriminalization

Cities pose the greatest challenge for decriminalization policies because they expose the most extreme harms that come from frequent drug use, and they also bring up public debates over the morality of recreational drug use. The high rates of overdose fatalities and crime in urban neighborhoods weaken the claims that recreational drug use is harmless. At the same time, other arguments assert that decriminalization provides necessary emergency services for people who are most at risk of being harmed by drugs, especially the users themselves. Overdose prevention sites clean needles, and easily accessible naloxone help to save people from death. The claims of both sides are publicly displayed through images from urban drug districts and are perhaps more influential than riots because they are seen more often.

Opponents of decriminalization usually admit that emergency services are very important. However, they argue that if fewer people were taking recreational drugs, there would be lower levels of addiction, and less need for such emergency responses. They point to the high crime rates and open-air drug markets as proof that law enforcement is necessary to curb extreme drug use.

For a variety of political reasons related to widespread urban rioting during the summer of 2020 and its association with critical social theory, almost all large cities launched some form of decriminalization or harm reduction policy by 2020. In every case, rates of drug use, addiction, and crime increased. This caused negative public reactions to city policies, often from people who do not live in those high drug-use neighborhoods.

By the mid-2020s, many cities reconsidered their drug policies to include more law enforcement tools. Mostly, these involved efforts to remove homeless encampments and make drug use less publicly visible. Some cities launched new efforts to prosecute open drug use in public parks and sidewalks and engaged in more public debate about making drug treatment mandatory instead of voluntary. These practices were more closely related to traditional law-enforcement measures. Nevertheless, harm reduction policies continued to dominate most large cities as late as 2025.

Ultimately, the effectiveness of any decriminalization or legalization policy requires some consensus of public will. The public needs to be more consistent in their views on recreational drug use, and cities need to make policy decisions about whether they believe drug use (casual or extreme) poses inherent risks to individuals and to society or whether it is truly morally neutral. Public opinion polls show great sympathy for compassionate harm-reduction polices, but they also show great frustration with increasing crime rates and overdose fatalities. It is difficult to support both goals with the same policies.

10

Legalization and the State

Cities may pose the most serious challenges for drug decriminalization and legalization policies, but states provide their greatest opportunities. Mostly, this is because the United States has fifty separate regional governmental units, and residents are allowed to move in and between them whenever they like. This means that populations within each state generally share some consensus with regard to moral values and social priorities related to drug policies. States also include both urban and rural districts, so they do not suffer from the same public image problems that cities must deal with when crime and addiction mortality rates are concentrated in small areas. State drug policies are more likely to have broader public support.

Each state passes its own laws that reflect the priorities of its population. The Fourteenth Amendment to the US Constitution requires every state to provide at least as much protection for their residents as is provided by the national government. However, the Tenth Amendment allows each state to provide greater protection for their residents than is guaranteed by the federal government if they choose to do so. That is why marijuana is legal in some states and not legal in others. The federal government designates marijuana as a controlled substance, but individual states may choose to allow their residents to buy, sell, and consume within their own borders. Drug policies reflect the particular priorities of the people living in each state.

State legislatures may pass laws about what is legal or illegal, but most examples of the priorities of their community can be found in their budgets. There is only a limited amount of taxpayer money to go around, so each state legislature must choose which programs should be funded and which ones should rely only on private support. The state budgets generally reflect the interests of the people during the budget-making process. As a practical matter, the budget process is a complex mixture of bureaucratic pressures and public interest groups, but in the end, if the budget choices made by the state government do not seem to reflect the general interest of the local citizens, the public will react. Either the majority of representatives will be voted out of office so that new budget priorities are enacted in the next cycle, or individual residents will "vote with their feet" and simply move to another state.

Interstate migration occurs every year, and housing prices, costs of living, and job availability are the three main reasons for moving. In many cases, state tax rates play a large role in determining cost of living and in encouraging interstate migration. People who remain in their state are more likely to support or be tolerant of their state's priorities. Generally, the decision to decriminalize or legalize certain drugs or to maintain criminal penalties generally reflects the will of the people who live in the state region. If certain policy changes lead to unexpected or negative results, the voters usually make their government aware that those policies should be altered or repealed.

Comparing American States to European Nations

Portugal and the Netherlands (especially the Dutch city of Amsterdam) are both frequently cited as models of successful harm reduction policies. Actual comparisons between these European examples may not always support the practical implementation in American cities and states. These two European nations share certain cultural characteristics that are not always shared by those other governments who seek to imitate their policies. In the United States, there are both similarities and some notable differences.

Both Portugal and the Netherlands enjoy relatively small populations that reflect more cultural consensus than differences. According to their annual budgeting reports, Portugal has a national budget of about $102 billion, which is roughly the same size budget as the state of Illinois ($109.5 billion). The Netherlands has a much larger national budget of $396 billion, which is less than the state of California but is roughly the same as both Texas ($185.2 billion) and New York ($212.8 billion) budgets combined. In terms of population, Portugal has a population of 10.5 million, which is a little larger than the greater Chicago metropolitan area (8.6 million). The Netherlands has a population of 17.9 million, which is just a little smaller than the greater New York City metropolitan area (19.4 million).

Population densities in Portugal and the Netherlands are widely apart. About two-thirds of the Portuguese live in urban areas, whereas nine out of ten Dutch live in urban areas. Between 84 percent and 88 percent of the people living in the

American states of Illinois, New York, California, and Texas also live in urban areas. In this way, Portugal has a much larger rural population than its American counterparts, whereas the Dutch tend to have higher urban populations.

Nevertheless, the most striking difference between the European examples of Portugal and the Netherlands and the American states is cultural diversity. In 2020, around 85 percent of Dutch population were native-born, while more than 90 percent of Portuguese population were native-born. By contrast, about one-third of Los Angeles area residents are foreign-born, and more than half have parents who were foreign-born, mostly from Latin America or Asia. Similarly, in Chicago about one in four residents are foreign-born (or are children of parents who were foreign-born), and nearly 40 percent of the residents of New York City were foreign-born. In both Chicago and New York City, immigrants come from all over, including strong percentages from every populated continent in the world. Cultural diversity is significantly higher in large American cities and states, than it is in either Portugal or the Netherlands.

Americans generally "celebrate" their cultural diversity. The phrase is a very common slogan for almost all educational facilities and large corporations. However, in terms of drug policies, cultural diversity generally poses challenges for decriminalization and legalization policies. Most drug laws reflect the majority values of a population, and societies that have higher cultural consensus usually exhibit less controversy over their drug laws. By contrast, population centers with greater cultural diversity, such as found in the United States, generally experience much more controversy when new drug policies (such as decriminalization or legalization) are introduced. In this way, the actual practice of implementing drug decriminalization in Amsterdam and Portugal is much different from the experiences of most American states who imitate those policies. There are more people who share common values in these European states than there are in the American examples.

The Netherlands originally justified its tolerance policies in the early 1970s on the presumption that existing cultural pressures would prevent youth from irresponsibly experimenting with dangerous drugs. The government of Portugal published similar explanations when they introduced their decriminalization policies in the early 2000s. In both cases, government policymakers believed that they could influence the habits of their residents by applying more informal social pressures that would limit the harm of recreational drug use and avoid other harms caused by heavy criminal prosecution of drug users. In that way, they could avoid the need for more law enforcement.

Part of the Dutch harm reduction strategies was to restrict access of recreational drugs to certain confined districts. Local police recognized certain "red light districts" where recreational drug use and prostitution were allowed to continue with very little police interference. Portugal followed similar tactics by limiting sales of certain drugs to particular urban districts. By contrast, the United States does not officially recognize red light districts. Police and news media are aware of where the open-air drug markets are, but most local governments are embarrassed by these districts and seek to limit or eradicate criminal activity in these sectors. American states have never officially instituted separate drug policies for differing population districts.

During the mid-2020s, both the Netherlands and Portugal began reconsidering their drug decriminalization policies. In both cases, increasing immigration and "drug tourism" were cited as causes. The Dutch government began exercising greater scrutiny over the sales of recreational drugs to foreign visitors and also began advertising and enforcing laws against public drug use. In preparation for their National Plan for the Reduction of Addictive Behaviors and Dependencies 2021-2030 and for their part of the United Nations Office of Drugs European Horizon Action Plan (2021-2024), Portugal debated serious changes to its policies in 2023 after immigration rates increased to their highest levels ever (10 percent) and the rate of recreational drug use increased from 7 percent (in 2001) to nearly 13 percent (in 2022). Portuguese drug users continued to be monitored by health professionals rather than law enforcement, but at the same time, Portuguese police devoted more resources to prosecuting drug dealers, especially those that have ties with international criminal organizations. The primary argument for change in both the Dutch and the Portuguese laws was that new drug users were no longer influenced by the local cultural pressures, and large drug-dealer organizations had no concern for preserving cultural priorities in either nation.

Variations among American States

There is great variety among the American states. California has about 39 million people, with a budget of $445 billion. By comparison to foreign nations, California's government spends just a little less than the entire nation of India (at $495 billion), which has the largest population in the world and the seventh largest land mass. The California budget is about the same as the budgets in the nations of Australia and Brazil. The second largest American state budget is New York at $212 billion, which is roughly the same amount spent by nations such as Austria, Mexico, Poland, Saudi Arabia, Sweden, Switzerland, and Thailand. The second and third largest American state budgets combined (New York and Texas) spend about the same amount of money as Canada.

Six American states have budgets of more than $100 billion, but most state budgets average about $55 billion. The US state with the smallest budget is Wyoming with annual expenditures of $5.7 billion and a population of only 578,000. Despite its small size, Wyoming's economy is still larger than more than 120 other nations in the world. No matter how small the population, none of the American states will ever be very poor because our federal system ensures that every state has a minimum amount of federal money passing through it.

A lot of federal money is authorized by the US Congress and then sent to state governments to administer in their own systems. In some cases, federal grants, loans, and other forms of aid may be given directly to cities or to agencies operating within the state. The largest percentage of federal money is sent to states for social security, healthcare, welfare assistance, education grants, and highway funds. Most federal assistance to low-income households come in the form of WIC (women, infants, and children) programs, food stamps (supplemental nutrition assistance programs or SNAP), temporary assistance programs (TANF), Housing and Urban Development (HUD) grants, and home energy assistance programs (LIHEAP) which have their origin in the federal budget, even if they are administered through the states. All Medicaid money begins in Washington, DC, and is then sent to state governments to manage and distribute.

Some larger states like California, New York, Texas, and Illinois have extremely high budgets, but that is mostly because they have large populations. On a per capita basis (that means, the amount of money spent per person living in the state), the five largest budgets are in Alaska (around $16,000), New Mexico and Vermont (each around $13,000), and Delaware and California (each at around $11,000). Of these, Alaska and Vermont are the second and third least populated states. In part, their per capita rates are high because they receive a lot of federal money that is passed through their state budgets. In the case of high-population states, such as California and New York (with a per capita rate just under $11,000), their rates are high because these state budgets have much higher-than-average tax rates, and the state legislature allocated a lot more money for public welfare expenses. Based on annual reports compiled by the Bureau of Fiscal Service within the US Department of the Treasury, in both California and New York, money spent on welfare is between 150 percent and 175 percent more than the amount spent on education. Except for Alaska, Vermont, and Delaware, most states spend 115 percent to 125 percent more on education than they do on public welfare. Since 2000, both California and New York have been losing residents who move to other states with lower living costs.

States with large overall budgets ($60 billion or more) tend to have large urban centers, for welfare tends to be concentrated in urban centers, because the signs of poverty are more visible to the public when populations are densely concentrated in small districts. Poverty exists in rural communities, but it is more difficult for state agencies to reach out to broadly dispersed populations. In many states, there is a public perception that the cities receive the most attention and the rural farm districts receive much less. This perception often causes tension during budget-planning processes. It also affects decisions related to drug decriminalization and legalization.

States with high concentrations of urban populations are more likely to approach drug policies that reflect urban concerns and which are reflected in their state budget priorities. With a few notable exceptions (like Montana), states with the largest urban population centers were the first to legalize recreational marijuana, while states with large rural areas resisted those policy changes.

State Budgets Reflect State Priorities

A state budget is a plan that legislatures use to decide how and where their government money will be spent. Most states use biennial budgets, which means they plan their spending priorities two years in advance. About a quarter of US state legislatures only meet in session every other year because that is when their budgets are discussed.

A budget is more than just deciding where the money goes; it often determines policy. If a program is fully funded, the purposes of that program become a priority for state lawmakers. If a program's funding is cut, or if the money is shifted over to another agency, lawmakers are indicating that they no longer support that policy approach. State legislatures pass laws that prohibit certain activities, but some of the most influential tools for policymaking come from their budget decisions. For this reason, the state budgets usually represent an overview of the cultural and social priorities of their communities.

Basic Process: In most states, the governor sends out a budget proposal to the state legislature around the start of the new year in January. This proposal reflects recommendations sent to the governor's office by each state agency during the months prior. The governor and their chief advisors look over each recommendation and then adjust these requests higher or lower depending on their administrative priorities. After the governor's budget proposal is sent to the state legislature, it is broken down into component parts and passed out to various committees to examine. Budget committees hold public hearings at various stages of the process as they work through different topics a few at a time. This process may take six to eight months.

As a general rule, almost every government agency and program asks for more money than they received in their previous budget allotment. This is because inflation always increases costs (called a "cost-of-living" adjustment). In many cases, some agencies seek substantial budget increases in order to pay for new programs or special projects like building construction. Since almost every agency asks for more money, and the rate of state revenue is usually only moderately increased, there is always some debate over budget priorities. Every state agency and related interest group must compete with others in order to guarantee their share of the state money during the budget process.

At various points during the year, committee members will formally meet with agency directors to discuss why they should receive their budget request. In addition, individual lawmakers generally meet with other special interest groups, including 501.c nonprofit organizations, private corporations, and private citizens at almost any time of the year.

People who meet with lawmakers to promote their issues are called lobbyists. Some lobbyists are professionals, which means they are paid directly by the special interest group that they represent. Other types of lobbyists are not paid, but they still represent particular interests through formal and informal meetings. Depending on the size of the state, the number of lobbyists that meet with lawmakers can vary from a few hundred to many thousands.

After the state legislature goes through the governor's budget items, making their own additions or subtractions, they vote on the final budget proposal. Throughout the process, representatives of both political parties and from the governor's office usually talk with key representatives of the legislature so that both sides know what to expect. If the full legislature approves a budget, it is sent back to the governor for his approval. If the governor vetoes the budget, the state legislature must try to either override the veto or make changes to the budget that the governor will support.

The entire process often takes close to a year and a half. For large states, like California, New York, Texas, Illinois, and Florida, there are billions of state dollars being distributed. For other smaller states, the amount of state spending above and beyond that provided by the federal government is more limited. Most federal money coming into the state is already marked for particular types of expenses by federal lawmakers. The state may select which groups receive those funds, but in many cases, the legislature has only limited control over that money.

Since the amount of money is counted in the billions of dollars in every state (even Wyoming), it is very rare that lawmakers can read through every budget item. Researchers estimate that about 80 percent of each state's budget is automatically determined based on the numbers used in the previous year. Only those programs that generate the most public interest (or attract the greatest public scandal) are closely examined. For this reason, it is most common for state budgets to grow slowly and rare for any budget items to decrease substantially.

It is easier for a lawmaker to announce support for increasing particular budgets than it is to declare that they will cut particular budgets. In every agency, there are people who work in the program and who receive benefits from the services. If a budget is cut, employees are potentially laid off and public benefits are reduced. Drug policies are often strongly associated with urban priorities, crime rates, health trends, and economic growth potential. For these reasons, they are often very controversial and usually receive much more public attention than other state priorities.

Popular Myths about Government Spending: News of projected budget cuts usually results in controversial stories that include very emotional appeals warning against terrible consequences if a particular program is no longer funded (or not funded at the same amount). In some cases, these fears are justified, and in other cases they are exaggerated in order to influence public opinion. This is a normal part of the political process in an open democracy with a free press.

Unfortunately, budget debates over drug policies at both the state and federal levels have generated many generalizations that are simply false. One of the most common myths is that the United States spends more money on the military than it does on education and helping the poor. (This assertion is frequently made on websites that oppose the drug war.) This emotional assertion may be satisfying because people do not like war, and most people have great natural sympathy for the disadvantaged. Yet, the generalization is not accurate at any level.

Based on US Census Data on State and Local Expenditures for 2022, the federal government typically spends trillions of dollars on public entitlements like welfare, social security, unemployment, healthcare, and education. During the mid-2020s, the Department of Health and Human Services received $1,720 billion ($1.72 trillion), and the Social Security Administration received $1,260 billion ($1.26 trillion). The Department of Defense and the Department of Homeland Security combined received only $460 billion, which is about one-fifth of the amount spent on health and welfare. The Department of Education by itself received about $100 billion, which is about six and half times (650 percent) more than the Department of Justice, which is the agency that funds almost all federal law enforcement, such as the Drug Enforcement Agency (DEA), the Bureau of Alcohol, Tobacco, Firearms, and Explosives (ATF), the Federal Bureau of Investigations (FBI), the Federal Bureau of Prisons, and dozens of other agencies that deal with law enforcement and training. At the federal level, our country spends many times more money on health, welfare, and education than it does on military and police.

The same priorities are also reflected in state budgets. Every state in the union spends about eight times (800 percent) as much on welfare and education as they do on law enforcement and prisons. During the mid-2020s, the fifty states combined spent a total of $1,800 billion on welfare and education and only $84 billion on police and corrections (about 1/20th of the budgets). States also spent a combined $223 billion on hospitals and healthcare, which is nearly three times (265 percent) as much as they spent on police and corrections. Part of the reason for their imbalance is that most of the state money used to pay for healthcare comes from the federal social security budget in the form of Medicare and Medicaid. This is especially important for drug policies because almost all drug treatment centers use Medicaid or Medicare for payment.

There are approximately 12,000 drug treatment centers around the country. If the user is sixty-five years or older, or is disabled, they may be eligible for Medicare-funded treatment programs. If the user is low-income, or disabled, they are eligible for Medicaid funding. In addition, since the Affordable Care Act was passed in 2013, all insurance companies are required to pay some portion of drug treatment for people of any income level. Some treatment facilities cater to wealthy clients, and they rely only on private insurance plans or out-of-pocket costs. However, the majority of treatment centers deal with ordinary users from middle to lower income brackets and almost all of these accept Medicare or Medicaid funding. In the extreme high-intensity drug-use districts, many charitable organizations also provide completely free treatment services and will use Medicaid funding as it is available and private donations when it is not. Each state manages its own share of the Medicaid and Medicare funds, including those that go to drug treatment clinics and other programs.

In terms of budgeting for drug-treatment facilities, there is no measurable competition between law enforcement, corrections (jails and prisons), and healthcare priorities. Oregon, Colorado, and Washington were some of the earliest states to legalize recreational marijuana. They were followed by California, New York, Alaska, and others. New York spends about 2.1 percent of its state budget on police and corrections, while Washington spends 2.7 percent, both of which are lower than average (3 percent). However, Oregon spends 3.4 percent and Colorado spends 3.6 percent which are both slightly higher than average, while Alaska spends 5.7 percent. The money spent on police and corrections is not really affected by drug legalization because there are many other crimes that are not based on possession or trafficking. Typically, crimes of violence and against property increase after legalization, so the demand for police and corrections remains just as high after decriminalization as before.

On the opposite side, the money spent on hospitals and healthcare is higher than average (8 percent) in New York (at 9 percent) and Washington (at 15 percent). It is slightly lower than average in California and Colorado (around 7.5 percent). Neither decriminalization nor legalization necessarily saves money in terms of state expenses. Much of the state money used for drug-treatment facilities comes originally from either local city or federal sources. Very little of the state money that would usually go to police and jails is ever spent exclusively on drug-treatment programs.

Decriminalization and Legalization as Budget Issues

Decriminalization and legalization do not substantially change the costs of healthcare, police, or corrections. Nevertheless, public debates over drug policies often play large roles in state budgeting decisions. Most harm reduction programs involve some form of relationship between public agencies and 501.c nonprofit organizations. If drug use and addiction are treated mostly as a health issue, any organization that treats physical, mental, or emotional health will be more likely to receive government funding. If more nonprofit organizations are funded, there is more public pressure on lawmakers to continue supporting these programs.

Traditional law-enforcement-based programs generally do not involve nonprofit organizations, so their only lobbying efforts come directly from the police agencies or related police associations. Legalization of marijuana does not take money away from police and corrections to give to healthcare. However, from a perspective of practical politics, the social-welfare policies that emphasize harm reduction generally encourage more funding to a broader base of nonprofit organizations, which guarantees more public funding overall.

Rather than taking money away from one priority and giving it to another, the result is simply more government money being spent.

States with large urban centers, who have the most 501.c nonprofit organizations, tend to more fully embrace decriminalization and other legalization policies. States that legalize or decriminalize certain drugs tend to also have higher ratios of budgeting dedicated to public welfare than to other priorities. Most states with drug decriminalization and legalization tend to also have higher tax rates.

New Funding Options: Perhaps the most obvious way in which the decriminalization of medical marijuana and the legalization of recreational marijuana impact state budgets is in the promise of added revenue streams from taxation. This opportunity is not new. During the economic depression of the 1930s, the Roosevelt administration joined most state governments in justifying the repeal of alcohol prohibition by claiming that new tax revenues would help state budgets. There was some hesitation to repeal the Eighteenth Amendment during the late 1920s on moral grounds, but that opposition was largely swept away when the national economy experienced sharp decline and recession. In a similar way, many states that had previously opposed decriminalization and legalization proposals became more receptive to these ideas after they reconsidered marijuana taxation as a potential revenue stream.

Legalization of Gambling: Alcohol was not the only product that had once been outlawed for moral reasons and later legalized for economic reasons. Gambling was also criminalized periodically during the nineteenth century and was prohibited in almost every state and local city around the same time that alcohol was outlawed. The one exception was Nevada, which allowed gambling in private houses in 1913. As the nation repealed Prohibition, Nevada officially passed a "wide open gambling bill" in 1931, which legalized gambling in commercial operations like casinos. For every other state, though, gambling was illegal and was strongly associated with organized crime for most of the twentieth century. Congress passed the Johnson Act of 1951 prohibiting the possession, operation, transport, and repair of any gambling devices. (Nevada was given an exception.)

Horse-race betting was legal at the race track, but off-site betting and all sports betting was illegal because lawmakers feared gambling would harm the integrity of sports. This fear was confirmed by the scandal of the 1919 World Series when members of the Chicago White Sox agreed to lose games in exchange for large bribes given to them by a famous gambler. Similarly, the reputation of boxing was tarnished by the involvement of gamblers who bribed managers and fighters. In 1959, the Department of Justice sued the International Boxing Club (IBC) for antitrust violations, but one of the real motivations behind the suit was to break the criminal involvement of gamblers fixing fights. During the 1940s and 1950s, gambling (far more than drugs) was viewed as the primary source of crime and moral decay in our nation.

Public tolerance for gambling changed in the 1970s when New York, Montana, and New Jersey legalized gambling in designated districts. New Hampshire introduced a legal state lottery in 1964, which replaced the "numbers" racket that frequently dominated organized crime operations in large cities. New York followed suit in 1975, and by 1983, seventeen states introduced legal lotteries. During the late 1980s and 1990s, states began legalizing gambling casinos—first on riverboats only (as a nostalgia practice), then in Indian tribal lands, and finally anywhere. By 1993, thirty-five states held legal lotteries and thirty-eight allowed legal gambling of one form or another. US Congress responded to this trend in 1992 with the Professional and Amateur Sports Protection Act (PASPA) that criminalized sports betting at the national level.

During the early 2000s, both legal and illegal gambling increased, becoming multibillion-dollar industries. Before social media was invented, Congress passed the Unlawful Internet Gambling Enforcement Act (UIGEA) which prohibited internet gambling. However, web servers were hosted offshore and still available to online US players, so most online gambling was mostly unaffected by the law. Rising smartphone use and wireless connectivity took gambling out of the casinos and placed opportunities in the hands of any Wi-Fi user. After the invention of cryptocurrency, players gamble anonymously whether it was legal or illegal. In 2018, the federal law prohibiting sports betting (PASPA) was ruled an unconstitutional violation of the Tenth Amendment in *Murphy v. NCAA*. Almost immediately New Jersey and West Virginia passed laws legalizing sports betting, followed by Delaware, Rhode Island, Mississippi, New Mexico, Arkansas, and Pennsylvania. By 2022, thirty states legalized sports betting, and all but five states operated lotteries. Gambling is the single largest source of tax revenue for almost every state.

Taxes Reflect State Priorities

Federal income taxes are established by the US Congress. However, in addition to federal tax streams, each state also establishes its own tax rates. These include sales taxes, income taxes, and property taxes. The amount and types of taxes reflect the priorities of each state.

Sales Tax: All but five states (Alaska, Delaware, Montana, New Hampshire, and Oregon) have statewide sales taxes. In addition, local counties or cities may also impose taxes. For example, Alaska has no state sales tax, but the cities of Palmer and Soldotna both impose local sales taxes. Sales taxes are usually paid by everyone because everyone purchases products. Some states provide exceptions for food and groceries so that the taxes are not necessarily paid by all buyers for all items. States that encourage tourism often have low or no sales taxes.

Income Taxes: All but seven states require state income taxes in addition to the federal income taxes. Alaska, Florida, Nevada, South Dakota, Tennessee, Texas, and Wyoming do not require state income taxes. Everyone who is employed must pay income taxes. If you have no job, you do not pay these taxes. If you are a low-income earner, you may belong to a tax bracket that also does not pay taxes. States that want to place the greatest tax burden on those with the most wealth generally have higher income tax rates at the top levels.

Property Taxes: Every state requires homeowners and other businesses to pay taxes on their properties. In addition, some states tax large moveable property items, like cars, boats, and recreational vehicles. If you do not own your home or have no other large pieces of property, you do not pay these taxes. States that do not want to place greater tax burdens on the poor will usually require higher property taxes.

The overall tax burden that any state resident must pay will be a combination of sales taxes, income taxes, and property taxes. According to the Tax Foundation, states with the highest per capita tax burden are New York (12.02 percent), Hawaii (11.8 percent), Vermont (11.12 percent), Maine (10.74 percent), and California (10.4 percent). Washington, Oregon, and Colorado are all around 8 percent, which is about the national average. The states with the lowest per capita tax burden are Alaska (4.93 percent), New Hampshire (5.63 percent), Wyoming (5.7 percent), Florida (6.05 percent), and Tennessee (6.07 percent).

Taxes reflect state priorities. Homeless people and lower-income earners often do not pay any taxes. High-income earners usually pay the greatest percentage of taxes. Social services that cater to homeless or lower-income people (like drug-outreach programs) are usually paid for by higher-income earners.

Dilemma of Taxing Vice

State legislatures spend a long time debating various tax policies because good intentions often lead to unintended results. For example, placing very high taxes on soft drinks will discourage people from buying sugary drinks. However, if the goal of the tax was to generate more revenue, discouraging people from buying soft drinks will result in less money. The goals of influencing behavior and generating revenue are mutually exclusive.

During the early 2000s, many states imposed very high "sin taxes" on cigarettes—increasing rates anywhere from 100 percent (twice as much) to 1,000 percent (ten times as much). Pennsylvania and New York were the first to impose these taxes, and their tax revenues increased by 50 percent and were nearly doubled (100 percent) by 2002. Pennsylvania grew its tax revenue from tobacco by three times (300 percent) between 2002 and 2004. Illinois, Florida, and California experienced similar outcomes. These states profited from taxing behaviors they were hoping to discourage and that represents a conflict of interest.

Tobacco use is no longer socially popular, but gambling has lost much of its social stigma. State tax revenues from gambling are about 500 percent higher than they are from tobacco and nearly 1,200 percent higher than from alcohol sales. Increasing sin taxes on certain items may discourage some use but they will still increase revenue. Conversely, decreasing tax rates may encourage use. In some situations, lowering taxes actually increases revenue (called the "Laffer curve"). Gambling enjoys widespread public favor, so states suffer little political costs from advertising and promoting state lotteries and gambling casinos as income generators. However, tobacco use is out of public favor, so states do not like to publicly encourage more tobacco use. Yet, they still rely on cigarette tax revenue to support state budgets.

Taxes on other products, like medical and recreational marijuana, are even more controversial. If the state earns tax revenues from the sources of addiction, they are in a position where they might want to discourage use, but they still benefit financially from increasing use. Unlike gambling, most residents would find state ads promoting marijuana use to be unsettling. If most marijuana users were from middle-income families who used the drug occasionally only for recreational use, the public would have fewer issues with charging such users higher taxes. However, if most marijuana users are from lower-income families, or if they turn to the drug because of their unfortunate socioeconomic conditions, asking them to pay more for the drugs that hold them in addiction may spark greater public reactions.

These reactions largely reflect different perspectives on recreational drug use. Libertarians would argue that all recreational drug use is a choice, so they would have few issues with raising taxes on the products to increase revenue options. However, libertarians also generally oppose all taxes on principle. By contrast, social-welfare advocates argue that recreational drug use is usually a by-product of poor living conditions and insufficient economic opportunities. Raising taxes on marijuana to generate more revenue that could be used to assist low-income neighborhoods is more problematic. From the traditional conservative viewpoint, no revenue should be generated from activities that cause harm to society.

Potential Tax-Revenue from Marijuana

When recreational marijuana was first legalized in many western states (Washington, Oregon, California, and Colorado), there were great expectations for large tax revenue streams. Each state experimented with various tax options—charging by weight, sales, or potency. By the mid-2020s, more than half of US states generated some tax money from either medical or recreational marijuana, and taxing plans have become more routine. In 2022, sales of marijuana generated $3.1 billion in new tax revenue.

The problem with marijuana taxation is that every state market must compete with a well-established illegal market. This means that if states increase tax rates on marijuana too high, people will avoid legal dispensaries and instead purchase their drugs from illegal dealers. This means that there is usually an upper limit to how much tax revenue can be generated from marijuana sales.

This phenomenon was most noticeable in the top marijuana sales states between 2022 and 2023. According to the Bureau of Fiscal Service's report on state revenues, California generated nearly a billion dollars ($920.6 million) in 2022, Washington generated $484 million, and Colorado generated $313.2 million, with Illinois coming in fourth at $284.7 million. These numbers seemed to promise continued growth. However, in 2023, each of these states earned less tax revenue: California fell to $567.3 million; Washington fell to $460.2 million; Colorado fell to $262.9 million; and Illinois fell to $278.1 million. The total tax revenue generated across all states from marijuana sales in 2023 fell to $2.9 billion, even though four new states were added to the total (Minnesota, Mississippi, Rhode Island, and Vermont).

There are two main reasons for the decline in tax revenue. The first is because marijuana has been outlawed for so long (more than 100 years) that there is already a very large, well-established illegal market system in place. When a state decriminalizes medical marijuana or legalizes recreational marijuana, illegal sources of the drug do not decline but usually increase. The number of illegal marijuana growers, sellers, and distributors increased by a factor of 300 percent to 400 percent. The cost of doing business without paying state licensing fees or taxes is much lower for illegal farmers and dealers, and therefore the end price for buyers is always less. When taxes or licensing fees appear to be too high, buyers (and some sellers) will move into the illegal market sector and the state loses out on all those taxes.

The other reason for the decline has to do with the nature of drug addiction itself. Marijuana is a gateway drug with (mostly) moderate effects. As users become accustomed to the drug experience, tolerance levels increase, and experienced users tend to seek out other types of more potent drugs. When a state legalizes recreational marijuana, users who had never tried recreational drugs (or did so only rarely) become more accustomed to purchasing and consuming drugs more frequently. Higher drug use leads to higher tolerance levels and addiction rates. Addicted users seeking more potent drugs must find their drug source through illegal vendors (who pay no taxes).

Polydrug use (taking more than one drug at a time) increased during the late 2010s and 2020s. Users frequently combined marijuana with fentanyl, alcohol, and xylazine. Unfortunately, polydrug use is also the leading cause of drug overdose mortalities. Heavily addicted users generally limit their marijuana use to moments of opportunity and rely instead on more potent drug options. In high-intensity drug use districts, marijuana sales at legal dispensaries do not increase with rising addiction rates. Instead, most drug sales occur illegally through dealers found in the open-air drug markets. In the four states mentioned earlier (California, Colorado, New York, and Washington), recreational drug use of all types increased between 2022 and 2023. People who used to buy their drugs from state-licensed dealers shifted to buying marijuana and all other drugs from illegal dealers. As an unintended consequence, tax revenues dropped substantially in all these states.

Marijuana generated its highest tax revenues in 2022 at just over $3 billion. That is a lot of money, but it is a fraction of the tax revenue generated by alcohol ($8.2 billion) and tobacco products ($19.1 billion.) Annual reports by the American Gaming Association indicate that gambling generates a little more than $13 billion in tax revenue, and lottery revenues are more than $90 billion (with 30 percent to 40 percent going into state budget streams). Revenue generated from gambling is extremely high, but like marijuana, it also faces natural limitations because illegal gambling also has a very well-developed infrastructure. Business research specialists estimate that the illegal gambling trade is about 500 percent more than the legal trade, and none of that can generate legal tax revenues.

The Story of Oregon's Decriminalization Experiment

Oregon was the only American state to decriminalize all drugs and to legalize both marijuana and psilocybin. These actions follow a long history of experimental drug policies. Oregon was the first state to decriminalize marijuana in 1973 and the second state to legalize medical marijuana in 1998. It was the third state to legalize recreational marijuana in 2014 (though it did originally include the measure on the 2012 election ballot, in the same year that Colorado and Washington passed similar laws).

Ballot Measure 110: In Portland, Oregon, the summer of violent protests and riots during 2020 began the day after they erupted in Minneapolis, on May 27, and continued for 173 days. Voters went to the polls on November 3 amidst protests but no violence. However, there was violence on the day before (Monday) and enough violence on the day after (Wednesday) that Portland police declared a riot emergency, and the National Guard was called in to restore order. A few final acts of violence (smashing windows, destroying ATMs, and burning cars) continued for about ten days following the election. Portland residents experienced their first full day without BLM protests on November 14, 2020. The continual presence of hundreds of protestors living in permanent encampments around Portland certainly played a role in influencing the results of the 2020 election.

Beginning in September, sympathizers of the protests began organizing new public initiatives to be included on the 2020 election ballot. Supporters of Ballot Measure 110 (BM110) the "Drug Addiction Treatment and Decriminalization" initiative collected $6 million in an effort to decriminalize drugs in Oregon. Most of the money ($5 million) came from the Drug Policy Alliance, which is a New York-based 501.c lobbying group that specializes in drug decriminalization and legalization. They were responsible for the 2012 and 2014 ballot measures that eventually legalized recreational marijuana in Oregon. Other donors for BM110 came from Facebook founder Mark Zuckerberg, who contributed $500,000, and George Soros's Sixteen Thirty Fund, which contributed $250,000 along with another $250,000 from the American Civil Liberties Union. The measure passed on November 3 with more than 58 percent of the vote.

BM110 decriminalized small amounts of any drug by removing all criminal penalties, and by shifting the enforcement of drug laws from the police over to the Oregon Health Authority. With the exception of marijuana, drugs were not legalized under the new law, and it was still illegal to buy and sell more potent drugs like amphetamines, cocaine, heroin, fentanyl, ecstasy, and others. However, possession and public use no longer resulted in criminal prosecution. Instead, police were authorized to give violators tickets of no more than $100, which included a hotline number that drug users could call if they wanted treatment options. There were no mechanisms to force users to seek treatment, and there were no punishments for failure to pay the fine.

In addition to the drug decriminalization measure, Oregon residents also passed Ballot Measure 109 ("Oregon Psilocybin Services Act"), which decriminalized psilocybin (magic mushrooms) and legalized its use for medical therapies. Another bill created a new civilian oversight body with the authority to fire Portland police officers independent of the Portland police commissioner. Afterward, Kayse Jama (director of Unite Oregon that supported decriminalization) said, "The reality is that systems of oppression always find different ways of incarcerating Black and Brown folks. I think [BM110] is a good step forward; it's one tool we want to remove from their toolbox. But we also understand that [law enforcement] will continue to target our community" (Cooper, 2020). For most Oregon residents, decriminalization was seen as a natural conclusion to the previous six months of BLM protests and rioting that preceded the vote.

There was a small group in opposition to BM110, led by Dr. Paul Coelho of Salem Health Hospital, who collected only $167,000 in contributions. On his "No on 110" website, Coelho warned that decriminalization removed "the threat of incarceration and abandon[ed] the collaboration between law enforcement, the judiciary, probation, and the drug court system [and would] result in a revolving door of drug abuse, treatment refusal, crime, homelessness, and ongoing costly health related expenditures for hospitalizations due to overdose, infections, and drug-induced psychosis." He said the primary problem with BM110 was that it assumed that people suffering from addiction "will naturally seek out and accept treatment for their condition. But I can assure you as a front-line provider this is simply not true" (Ballotpedia, 2020).

Changing Drug Conditions between 2020 and 2023: Supporters of BM110 argued that the drug war failed, and drug overdose deaths and addiction rates in Oregon were higher than national average. The theory was that if drugs were decriminalized, the stigma of drug-use would be removed, and therefore drug-users would be more willing to seek out treatment if their drug-use grew out of control. This theory did not prove to be true.

After Oregon passed the decriminalization law, drug overdose rates increased 75 percent, which was 57 percent higher than the overdose rate increase nationwide (18 percent). Unfortunately, nearly 90 percent of the people who died from overdoses were already dead before emergency responders arrived on the scene. Also, the number of out-of-state visitors dying from drug overdoses doubled, which indicates a higher rate of "drug tourism" coming into Oregon from other states. Though drug decriminalization was originally intended to better protect people of color, by 2022 the rate of overdose deaths among Black drug users increased 136 percent, which was nearly twice as high of the increased death rates among white users (69.9 percent, see Kubeisy, 2024).

The number of nonfatal emergency room visits due to drug overdose increased 200 percent over national average, and Portland had the highest nonfatal overdose rates among cities of similar size in the nation. All the western states (Washington, Oregon, and California) saw higher than national average increases in use of any recreational drugs, addiction rates, and overdose fatalities. However, Oregon's rates were significantly higher than both Washington and California. Oregon's rates of monthly illicit drug use increased 6.9 times higher than national average. More than one in five people in Oregon used recreational drugs, including marijuana in the past month—which is higher than Washington's rate of one in six and California's rate of one in ten.

Perhaps most notable was the success of BM110 to change public attitudes toward illicit drug use. Prior to 2020, Oregon had the eighth lowest number of people who thought trying heroin once or twice was harmful and the third lowest number of people who thought experimenting with cocaine was harmful. These rankings indicate that the stigma of drug use had already begun to change in Oregon following their earlier legalization of marijuana in 2014. After two years of decriminalization, though, the public perception of recreational drug use of all kinds had become more normalized. In 2022, Oregon had the lowest number of people in the nation who believed heroin or cocaine was harmful. Police gave out nearly 6,200 tickets for drug violations, but only fifty people took advantage of the drug treatment hotline. A later NSDUH survey of drug use indicated that the number one reason why people in Oregon did not use drug-treatment services was that they were "not ready to stop using" the drugs.

During the period from 2020 to 2023, homelessness in Oregon increased by 10.8 percent, which was higher than similar increases in Washington (at 4.8 percent) and California (at 3.5 percent). Drug trafficking continued to be illegal in Oregon, but law enforcement officers were reluctant to make arrests. Seizures of illegal drugs increased substantially (by 4,352 percent of fentanyl), but the number of arrests fell from 698 in 2020 to 585 in 2021 and 404 in 2022. On the federal side, the number of interstate drug-trafficking cases increased substantially. In addition, violent crimes increased more than 17 percent (which was three times higher than the 4.5 percent national average). Oregon Department of Transportation also noted substantial increases in the rates of impaired driving accidents, especially from polydrug combinations (Kubeisy, 2024).

HB4002: By the end of 2023, the public opinions on drug decriminalization in Oregon changed dramatically. A poll from August 2023 indicated that 61 percent of the state thought BM110 was a failure. (This is compared to the 58 percent of voters who agreed to pass the law less than two years earlier.) The opposition was highest among people who had prior experience using drugs, and 76 percent of this group believed drug possession should be recriminalized and 78 percent believed drug treatment should be mandatory (and not voluntary). The former Democrat Governor, Kate Brown, who signed BM110 into law commented that the decriminalization bill "was a theory that was put into practice in a state that was probably one of the least prepared to be successful" (Schick and Wilson, 2024).

A new 501.c group was formed to prepare a new ballot initiative for 2024. The "Coalition to Fix and Improve Ballot Measure 110" collected $700,000 to solicit the signatures necessary to put a new measure on the ballot for the next statewide election. Though far less than the $6 million that was spent to pass BM110, the movement to revise the bill still had a lot of public support. Max Williams, who led the coalition, explained, "We strongly support the parts of Measure 110 that are putting resources into moving people into treatment and recovery … That's why this isn't a repeal. But what we're trying to do is actually make 110 better and really fulfill its promise, which is more people into more treatment quickly" (Parfitt and Dooris, 2024).

Oregon state lawmakers responded to the strong public pressure to revise the existing laws with House Bill 4002 (HB4002). By February 2024, the bill was passed by large margins in both houses (51–7 in House and 21–8 in the Senate) and signed by Governor Tina Kotek on April 1. The new law recriminalized drug possession of all Schedule I through IV drugs as a Class A misdemeanor. Drug manufacturers and traffickers would face Class C felony charges with penalties ranging from three years to eleven years (if the trafficking resulted in someone's death).

The law also encouraged police to offer violators "diversions" to incarceration—which means mandatory treatment rather than going to jail. The state spent $211 million to create new drug courts to deal with the influx of offenders and also added $30 million to help cities and counties develop new diversion programs. These diversion options were intended mostly for first-time offenders or for those who had never participated in a treatment program before. The new law also explicitly outlawed public use of any illegal drug. The most significant change was that Oregon's experiment with drug decriminalization was officially ended.

During the 2024 presidential election cycle, California also chose to reverse many of its decriminalization policies by passing Proposition 36, increasing sentencing for certain drug and theft crimes by reclassifying many misdemeanors as felonies. The new law overturned previous decriminalization measures passed in 2014 (Proposition 47) and upgraded criminal penalties for thefts of $950 or more in property loss, which meant violators would face a year or more in prison upon conviction for many crimes that are most associated with drug addiction. The law passed with more than 68 percent of the vote on November 5, 2024.

Ideological Postmortem: Oregon ended its decriminalization experiment in 2024, but that does not mean that the state gave up its predominant libertarian and social-welfare ideological perspectives. The greatest source of debate over the failure of BM110 was over implementation and not necessarily over the intended goals of harm reduction. Very striking differences exist when reflecting on the lessons learned from Oregon's decriminalization experiment.

Libertarian View: From a libertarian perspective, the Oregon decriminalization law failed because it only decriminalized drugs. Libertarians do not believe that any substance is biologically addictive and that the decision to use or not to use recreational drugs is a matter of personal free will and is, therefore, a human right of preference. *Reason* magazine, which is a main resource for libertarian ideas, argued that Oregon would have had better success if they legalized all drugs and removed all government regulations. That would have undercut the illegal drug markets and given citizens the freedom to choose their options without inflated prices of government-regulated drug dispensers or the other inflated prices of international drug cartels. The libertarians are consistent in these positions that they have held since the early 1970s. However, their views were not supported by most Oregon voters or most Americans.

Social-Welfare View: The most dominant perspective in Oregon remains the social-welfare harms-reduction approach to drug policy. As in 2014 and 2020, the advocates for HB4002 cited Portugal, Amsterdam, and Spain as effective examples of drug-control policies. The revision of BM110 did not shift drug enforcement authority back to law enforcement, but instead created a new agency called the Alcohol and Drug Policy Commission, which was responsible for budgeting the diversions programs and facilitating cooperation between social services and law enforcement. This is similar to the bureaucratic model used by Portugal. The new law does not apply traditional law enforcement strategies to drug control but mostly changes tactics to better accommodate compulsory treatment. The law explicitly declared that the first priority should be moving drug users into treatment options (diversions) that do not include incarceration. However, incarceration was included as a last-recourse option. Advocates for this position believed that adding more money to facilitate social-welfare alternatives would fix the earlier experimental approach.

An online article written by "Sisters of the Road," which had been a major supporter of the BLM riots during the summer of 2020, listed three reasons why BM110 failed (and which reflected many similar views of those who did not want recriminalization). First, they argued the public was not accurately informed about the causes and extent of drug use under BM110. The article claimed that Oregon's increasing drug rates were part of a national problem and that BM110 helped prevent the problem from becoming worse. Second, they argued that there was not enough government funding given to fix the homelessness problem (through free or reduced housing) or to develop more detox and other treatment options. Third, they argued that BM110 was never really implemented because of general government mismanagement, which failed to provide the facilities and necessary training options. They concluded that HB4002 may lead to a revival of the War on Drugs and predicted that recriminalization will continue to hurt people of color most. Though the more extreme rhetoric of the BLM movement no longer dominated Oregon cultural politics in 2023, some of their assertions regarding systemic racism continued to frame some public viewpoints.

Traditional Conservatives: Oregon has had a mixed tradition of traditional conservative viewpoints. Since 1988, the state has supported the Democrat president candidate in every election. However, up to 1984, Oregon voted mostly Republican. Their traditions have usually reflected either slight libertarian or social-welfare priorities since 1988. However, at the national level, other traditional conservative voices freely commented on Oregon's decriminalization experiment.

Most conservatives (such as David Horowitz and Wilfred Reilly) disagree that law enforcement is motivated by race. They admit that people of color are disproportionately arrested for certain drug crimes, but they explain that is because the majority of international drug cartels are based in Central America and Asia. In terms of actual enforcement, as a percentage of police encounters, white drug users are more likely to be arrested and incarcerated when found with drugs than Black users. The traditional conservative view rejects the assertion that the United States suffers from systemic racism. They also note that the Portugal harm reduction models exist in social environments that enjoy much stronger consensus of cultural values than in the United States. The assertion of "systemic racism" and the waves of BLM protests and riots between 2014 and 2021 prove that there is much less cultural consensus about social priorities. Therefore, traditional conservatives do not believe drug decriminalization will ever work in the United States.

In terms of Oregon's experiment, traditional conservatives argued that it removed penalties for illegal drug use and removed all incentives for encouraging drug treatment when it deliberately removed the stigma associated with recreational drug use. Also, when drug crimes were redefined in terms of racial inequality, the new cultural environment failed to account for medical and biological pressures of addiction. Conservatives argue that Oregon's decriminalization encouraged more drug use, which led to more addiction, which led to higher unemployment and homelessness, which led to higher crime rates involving property, violence, and drug fatalities. They claim that the most compassionate policy for addicted users is to use police officers to investigate, apprehend, and arrest drug offenders. Users should be sent into compulsory treatment, while the dealers and traffickers should be removed from society through extended periods of incarceration (the law enforcement model).

Drug abuse and addiction are complicated by the fact that humans act from a complex web of interrelated motivations. Libertarians do not believe that addiction plays a relevant role in individual motivation. Social-welfare advocates recognize addiction but believe it should be treated using health care alone. Traditional conservatives also believe in the power of addiction but argue that incentives for positive treatments must be balanced with disincentives for egregious drug violations (especially illegal dealers).

One of the lesser-considered implications of Oregon's decriminalization experiment is what it may suggest about other recently decriminalized activities, particularly gambling, pornography, and prostitution. Unlike drug addiction, users do not suffer fatal overdoses from these behaviors. However, some observers might argue that suicide rates are at their highest levels in American history, partly due to increased habits of vice. Again, human motivations are complex, and it is impossible to establish any causal connection between the despair linked to potentially self-destructive habits from gambling, pornography, or prostitution. However, if one of the lessons from Oregon is that decriminalization may unintentionally encourage more drug use, it is not unreasonable to assume the same upward trends would occur with other behavioral vices. Another potential lesson from Oregon could be to recognize that neither legalization nor criminalization is sufficient to curb behaviors. Laws must be accompanied by cultural pressures that also emphasize the dangers of such actions. If vice is normalized, and the public shame (stigma) for self-destructive actions are removed, there is very little chance that the vices will reduce on their own. Recriminalizing gambling, pornography, and prostitution would require more consistent cultural messages about the self-destructive nature of vice.

Conclusion: State Priorities and Decriminalization and Legalization

Decriminalizing medical marijuana or legalizing recreational marijuana does not generate more money for states. Increases in tax revenue are relatively small compared to other state expenses. For comparison's sake, we can see $3.1 billion from marijuana taxes, but we should also see that states and private companies spend about $2.6 billion on drug screening, and the national expenditure on substance-abuse treatment programs is about $11.8 billion. The state is not required to pay the entirety of these two types of expenses, but it is easy to see that income generated from one source does not always match new expenses that may follow legalization. Overall, the Centers for Medicare and Medicaid Services report that the national health care expenditures generally increase by 4 percent or 5 percent each year. As recreational drug use increases, these health expenses will generally also increase at higher rates.

The decision to decriminalize or legalize certain drugs reflects priorities of each state that extend beyond issues of tax revenue and finances. California, New York, and Illinois have very high overall tax rates that are near or above 10 percent. Likewise in Europe, Portugal has an average effective tax rate more than 14 percent, and the Netherlands' effective tax rate is nearly 18 percent. By contrast, Texas and Florida have not implemented any harm-reduction policies at the state level and have not legalized recreational marijuana. Their effective tax rates are 7.5 percent and 6 percent, respectively. In those states, social-welfare objectives are at a lower priority than in California or New York. People who disagree with state priorities generally leave, and Florida and Texas are the two states where most people who move out of California and New York end up residing. People who remain living in California and New York generally support their state's social-welfare priorities and continue to vote for harm-reduction policies.

State residents consider some of the following questions when evaluating their drug-policy priorities:

1) How important is the freedom for individuals to use recreational drugs?
2) Should state and local governments plan to provide most social-welfare obligations for their residents (healthcare, education, job services), or should individuals plan to take care of these issues for themselves?
3) How important is the protection of private property and public safety?
4) Should state and local governments promote common standards of moral conduct or faith-based expectations of individual character?
5) Should we invest in state-based programs, or should we rely on private enterprises to facilitate social change?

Honest and intelligent people often find themselves on opposing sides, when answering these questions.

Libertarians generally argue in favor of the decriminalization and legalization of all drugs because they do not want the government overseeing any individual choices. For these reasons, they oppose using police to monitor drug use. They do not, however, support higher taxes or larger percentages of state budgets going to welfare programs to care for addiction treatment because they argue that if you choose to take drugs, you also choose to pay the consequences. Libertarians would argue for privately funded treatment facilities and privately funded services that care for the poor.

In many ways, people who adopt social-welfare viewpoints agree with libertarian views in so far as they support the decriminalization and legalization of certain drugs. Both libertarians and social-welfare advocates believe that personal morality and individual lifestyle choices should be outside the domain of government policy. However, in stark contrast to the libertarians, the social-welfare supporters believe that most of the state budgets should be spent on providing basic needs of healthcare, housing, food, and income assistance. Decriminalization policies shift most burdens of drug policies from the police to healthcare and government-funded social services and generally result in larger governments and higher taxes. Social-welfare advocates believe those are important priorities.

Traditional conservatives also believe that governments should provide necessary protections for individual choices and private property. They disagree with libertarians who believe the government should play little or no role in the economy or basic social services. However, they also disagree with social-welfare advocates about the kind of role that governments play. Laws should provide clear standards for moral conduct and ensure individual accountability by encouraging self-restraint. They oppose the decriminalization and legalization of recreational drugs because that sends the wrong message about the importance of sober living and because it forces the government to assume a larger role in managing the welfare of its citizens. For these reasons, they believe it is an inappropriate priority to permit higher taxes to support and possibly encourage personal recreational choices that are often self-destructive.

The general consensus of the majority of residents in each state usually promotes a common cultural preference on one side or the other. It is very difficult to find policy options that attempt to cater to all sides. When state legislatures debate drug policies, they usually argue from larger moral presumptions that are not always transparent. In part, this is because the state budget process involves complex combinations of pressures from bureaucratic and special interest groups. Nevertheless, the people who decide these policies are usually quite aware of the social priorities that they rely on—that is why we have political parties and other special interest coalitions who self-identify as "libertarian," "liberal," or "conservative."

Drug policies often shift as these ideological preferences change over time. Policies of the 1960s and 1970s were changed slightly in the 1980s and 1990s to reinforce traditional enforcement-based methods. By the 2000s, these policies shifted again, and the 2010s were almost completely different with more drug decriminalization and legalization at the state level. By the 2020s, cultural reactions shifted once more, and decriminalization and legalization were reconsidered. At no point during these decades was every state completely in agreement with one another on drug-policy priorities. The nation had a consistent policy, but states often adjusted the precise details to fit their regional cultures. The main change that occurred in the 2010s was that the federal government no longer promoted consistent policies for all states to follow. That left each state to begin to develop their own unique policy preferences.

One of the advantages of the American federal system is that people are free to move from one state to another. States generally pass laws and craft budget priorities that reflect the priorities of their residents. If policies begin to turn in ways that certain segments of the public oppose, and if there are not enough votes from that segment to change policy (or influence the budget decisions), residents simply move. This means that each state gradually develops stronger bases of consensus within its own region. In this way, decriminalization and legalization policies are most successful at the state and local levels, even if they continue to face greater difficulties at the national level.

Part III

Scenarios

Case 1

Becky and Linda in Medford, Oregon

Becky is forty-three years old and operates a 501.c nonprofit organization called the "Clean Junk-Wagon." She and her assistants drive around in a white van as outreach workers for people living in Medford, Oregon, who may not have a permanent house and who suffer from addiction.

Medford is a small college town in Oregon near the southern border. It is located just south of the mountain passes and opens into a wide agricultural plain. The town has about 80,000 people, but it is situated along Interstate Highway 5 that runs from Canada through Bellingham, Washington, Seattle, Portland, Oregon, and Medford and then continues south into Sacramento, California, and on to Los Angeles, San Diego, and into Mexico. It is a long highway known for drug trafficking since the 1960s. Medford also has a smaller interstate highway that runs eastward toward Idaho and Utah. Highways connect Medford with Ashland about ten miles away, creating a larger metropolitan area of about a quarter of a million people. Ashland is dominated by the local Southern Oregon University, and in Medford, healthcare is the largest legal economic industry, followed by agriculture. The soil is good for many kinds of crops, including marijuana.

Marijuana has only been a legal crop for about twenty-five years. Marijuana possession was decriminalized in 1973, but it was not approved for medical use until 1998. Nevertheless, marijuana has always been Medford's leading illegal industry since the 1970s. After decriminalization, Oregon Health Authority authorized legal cannabis farming according to particular guidelines. Many new farms grew marijuana openly for medical use. Many of these farms also sold the drug illegally for recreational use. The state did not approve legal dispensaries until recreational use was legalized in 2014. Since then, there have been more marijuana dispensaries than there are fast-food restaurants in Oregon.

The number of marijuana farms grew substantially after 2012—some legal and some illegal (unlicensed). Most of the marijuana is cultivated for out-of-state export, even though interstate trafficking remains illegal. It is difficult for inspectors to track whether the harvests end up going to legal dispensaries or whether they end up going to illegal vendors or out-of-state.

Most of Becky's job involves intervention for other forms of drugs. She drives to key neighborhoods where illegal drug use is most common, and then stops to talk with potential clients who may need her help—most of these do not live in permanent housing, so she first hands out hygiene kits that includes toilet paper, tissue paper and hand wipes, toothbrush–toothpaste sets, bandages, sunscreen, and lip balm. In addition, she hands out overdose prevention kits that include free sterilized needles, fentanyl testing strips, clean pipes and metal containers for mixing heroin, Narcan nasal sprays, and a card that includes telephone numbers to free health clinics, some of which provide drug-counseling services. For those who have not eaten recently, she also provides free meal kits with granola bars, gum and candy, peanut-butter crackers, and a water bottle.

Most of her time is spent organizing supplies in the morning and then packing the vehicle to drive along specific routes in town around noontime. She knows most of the people but always encounters new faces. Her primary goal is to help prevent drug overdose, so she sometimes sits with users as they prepare to take their drugs—she does not tell them what to do, but she will help with the process if they ask her. In some cases, she will be notified that there is someone on the street or in a park who appears to be experiencing a drug overdose, and she is always ready to administer Narcan. She says she has saved dozens of lives and has never lost a client due to a drug overdose while she was there beside them. However, in some cases, she arrives too late and must notify authorities that one of her clients has died and needs to be picked up.

Becky is a recovering drug user. She grew up in Medford, and when she was a young girl marijuana was the most common drug in her school. However, she got involved with black tar heroin shortly after she graduated and suffered from about five years of addiction. She was eventually arrested and sent to mandatory treatment facility that used a twelve-step program and methadone to help cure her addiction. She credits the access to methadone for saving her life, which she believes was beginning to spiral out of control. Since then, Becky has dedicated her life to trying to help others who are in situations similar to her own past. She formed her 501.c corporation just after Oregon passed Measure 110, which decriminalized all forms of drugs, and provided $300 million in grant money to help addicted users. Her organization is small, but it is almost entirely funded through state grant money, which amounts to several hundred thousand dollars per year.

One of Becky's friends is Linda—a lieutenant in the Medford Police Department. Linda was the one who arrested Becky for theft and who also found a small amount of heroin among the belongings. Because of the heroin, Becky was able to avoid jail for theft and go straight into a mandatory treatment program. Linda arrested Becky, but after finishing treatment, Becky thanked the officer and the two developed a long friendship. Becky does not reveal who she talks to or who she helps administer heroin injections because, technically, Becky's facilitation of drug use is illegal. However, both Becky and Linda are dedicated to helping solve the same problems, so they often get together outside of working hours. Neither one talks openly or specifically about their work to the other.

Linda is fifty-four years old and has served in the Medford Police Department since graduating from Southern Oregon University in Ashland thirty years ago. She has been promoted several times and now works with MADGE (Medford Area Drug and Gang Enforcement) which is an interagency task force that brings local, state, and federal investigators together to intercede and dismantle interstate drug trafficking and organized drug gangs in the area. The I-5 corridor from Portland to Medford was designated a high intensity drug-trafficking area, and her unit focuses most of their attention on growing crime rates in Medford and the surrounding areas.

Medford has one of the highest crime rates in Oregon, mostly for theft and also for gun violence in connection with drug gangs, which has become increasingly more common. The area also has a large homeless population, which has increased in size since decriminalization laws were passed. When Linda began working as an officer, the biggest source of addiction was alcohol and marijuana was second. Property crimes were higher than average, but the problem was not noticeable to the public. After marijuana was legalized, the rates of illegal drug trafficking increased substantially. Mostly, the marijuana that is grown in plain sight in Oregon is transported into states where it is still illegal. In addition, the people operating legal and illegal marijuana farms are not from the area—many are from Mexico (now about 12 percent of the population), Asia, and other states. After decriminalization from Measure 110, her contacts with members of organized crime increased noticeably. Linda has also seen a 3000 percent increase in the amount of illegal fentanyl seizures and has been particularly disturbed by the ratio of xylazine content discovered in the counterfeit pills.

Becky and Linda have different opinions about marijuana legalization and about Measure 110. Becky genuinely believes her work saves lives, and she counts her clients on the street as her friends. Yet, she also knows that her friends are frequently dying, and very few are seeking the same treatment options that helped Becky overcome her own addictions. She also feels a little uncomfortable that her job depends on high rates of drug addiction. She also sometimes feels like she is not making enough of a difference. Becky hopes that with more state funding, there could be more people like her working in outreach programs, and that may help to turn the tide of drug-overdose fatalities.

Linda does not like arresting people for drug possession, when she knows that they are suffering from harsh addictions that make it difficult to live normal lives. She deals with a lot of other crimes and knows that 60 percent to 90 percent of that crime is tied to drug addiction. Linda believes that mandatory treatment requirements are necessary to be truly helpful because users will not take the programs voluntarily. She does not know if marijuana legalization is the answer or the cause of the problem, but she feels strongly that a growing culture of recreational drug use has changed the city and is the main reason behind the crime and homelessness in her district. Linda believes that a more consistent anti-drug message would help more people.

Analysis

This story is about two friends who approach drug addiction from opposite viewpoints and who both live in a region of Oregon that spans both rural and urban cultures. Becky runs a 501.c nonprofit funded by Oregon's decriminalization Ballot Measure 110. Her mobile safe-consumption site provides homeless users with food and medical supplies, but mostly provides drug tools and access to naloxone as needed to prevent overdose fatalities. Becky's experience is based on her former drug use. She acts out of sincere compassion based on these personal experiences. Like most former drug users, Becky began her drug use with marijuana. Her facilitation of drug use is technically illegal, but she does not worry about enforcement. She cannot be explicit about her work with her friend Linda.

Officer Linda works on a federal Joint Task Force that was developed because that stretch of Oregon's interstate highway is designated as a High-Intensity Drug Trafficking District. A lot of drugs that are hidden among legal licensing fronts and are sold illegally over interstate highway system. Officers generally encountered increased homelessness, drug use, crime, and increased presence of drug cartels after both decriminalization and legalization laws were passed.

Officers believe they are necessary to bring drug users into treatment, which is how most users escape their drug addictions. Officers and outreach workers often work on opposing sides of the problem, but they also both share similar compassion for users and often develop working friendships with each other. It is rare that police or outreach workers have antagonist relationships with each other.

Case 2

Tim and Alta-Mae in Chico, California

Tim is eighty years old and lives with his seventy-seven-year-old wife, Alta-Mae, in Chico, California. He was a career army man for nearly forty years, working in mechanics and eventually specializing in computer networking systems. After retiring, Tim served as the technical director for a new Native Casino that was being built just outside of town, and he has worked there for more than twenty years.

Chico is a medium-sized college town of around 100,000 people located in northern California. Its primary economic activity has always been almonds, walnuts, and pecan orchards, alongside rice and other agricultural products. Aside from his job at the new gambling casino, Tim also owns a small farm plot on the edge of town with a few acres of olive trees, which he still cares for with a few hired hands during harvesting times.

The local university, California State University Chico, is known for education, business and computer sciences programs, and agriculture. During the late 1980s, however, the school was also recognized as the "Number One Party School in America" by *Playboy* magazine. The cable music video channel MTV hosted a special event there during the annual Pioneer Days, and the street party turned into a riot, which shut the production down and brought in many police, resulting in considerable property damage. The reputation of the school changed very quickly, and for the next twenty years, fraternities and sororities seemed to want to live up to the playboy designation by hosting increasingly more public displays of drunken festivities. During the 1990s, the Halloween week street parties drew in twice and three times the number of regularly enrolled students (up to 30,000 people). Local citizens finally reacted, and in early 2000s, the Chico police department began cracking down on these public displays of intoxication. Most street-based college drinking events ended by 2002, but the reputation as a party school continued. The actual college culture gradually settled into more sober habits by the 2020s.

Tim and his wife were living away on army bases overseas and elsewhere in the United States during these years. When they were both young, during the 1950s, Chico had only 12,000 people and most of them worked in the nut orchards. They remember their hometown as being very quiet and peaceful. Churches frequently held citywide activities for the youth, regardless of the denomination, and there were very few visitors coming into town to cause any public disruptions. Right after they left in the late 1960s, illegal marijuana farmers were beginning to emerge in the counties north and south of them, but Chico was mostly left alone until the 1980s. Tim and his wife mostly remember occasional alcohol abuse as the main cause of scandal.

When they returned to the area in 2000, Tim and Alta-Mae chose to move to the outskirts of Chico because there were fewer people living there and because they had been warned by relatives that the small-town culture had changed since they last lived there. California had recently legalized marijuana for medical use, but it was common knowledge that most of the legal marijuana was being sold for illegal recreational purposes. College students were more open about their marijuana use, but most of the changes were seen off campus in the city center and in the public parks. There were many more public displays of intoxication, and the town square drew a large homeless encampment. Bidwell Park, which had previously been known for its family-friendly swimming holes and jogging trails was now becoming known for its drug trafficking. News reports of increasingly large seizure of illegal marijuana and methamphetamines becoming more common, with Butte County police uncovering more than 100 methamphetamine labs between 2005 and 2010.

Safety became a growing concern for Tim and Alta-Mae during the 2010s, even though they lived in a farming district. In-town rates of home invasion became more common—most of these were cases of drug users robbing other users at gunpoint to steal their supplies and money. However, other property crimes such as car break-ins and auto thefts also became well-publicized in the papers. The fear of heightened crime became so strong that Alta-Mae preferred not to visit the town center without her husband. Tim eventually bought five large dogs who barked at any intruders and also installed security cameras along his driveway that were connected to his smartphone so that he could keep eyes on his property while his wife was home alone during the day. During the late 2010s, he noticed many times when people would enter the driveway part way, and then back up and leave once they saw the dogs.

At one point, a neighbor who owned twenty acres in the adjoining property put up high fences all around the perimeter, right next to where Tim and

Alta-Mae were living. Tim grew suspicious and flew his drone to video-record what was going on inside the compound and discovered the rapid construction of a large marijuana facility. Marijuana is legal to grow with special licensing in California, but it is not legal in Butte County. Tim turned his recordings over to the Butte Interagency Narcotics Task Force (BINT) unit in charge of drug interdiction in the Chico area, and they obtained a warrant and entered the compound and seized the illegal marijuana plants. The property residents fled the scene and were not apprehended.

After legalization of marijuana in 2016, the general rate of recreational drug use increased substantially in Chico. Mortality rates from fentanyl drug overdoses increased 150 percent between 2017 and 2022, and the Northern Valley Harm Reduction Coalition (a 501.c nonprofit organization) began distributing overdose prevention kits in the parks on Saturdays. They handed out free syringes, fentanyl test strips, first-aid supplies, free syringes, and other items. The Chico City Council met to discuss whether the organization should be prohibited, and several members were strongly in favor of the ban. Tim and Alta-Mae were also opposed to the establishment because they feared it would only promote more drug use rather than reduce it. However, the council took no action and state authorities continued to provide grant money to fund their operations.

Tim served in the military for nearly forty years and lived in a wide variety of communities, so he is not easily surprised by alcohol abuse or other forms of addiction. Neither he nor his wife has many moral qualms about recreational marijuana use, but they are strongly opposed to criminal activity, especially property crimes and potential gun violence. They never used drugs personally, but they have family members who suffered from addiction, and so they are highly sensitive to the struggles and the dangers of drug addiction. Drugs seemed to be transforming their hometown. Tim and Alta-Mae both vote, but they do not really believe that their voice matters as much as those special interests that come from large urban centers of the state—especially the Bay Area, Los Angeles, and San Diego. Whether or not they supported decriminalization or legalization, Tim and Alta-Mae felt like these policies were going to be determined by special interests in the big cities. Their small-town farm seems far removed from those areas.

At eighty years old, they both most notice that their small town of Chico, which they once used to run around carefree as children, was no longer what it once was. They love the town, and they do not want to move away at this time of their lives. However, they are sad to see the damage caused over the past few decades by illegal drug use. In 2023, the Federal Drug Enforcement

Agency recognized Chico and Butte County as a new district to be added into the already existing Shasta and the Sacramento Valley region that is called the Northern California High Intensity Drug-Trafficking Area.

Analysis

This story is mostly about how recreational drug use can transform the culture of smaller rural communities, which is especially noticeable for older residents who remember conditions before drugs became common. Elderly residents are often more concerned about their physical safety, and increasing recreational drug use usually increases crime and the rate of property violations. The cultural consensus of post-Second World War towns can change quickly, especially if a town's reputation for vice attracts out-of-state visitors. In Chico, the reputation of the college campus as a party school set the stage for a parallel reputation later for drug use. Though college students may experiment with drug use, most serious addiction rates occur among nonstudents.

Local governments that previously dealt mainly with alcohol addiction are often slow to refocus on drug addiction and in both cases usually only react when intoxication (whether from alcohol or drugs) reaches public notice. Interstate highways connect rural and urban communities together, and most stretches of Interstate-5 along the West Coast are designated as High Intensity Drug-Trafficking Districts. International drug cartels can be found even in small rural farming districts where marijuana cultivation is easier. The federal Joint Task Forces usually react to interstate drug trafficking before city governments.

Legalization of gambling occurred shortly before the widespread movement to decriminalize medical marijuana. In states where private casinos are not legal, Native casinos become more common. Legalized marijuana, though, caused the most noticeable cultural changes because they impacted public perceptions in the form of increased homelessness, drug-related crimes, and the sense of heightened threats to personal security. The presence of new 501.c organizations to deal with more potent drug addiction is usually seen as a sign of big-cities drug problems transforming small-town culture.

The two characters are on the old side of the baby boomer generation and are less concerned about morality of drug use than they are about its associated crime. They have differing thresholds of personal security and react differently to cultural changes. Rural voters often feel unconnected to state political decisions. Not all people are able to leave the state, especially older residents.

Case 3

Jennie and Brett in Louisville, Colorado

Jennie is twenty-three years old and works at a coffee shop in Louisville, Colorado, which is a fairly affluent suburb of Denver. The larger metropolitan area has a population of three million, but this little township only has a few more than 21,000 people and is filled with residential houses, churches, schools, retail shops, and general suburban living. She lives with her two best friends from high school and her apartment is situated between Highway 36 that goes through Boulder to the Rocky Mountain National Park and Interstate 25 that goes north through Fort Collins and into Wyoming. Brett is Jennie's boyfriend. He is twenty-eight years old and lives in his own house a few miles away from Jennie.

The two are different in many ways. Jennie was born in Denver, and her parents raised her to appreciate the mountains and the environment and take life at a slower pace. They considered themselves to be religious, but they did not attend any particular church. For his part, Brett is not from Colorado but was originally born and raised in a small farm community in Iowa. His father worked as an emergency first responder, while his mother mostly worked at home as a fulltime mother, homeschooling Brett and his four siblings. Their church played an important role in their weekly routine, as did the grandparents, uncles, aunts, cousins, and other extended family relations who all lived in the same general area.

Jennie and Brett met at a Church function—which was unusual because Jennie rarely went to Church. She went that Sunday because a friend from her work encouraged her to do so. She and Brett were instantly drawn to each other and almost immediately started spending a lot of time together with the same church friends. It took a few weeks, though, before they went on private dates alone and had a chance to really talk. By that time, they were both fairly smitten with each other, so the deeper conversations were somewhat difficult.

The first issue of surprise was about drugs. Brett lived in a town where drug use was kept in the margins of society, and he had very little experience with either heavy drinking or marijuana use, which is illegal in Iowa except for medical use. Brett knew that some people in Iowa cities had medical marijuana cards, but he did not travel in those circles and never met anyone personally who had one. He never even experimented with marijuana. His family was strongly against recreational drug use on moral and practical grounds. Since he was homeschooled, he was largely kept away from public examples of drug use until he went to college. Even at the university, he stayed away from those students who devoted their weekends at the bar or to video games. He belonged to a Christian fraternity, lived a sober life, and deliberately kept himself separate from the temptations of intoxication.

Jennie was not a heavy drug user in any sense. Her parents also taught her about the dangers of drugs and alcohol, and there was only occasional drinking in the household. Marijuana and other drugs were clearly forbidden, and her parents assumed that Jennie held the same values. However, when Jennie was in her later high-school years, it was not uncommon for one or two of her friends to bring a small amount of marijuana to parties. She infrequently used the drug without her parents' knowledge, but it was legal in the state, and though she was underage, she did not see it as any different from drinking beer at a party—which she usually did not do. When Jennie turned twenty, her parents moved out of state to Florida, and she stayed behind. One of her roommates, Sarah, was always sober—she was an outdoors nature girl who did not eat meat, drink alcohol, smoke, or take drugs. However, Jennie and her other roommate, Rachel, occasionally liked to drink and sometimes took marijuana when they were watching movies together. Sarah did not mind but also never joined in.

The topic of marijuana came up when Brett and Jennie started talking about their weekend plans, and she invited him to a movie night and described the routine. Brett was surprised when Jennie admitted that she occasionally smoked marijuana. Frankly, Jennie was surprised that Brett reacted that way. From there, they went on to discuss other topics about religion, morality, and differing political values. Since her parents were not very political, nor were they tied to any particular church, she found she was open to most of the same values as Brett—though, she usually did not think about faith, religion, and morality in the same way as he did. They continued to see each other, and Jennie simply avoided talking about marijuana. Brett did not ask directly about it.

Jennie was only eleven years old when Colorado passed its recreational marijuana law, and she remembers that her parents said very little on the topic except to warn her not to get involved with drugs. Brett never faced the issue of marijuana on an election ballot because it was never voted on in Iowa, and it had already been passed in Colorado six or seven years before he arrived. Legalization never entered his thinking when he applied for the engineering job, and when they asked for a drug test, he assumed it was a routine request. Only later did he learn from his coworkers that many applications never reached the final stages at his company because so many people from Colorado failed their drug tests. Brett realized that he benefitted in some small way from marijuana legalization because he was more in demand as a new hire for being drug free. For Jennie, part of the reason why she worked at the coffee shop is because they did not have any drug tests. She did not face many employment difficulties, but the drug-testing requirement and her lack of college education did limit her options.

About six months into their relationship, Brett asked if Jennie was still taking marijuana. She admitted that she was, on occasion. He asked if she would be willing to end the habit. After thinking a moment, she agreed that she could if he wanted her to. And she tried. She resolved to stop using it as soon as her current supply of marijuana ran out.

Two weeks passed, and her supply ran out, and Jennie found that she did not want to stop using. She ordered a new supply—Colorado permits buyers to purchase 1 oz at a time (about twenty-eight cigarettes). She promised herself, it would be the last one. A month more passed, and she found herself in the same situation. Colorado legalized online marijuana sales in 2024, so ordering more drugs was as easy as ordering a pizza. Jennie finally had to admit to herself and to Brett that she was finding it very difficult to stop taking the drug because it was also so easy to replenish her supply. This caused her to consider other areas of her life that seemed to be at a standstill—no college, she was in a low-paying job, and she had no plans for future improvement.

Denver has a serious drug problem among the homeless encampments in the downtown area. Louisville was mostly removed from the open-air drug markets found in the Ball Park District, along Broadway. Nevertheless, crime rates in the state had increased about 50 percent between 2011 and 2022—compared to national ranking, Colorado moved from twenty-seventh lowest overall crime rate in 2010 up to fourth highest overall in 2022. During the time that Brett first arrived in Colorado, he noticed many more homeless encampments appearing under overpasses and along certain corridors. He also saw actual evidence of property crimes, with smashed windows of businesses along certain streets. The police issued public alerts about auto-theft rings, and the blotter reported an average of three people dying from overdoses per day—mostly fentanyl but also from heroin and other drugs. Public drug use was illegal, but there were certain sections in town where it was open and obvious. Also, the DEA announced the arrest of a dozen leaders from a Mexican Drug Cartel who were operating in the Denver area when they were arrested. All these things made Brett much more sensitive about drug use.

Iowa has several areas where drugs are more noticeable—especially in certain urban districts in Des Moines, Cedar Rapids, and Sioux City, but Brett never spent much time in those areas. In Denver, his job took him through the downtown district regularly and the public displays of drug use, especially around the Ball Park District. He enjoyed his job, but he began to seriously consider relocating.

Brett and Jennie were growing more serious, and her drug use was a stumbling block in their relationship. After years of conversation with friends and colleagues in Colorado, he realized that the recreational marijuana law would never be repealed. He asked Jennie if she would consider moving to another state where marijuana was illegal. Jennie might have initially rejected the suggestion as unnecessary a year or two earlier, but she was also beginning to think that she might need a new location and new circumstances to help her refocus her priorities. She told Brett that she would seriously consider the idea. Jennie was not a serious drug abuser, but the more time she spent with Brett, the more she began thinking that a drug-free community would be a healthier option.

Analysis

This story is mostly about interstate migration and the importance of subcultures in tolerating or discouraging drug habits. People who use no recreational drugs still live in states where marijuana is legal. In every state, there are more people who do not use recreational drugs than those who do. Legalization and decriminalization do not force people into drug habits, but laws can change the local culture and attitudes toward intoxication, which includes believing that marijuana use is less dangerous than alcohol or tobacco. Legalization usually results in increased rates of illegal drug use at the state level but may not change individual drug habits.

People who occasionally engage in recreational drug use may live in any neighborhood. Most people living in large metropolitan areas usually live in a suburb, and residents may interact professionally without ever knowing about their neighbor's drug habits. Drug addiction is most often symbolized by public vandalism and other obvious signs of intoxication in high-drug use districts, but actual drug use frequently occurs in private.

Friends and family religious traditions play major roles in defining individual views about (and habits with) recreational drug use. Similar views on the morality of drugs play important roles in relationship success. Users and nonusers often develop like-minded circles of friends, so those who do not use drugs are often less aware of the habits of those who do. Microcultures often separate peer groups where drug use is present from peer groups with no drug use.

People who take marijuana only once or twice per month may not realize their dependency or addiction until they try to stop the habit. Ease of access to marijuana makes ending the habit more difficult, even for very occasional users. It is not uncommon for people who are trying to live sober lives to move into completely new surroundings, where drug use is less accessible. It is usually easier to move into a nonlegal state than it is to change existing drug laws.

Case 4

Michael and Alice in Anchorage, Alaska

Michael is a forty-one-year-old Yupik Native who was originally born in the small village of Kwethluk along the Kuskokwim River. It is only 12 miles upriver from Bethel, which is the largest village in Alaska unconnected to the road system, with about 6,000 people. Most of Michael's earliest memories were in and around the river villages, which he (and most of his relatives) refer to simply as "Bethel."

Michael's mother had a history of alcohol issues, and many of her six children were given in adoption to aunts and uncles. When Michael was about ten, he was adopted by a non-native family in Anchorage, though he still returned to Bethel periodically to visit with his Native Yupik relations. Michael felt strongly attached to both his native relations and his non-native family relations in Anchorage.

Life in Anchorage was much different from life in the Bethel river district. Even though it is surrounded by many native villages along the river, Bethel is not a native town. It was founded by Moravian missionaries in the late 1800s, and though most of the residents are native, they do not have a tribal connection to the town. Most lived in Bethel because they were too disruptive in their home villages and were forced to live in exile away from their original homes. Bethel has little cultural cohesion and suffered high rates of violent crime and alcohol dependency for most of its history.

Most Alaskan natives live in tribal villages of a few hundred people that are not connected to the road system and are accessible only by boat or airplane. Such isolation gives villages some control over goods that come into town. The state gave local village councils special authority to decide whether or not to restrict alcohol in their communities through a policy called "local option." There are three local options: villages could prohibit all sales, possession, and importation of alcohol to become "dry villages." Or they could allow limited sales, possession, or importation to become a "damp village." Or they could place no restrictions at all to become a "wet village." After 1977, Bethel was a damp village, which meant there were no liquor stores or bars, but residents could legally import alcohol from Anchorage.

Throughout the 1980s and 1990s, Bethel residents often ordered large amounts of alcohol, which was then illegally transported by boat or snowmobile to dozens of dry villages up and down the river and in surrounding areas—bootleggers could make up to 300 percent profit. Bethel's illegal alcohol market was notorious, and almost all crimes in the district were alcohol-related. Michael lived in Bethel as a child during the height of this period.

Bethel voted to become "mostly wet" as a crime-control measure in 2007, which meant the city council allowed two liquor stores and two bars. The goal of this decriminalization reform was to break the hold of illegal bootlegging that seemed to dominate the economy. Unfortunately, the new legalization did not change the illegal markets or alcohol consumption. Rates of violent crime continued to increase both in Bethel and in the surrounding areas. With drug overdose fatalities reaching record highs during the late 2010s, Bethel once again voted to become "damp" in 2020. Liquor stores were shut down, and a single liquor store operated by the village council was located right next to the village jail. Anyone wanting to buy or import alcohol had to register with the city, and they were restricted to small amounts of alcohol per day and per month. Violations could lead to fines of anywhere from $150 to $1500 for each count, and potential charges with a Class C Felony and up to five years in jail.

Michael's memories of living in Bethel were mixed. He enjoyed the outdoor experiences of working hard at fishing camps, but he also had darker memories of violence committed by friends and relatives when they were drunk. He did not experience any violence living with his family in Anchorage, but he was reexposed to the binge-drinking culture every time he went back to Bethel for summer visits. Anchorage was not free from peer pressure, and when Michael entered his late teens and early twenties, he developed his own habits of binge drinking with both native and non-native friends. However, he never let the drinking impact his job.

Michael married Alice around this time. She is also Yupik but was born and raised in Quinkalak, which is a dry village of a few hundred people spread across a wide district and is located about 70 miles south of Bethel. The economy relies mostly on fishing and subsistence, though most residents also have shares from the local mining district around Goodnews Bay. For most of her childhood, Alice worked hard in the village because it lacked basic necessities that are common to cities—most electricity came from local generators, and not all houses had indoor plumbing. There was no internet or cell phones when she was young, and communication often relied on CB radios. Residents were not poor but rarely had anything to spend their money on unless they left the village. Summer months were devoted to the fish camps, but villagers often left during the winter to visit Bethel and Anchorage or other larger villages.

Quinkalak is dry, but alcohol and drug abuse were still problems. Local culture stressed sobriety, and strong social pressure discouraged public intoxication in the village, but it was not uncommon in private homes. During visits to Bethel, and especially during the Fur Rendezvous festivities in Anchorage, habits of binge drinking were common. Alice's parents were sober, but after she left the village to live in Anchorage during her early twenties, she fell into the same habits of binge drinking as her friends. After many years in their marriage, Michael and Alice realized how much more vulnerable to alcohol addiction they were while living in the city, as compared to a dry village. They both cut down their drinking habits considerably and reduced the amount of available alcohol that was kept in the house.

As married adults, Michael worked as an orderly at a local hospital, and Mary worked as an aid in another medical center. They frequently came into contact with people who struggled with illness. In 2012, when the question of decriminalizing medical marijuana was brought to a vote, they had few strong opinions. They felt the same way in 2014 when recreational marijuana was brought to a vote. These views changed in the years that followed—mostly because of what they saw happening in Anchorage. There was a sharp increase in homeless encampments and an increasing number of reports about property thefts and violent crimes near their own neighborhood. They were especially concerned by the spike in sexual assaults and sexual trafficking because their daughter was entering into her teen years.

In 2020, Michael switched jobs to take a position for the Cook Inlet Tribal Council as an outreach specialist. His new job involves walking in and around homeless encampments asking natives if they need assistance with housing, healthcare, or addiction treatment. About 80 percent of the homeless in Anchorage are natives who come in from the villages for extended visits. They often live with friends or relatives periodically, but many will prefer the homeless encampments because of the easier access to alcohol, drugs, and other illegal activities. In some ways, the homeless camp is a little like a native village without any work obligations—but they are also much more dangerous. Drug use, crime, and victimization rates are very high, as are rates of sickness, accidents, and violence. Michael had firsthand experiences with binge drinking, and he understood the cultural issues that natives face when coming into Anchorage.

However, he was not prepared for the unsanitary and unhealthy conditions in the camps, especially the signs of violence and rampant drug use. He often felt unsafe in his job.

As per policy, Anchorage police patrols do not interfere with homeless encampments until they reach twenty-five dwellings or more or if there are violent incidents that require their presence. However, when police hear that outreach workers like Michael begin to feel unsafe walking into a particular encampment, they designate it as a high-priority problem. Most dangerous encampments are taken down—especially toward the end of summer when temperatures fall, and the risk of exposure becomes dangerously high. During these sweeps, residents are either moved into other shelters or are sent back to their villages.

Michael sees about 2000 clients per year, and he typically offers housing and treatment options during almost every encounter. Only about 1 percent of his contacts accept his offers. There are dozens of treatment facilities in Anchorage, and the bed vacancy rates are usually around 30 percent. Many resources are available, especially for natives. Nevertheless, Michael has a difficult time convincing his clients to use the resources because (and this is what frustrates him) they simply prefer the intoxicated lifestyle. He personally believes that most of the natives he meets on the streets would be much safer and healthier if they returned to their villages where they are known to family and friends and where they are more subject to restrictive cultural pressure of small village life. Many natives return eventually. However, with increasing overdose fatalities (which is about three times the rate of non-native Alaskans), many natives will never go back home.

Michael is unsure about whether legalization was a good policy decision for Alaskan natives. He owes his job to the massive increase in funding for outreach programs since 2020, and he is routinely told by his superiors that more funding is still needed. However, he also sees that general rates of drug addiction among natives have skyrocketed since decriminalization. He believes more natives should be forced into treatment, and police action is usually necessary for that to happen.

Alice strongly opposes legalization and decriminalization because she is afraid for her children. In 2024, every school in the state was equipped with opioid overdose kits, and she worries that recreational drug use will become normalized. Their children do not have smartphones, but the constant access to internet culture is present everywhere, and the traditional native values of hard work in the outdoors are nowhere to be found online. Neither Alice nor Michael use drugs, so they view the role of police from a much different perspective as the natives living in the homeless encampments. Reports of international drug cartels from Mexico operating in Anchorage make them both fearful about how easy it is for their children to gain access to marijuana and much more dangerous drugs, like heroin and fentanyl. They would be horrified if their children were someday drawn in among the natives who live in the homeless encampments around Anchorage.

Analysis

This story is mostly about drug policies at the local level, with special attention given to the unique autonomy of Native-American villages and other tribal districts. Native culture is known for hard work associated with subsistent lifestyles. Communal culture is strong among natives both in and outside of villages and tribal lands, and Natives are often more vulnerable to addiction when they are removed from their local tribal community. Most states and federal authorities rely on local tribal governments to handle law enforcement and other cultural issues. Drug laws have less impact on illegal markets than cultural consensus, and native villages use local option laws to reflect their cultural priorities.

Individual poverty is not always due to the lack of money but mostly due to the lack of access to certain urban conveniences. Native corporations and villages often have a lot of available money and resources, but individual members are not compelled to use them. Addiction is a leading cause for leaving the village and refusing treatment options. It is also the leading cause of homelessness among natives who find themselves outside of village social controls and removed from the natural requirements of subsistence lifestyles.

Crime rates, prostitution, violence, suicide, and drug use in homeless encampments are much higher than found in any native village, as are the rates of illness and premature death. Police usually do not interfere with homeless encampments until the crime rates become noticeable to the outside public or when organized crime operatives begin to set up collection points. International drug cartels can range from just over the southern border to as far north as Alaska. Outreach workers usually rely on police to help secure the environment and look to police as primary agents for compelling users into treatment options.

Case 5

Tom and Juanita in Dallas, Texas

Tom is a 51-year-old senior project engineer for the Texas Department of Transportation office located outside of Dallas. He is in charge of maintaining the state highways and often has anywhere between 5 and 500 people working for him on any given project. He works in an office some days but is out on the worksite most other times.

All Texas employees working for state and local agencies must undergo drug screenings prior to being hired. People who work in transportation departments, and especially those who operate heavy machinery are subject to random drug test periodically throughout their employment. Tom does not mind these rules because the jobsite is often dangerous, and he wants his people to be safe. He is an engineer with a college degree, but his full-time and part-time employees may come from anywhere—some of them only have high-school diplomas. Tom knows that heavy drinking is often part of the weekend celebrations, but he warns his people to be completely sober come Monday morning and not to get caught using any illegal substances—which includes marijuana.

The job of roadside construction involves a lot of heavy lifting, and Tom remembers a time about fifteen to twenty years ago when many of his workers were using doctor-prescribed Oxycontin to help relieve back pain. If the drugs were legally prescribed, and if the worker was not using them while operating any vehicles, there were few risks. The problem occurred when his workers became addicted to opioid and were caught using them during times when they clearly should not. In some rare cases, he remembers employees shifting from opioid use into heroin use when the doctor prescriptions became too difficult to legally procure—the illegal dealer always had heroin, which has similar effects. He had to fire good employees when they were unable to stop their drug habits.

By the early 2000s, his department began providing drug-treatment programs as part of their state-based insurance plans. This was welcome news for Tom because he did not want to lose a good worker. As rates of drug addiction increased, it was often difficult to find reliable workers. During the 1980s or 1990s, addiction treatment programs were very expensive, and workers often lost their jobs when they admitted their addiction. The new state programs provided more coverage and allowed for special leave options to help employees to undergo treatment and keep their jobs. After a 30-day inpatient or a 180-day outpatient program, his workers could go back to the job, and Tom was happy to keep them.

Marijuana is illegal in Texas—however, it is commonly used. The northern portion of the state is a major drug corridor called the Texaoma High-Intensity Drug-Trafficking Area (HIDTA) that spans across seventeen counties between Dallas and Oklahoma City. The proximity to Mexico makes Dallas a perfect hub for international drug cartels to import their drugs, process them, and the repackage them before they are shipped in all directions along the interstate system. The Sinaloa and Jalisco drug gangs compete with between 200–400 smaller criminal groups to facilitate their international trafficking operations. They bring in black tar heroin, cocaine, crack, China-white heroin, Xanax, ecstasy, and especially fentanyl. Local law enforcement agents seized more than 100 pounds of fentanyl in 2023, which was enough to kill 24 million people. These drugs are sent along the I-20, I-35, and I-45 highways on their way to every state in the South and Midwest.

Drug addiction rates in Dallas are higher than average, and the region ranks second in the nation for its illegal human trafficking problems. However, law enforcement is also well supported and very active. A few local governments declared themselves "sanctuary cities" for marijuana possession—particularly Denton, which is a small city north of Dallas, and a few smaller towns in and around the state capital of Austin. These were not reflective of many rural Texan cultural traditions, and the State Attorney General filed a suit against these cities in 2024 claiming that they were violating Texas constitutional law. Texas is not likely to overturn its marijuana criminalization policies. Tom and many of his colleagues like to drink alcohol, and they get intoxicated from time to time, but they have less sympathy for marijuana use and other more potent drugs. Tom especially blames the drug problem for most of the inner-city crime and homelessness issues that he sees in the Dallas-Fort Worth area.

In part, Tom's hostility is due to conversations with his wife, Juanita. She is forty-eight years old and works as a Victim's Advocate for Refugee Services office of Catholic Charities Dallas. Her views on international drug cartels are based mostly on her interactions with collateral victims, who often have nothing to do with drugs or who became victimized by drugs unwillingly. Since 2012, major surges of migrants have come across the southern border from Mexico into Texas. By 2023, the United Nations International Organization for Migration designated the Mexico–US border as the largest migration corridor in the world, with more than 11 million people passing through that district. In a single year, US Customs Border Patrol agents made contact with more than 2.5 million people as they entered Texas. Many of these migrants were victims of human trafficking. Juanita's job is to serve as an advocate for those victims, when they are rescued and presented to the immigration courts. She is deeply moved by their stories of fear, abuse, deprivation, and intimidation.

As an advocate, Juanita works with attorneys to get U-visas or T-visas for her clients. These are special permissions that allow immigrants to avoid deportation, even if they crossed illegally. A U-visa is given to the victims of human trafficking who are willing to provide evidence against their abusers, and the T-visas are given to any other victims of human trafficking who do not give evidence.

In most cases, the victims of human trafficking are women or children who have been forced into sex work by fear or intimidation. In other cases, they are men who have been forced into slave-labor conditions to work in farms, construction, or even factories. It is rare for Juanita to help with U-visas because the victims are too frightened to cooperate with the police against their abusers—most of whom have been repeatedly threatened that any testimony to the police will result in their being killed and their friends and families back home being killed or tortured. More often, Juanita works to compile paperwork evidence needed to support T-visa applications. In those cases, victims must explain the severe conditions of abuse that they suffered and do not have to testify or cooperate with police (the process takes about eight months).

Juanita is of Mexican descent, but her family has lived in Texas for so many generations that she does not know exactly when they arrived. She speaks Spanish but only because she learned it in school—she and her family have accents, but none of them speak Spanish at home. Nevertheless, her language skills combined with her ethnic background help her to better communicate with the thousands of refugees who come in contact with Catholic Charities. She shares many of the same cultural traditions as the refugees she works with, and she feels as though they are her people.

Tom does not support drug decriminalization or legalization in Texas because he thinks it hurts his workplace. However, Juanita is especially forceful on this subject—even though she is often trying to protect her clients from possible deportation by law enforcement authorities. For Juanita, she views the

Dallas Police Department as one of her strongest allies. They are the ones who investigate the drug dealers and the ones who most often find and rescue victims of human trafficking.

The biggest hurdle she faces in her job is simply finding people who need to be rescued. It is common knowledge that among the millions of refugees, there are probably tens of thousands of trafficking victims. However, Juanita only sees a few hundred in a given year—most are hidden from view. They are victims of human trafficking precisely because the drug cartels threaten them with grave physical harm—mass murders and mutilations are common on both sides of the border. It takes a lot of courage to break free from their oversight and for victims to make contact with someone who can help them. In her district, the Dallas police are the ones who most often make those contacts when they enter into the dangerous drug subculture in the process of prosecuting drug crimes. If drugs were decriminalized in Dallas, the police would no longer be able to make those contacts.

Tom and Juanita are not political advocates, but they would like some laws in Texas to change. Juanita would like additional regulations that require more training for local law enforcement officers in how to identify and detect human trafficking victims. Tom also supports more resources for drug-treatment facilities, which may be most helpful for his workers. At the same time, they both believe that strong anti-drug education programs in the schools would be most helpful in limiting local demand for recreational drug use. This drug-free goal is often supported in rural and suburban communities. It is not as strongly reinforced in urban centers, where the compassionate efforts to decriminalize or legalize certain drugs tend to weaken those messages.

Analysis

This story is mostly about the intersection between smuggling and legitimate business culture. It also shows how people may agree on the same conclusions but for entirely differing reasons. Texas is a hub for smuggling drugs and people from Mexico to the rest of the contiguous states. Texas is also unusual for having both very large urban districts as well as very expansive rural districts. Methods for treating illegal drug gangs differ for both types of communities. Texas also has a large population of people with Mexican descent, but that does not mean that they are all recent immigrants or that they even speak Spanish. Catholic cultural identity is usually more transcending than language among Hispanics along the southern borders.

No international drug cartels have a complete monopoly, and violence often arises between rival factions. Human trafficking is almost as common as drug trafficking and includes both forced prostitution as well as other forms of forced labor. Victims are held by threats of violence and deportation, both of which are routinely carried out. Most human trafficking victims go undetected unless police meet with them directly during criminal enforcement operations. Victims are eligible for sanctuary status of one kind or another, but most successful T-visa applications require attorneys to help process the materials.

Drug trafficking expands access of illegal commodities to legitimate workers. Most large businesses and almost all government agencies require some drug screening, especially for jobs related to transportation and heavy equipment. Many opioid addictions began from legitimate prescriptions, which can lead to heroin addiction if left untreated. Most insurance plans provide employees with drug-treatment options at significantly reduced costs. Employers generally prefer to keep well-trained staff rather than having to fire them for drug addiction.

Tolerance for alcohol abuse is not always carried over into tolerance for recreational drug use, especially in rural community cultures. People generally oppose the side effects of drug culture, especially when publicly exposed in urban districts. Supporters of the drug war often advocate for both increased law enforcement as well as increased training and education opportunities to lessen those side effects.

Directory of Resources

Books

General Information

Doweiko, Harold E. (2009), *Concepts of Chemical Dependency*, 7th ed., Belmont, CA: Brooks/Cole Cengage Learning.

Textbook on pharmacology, which takes addiction at face value and recognizes the biological dangers of drug abuse.

Meier, Robert, and Gilbert Geis (2006), *Criminal Justice and Moral Issues*, Los Angeles: Roxbury.

Provides a general overview of crime and law. Mostly balanced, but generally tends toward social-welfare presumptions about natural law and social harm.

United National Office on Drugs and Crime (2008), "A Century of International Drug Control," *World Drug Report*, New York: United Nations Publications.

Provides a succinct history of International Drug Controls since the late 1800s.

Traditional Conservative Perspectives

Berenson, Alex (2019), *Tell Your Children: The Truth about Marijuana, Mental Illness, and Violence*, New York: Free Press.

Argues that the pro-marijuana lobby has created a mythology about the harmless nature of the drug, whereas most evidence suggests that (among other problems) there is a strong link between marijuana use and psychosis and schizophrenia. Written by a journalist.

Califano, Joseph A. (2007), *High Society: How Substance Abuse Ravages America and What to Do About It*, New York: Public Affairs.

Founder and Chair of National Center on Addiction and Substance Abuse and served under Democrat and Republican Presidents. Strong representation of traditional perspective on drug policy based on dangers of drug abuse and addiction.

Horowitz, David (2021), *I Can't Breathe: How a Racial Hoax Is Killing America*, Washington, DC: Regnary Press.

Traditional conservative perspective from a former member of the Students for a Democrat Society (in the 1970s), which gives details on the Black Lives Matter 2020 riots.

Inciardi, James, and Karen McElrath, ed. (2011), *The American Drug Scene: An Anthology*, 6th ed., New York: Oxford University Press.

An anthology of historical essays. Mostly concludes with balanced interpretations that recognize social harms caused by drug use and addiction. Inciardi was the founder and codirector of the Center for Drug and Alcohol Studies at the University of Delaware.

Jonnes, Jill (1996), *Hep-Cats, Narcs, and Pipe Dreams: A History of America's Romance with Illegal Drugs*, New York: Scribner.

A history of recreational drug use with a clear appreciation of the danger of drugs and addiction. Reflects a traditional conservative view of drug abuse.

McCaffrey, Barry R. (1999), *The Destructive Impact of Drugs on the United States: How the Legalization of Drugs Would Jeopardize the Health and Safety of the American People and Our Nation*, Washington, DC: US Government Printing Office.

Policy position taken from the director of the Office of National Drug Control Policy published at end of Clinton administration, but still strongly reflective of traditional views of drug addiction and law enforcement drug controls, with some very early social welfare conclusions.

Sowell, Thomas (1994), *Race and Culture: A World View*, New York: Basic Books.

A fellow of the Hoover Institute and Stanford University who specializes in economics and social theory. He is African American and reflects a distinctly traditional conservative perspective.

Libertarian Perspectives

Boggs, Carl (2015), *Drugs, Power and Politics: Narco Wars, Big Pharma, and the Subversion of Democracy*, Boulder, CO: Paradigm Publishers.

Mostly libertarian-based argument but concludes with strong social-welfare positions.

Greenwald, Glenn (2009), *Drug Decriminalization in Portugal: Lessons for Creating Fair and Successful Drug Policies*, Washington, DC: Cato Institute.

Libertarian summary of Portugal's harm reduction drug decriminalization policies, which was widely used as a model for American and other European State drug policies.

Lynch, Timothy, ed. (2000), *After Prohibition: An Adult Approach to Drug Policies in the 21st Century*, Washington, DC: CATO Institute.

Anthology of libertarian arguments presented during the height of their influence.

Szasz, Thomas (1992), *Our Right to Drugs: The Case for a Free Market*, Westport, CT: Praeger.

One of the earliest libertarian arguments present in mainstream press.

Schaler, Jeffrey, ed. (1998), *Drugs: Should We Legalize, Decriminalize, or Deregulate*, New York: Prometheus Books.

Anthology of twenty-nine essays written by a mixture of conservative, libertarian, and liberal academics, policymakers, and journalists. Editor is a leader of libertarian ideology. Good source for understanding drug policy debates between 1988 and 1997.

Social-Welfare Perspectives

Babor, Thomas, Jonathan Caulkins, Benedikt Fischer, David Foxcroft, Keith Humphreys, Maria Elena Medina-Mora, Isidore Obot, Jürgen Rehm, and Peter Reuter. (2018), *Drug Policy and the Public Good*, 2nd ed., Oxford, UK: Oxford University Press.

Anthology of essays that rely on evidence-based ideologies of harm reduction. Traditional conservative viewpoints were not seriously considered.

Decorte, Tom, Simon Lenton, and Chris Wilkins, ed. (2020), *Legalizing Cannabis: Experiences, Lessons and Scenarios*, New York: Routledge.

Anthology of essays from a social-welfare perspective, which assumes legalization of marijuana is inevitable and addresses practical questions about best policy.

Dufton, Emily (2017), *Grass Roots: The Rise and Fall and Rise of Marijuana in America*, New York: Basic Books.

Asserts social-welfare approach as a foregone conclusion and strongly opposes traditional conservative ideological perspectives. Reflects academic presumptions of modern cultural criticism.

Reznicek, Michael (2012), *Blowing Smoke: Rethinking the War on Drugs without Prohibition and Rehab*, Lanham, MD: Rowman & Littlefield.

Clear social-welfare and harm reduction oriented.

Room, Robin, Benedikt Fischer, Wayne Hall, Simon Lenton, and Peter Reuter, eds. (2010), *Cannabis Policy: Moving beyond Stalemate*, Oxford, UK: Beckley Foundation Press.

Self-described as evidence-based policy guidebook by a UN-accredited Non-Government Organization, with a large collection of topical essays. Strongly favors social-welfare and harms reduction approaches. Traditional conservative viewpoints are not seriously considered.

Takahashi, Saul (2016), *Human Rights and Drug Control: The False Dichotomy*, Portland, OR: Hart Publishing.

Takahashi works with numerous international Non-Government Organizations and United Nations subagencies. Strongly opposed to George Soros attempts to equate drug use with human rights but otherwise supports social-welfare premises.

Tate, Katherine, James Lance Taylor, Mark Q. Sawyer, eds. (2014), *Something's In the Air: Race, Crime, and the Legalization of Marijuana*, New York: Routledge.

A social-welfare approach to drug policy based on cultural criticism, which reflects the growing Black Lives Matter movement of the time.

Vitale, Alex S. (2017), *The End of Policing*, New York: Verso.

Presents a modern cultural criticism (Marxist) argument that claims the police are agents used to support power relations related to race, class, and gender oppression. Extreme version of social-welfare position.

Websites

Government Primary Source Data

European Union Drug Agency, https://www.euda.europa.eu/index_en.

The European Union Drugs Agency which is responsible for reporting on implementation, changes, and proposals for drug policies among the twenty-seven states of the European Union, as well as other candidate nations who want to be recognized by the European Union.

Federal Bureau of Investigation, Uniform Crime Reporting Program, https://www.fbi.gov/how-we-can-help-you/more-fbi-services-and-information/ucr.

Annual Crime Reports from the Federal Bureau of Investigations with the US Department of Justice.

National Institute on Drug Abuse, Monitoring the Future Program, https://nida.nih.gov/research-topics/trends-statistics/monitoring-future.

Monitoring the Future Survey (since 1975), administered by the National Institute on Drug Abuse, within the US Department of Health and Human Services.

Substance Abuse and Mental Health Services Administration, National Survey on Drug Use and Health Program, https://www.samhsa.gov/data/data-we-collect/nsduh-national-survey-drug-use-and-health.

National Survey on Drug Use and Health implemented annually by the Substance Abuse and Mental Health Services Administration, within the US Department of Health and Human Services.

United Nations Office on Drugs and Crime, https://www.unodc.org/.

United Nations Office on Drugs and Crime, which reports on implementation, changes, and future proposals for international drug conventions.

United States Census Bureau, https://www.census.gov/.

US Census Data for demographic information about urban and rural changes.

United States Drug Enforcement Administration, https://www.dea.gov/resources/documents.

US Drug Enforcement Agency, which is responsible for the Annual National Drug Threat Assessment (requires a search for current and past year threat assessment reports).

USASpending.Gov, https://www.usaspending.gov/.

USASpending.Gov, a service of the Bureau of Fiscal Service, within the US Department of the Treasury for information on government spending at the state and federal levels.

501.c Nonprofit Foundations and Organizations

Foundation for Drug Policy Solutions, https://gooddrugpolicy.org/.

Policy lobbying group that lies somewhere between traditional moral conservatives and social welfare, but with a strong emphasis on the need for clear antidrug messaging and consistent law-enforcement policies.

Open Society Foundations, https://www.opensocietyfoundations.org/.

Open Society Foundations is an umbrella group that sponsors hundreds of like-minded organizations and largely funded by George Soros for the purposes of promoting drug decriminalization and other harm reduction strategies. Two relevant suborganizations include:

Drug Policy Alliance, https://drugpolicy.org/.

Drug Policy Alliance is largely responsible for promoting marijuana legalization and other decriminalization laws at the state levels.

National Harm Reduction Coalition, https://harmreduction.org/.

National Harm Reduction Coalition is a collection of 501.c organizations that lobby for and implement harm-reduction strategies at the local, state, and national levels.

Tax Foundation, https://taxfoundation.org/.

Research Institute that has operated since 1937, which tracks tax policies at the state and federal levels.

The CATO Institute, https://www.cato.org/.

Research institution devoted to libertarian ideals that emphasize private enterprise and individual freedom and de-emphasizes the role of government as a potential infringement on individual liberties.

The Heritage Foundation, https://www.heritage.org/.

Research institution devoted to promoting American democratic values. Reflects traditional conservative ideology.

Glossary

Addiction A physical and psychological compulsion that encourages a person to continue taking a substance or continuing a behavior that is harmful to self or others. Dependency becomes addiction when the person tries to stop the behaviors but is unable to.

Baby boomer The generation of children born after the Second World War. The particular dates often vary, but generally it refers to any person born between the years 1943 and 1957.

Binge drinking Drinking alcohol for the purpose of becoming intoxicated. Typically, this involves drinking three or four (or more) servings of alcohol per hour.

Convention (International) An agreement between nations to limit or encourage certain trade practices.

Corporal punishment Any punishment that inflicts some pain to the physical body.

Damp villages A designation used in Alaska to indicate a village that has voted to allow some alcohol but still restricts sales or consumption within village jurisdiction.

Demand control Any drug policy that seeks to limit the demand of drug users from wanting to seek out illegal vendors.

Dependency A condition when an individual has developed a biological or psychological need for a substance or behavior. Usually defined by the appearance of withdrawal symptoms that occur when the individual stops the behavior or no longer consumes the substance.

Detox center A place set aside for intoxicated individuals to safely return to sobriety. Often connected with a treatment center, but not always.

Digital Addiction Any dependency on the stimulation derived by electronic sources (cellphone, laptop, tablet, or computer). Typically involves a compulsion for continuous stimulation through online (internet-based) activities.

Drug Court A legal entity that deals in violations of drug law and which usually provides first-time offenders with opportunities for treatment and with pathways for expunging their records after successful fulfillment of obligations.

Dry villages A designation used in Alaska to indicate a village that has voted to prohibit sales or possession of all alcohol.

Evidence-based policies Policies that do not consider moral values or the impact of activities on individual character. Instead, policies are based on evidence of potential physical or psychological harm to the individual drug user and to the community.

501.c.3 or 501.c4 nonprofit An organization formed for the purpose of helping the community or society in some way. The numbers refer to the location in the federal tax code referring to tax-deductible organizations. Sometimes referred to simply as a "501.c."

Hallucinogens A classification of drugs that impair ordinary sensory perceptions to the point that the user experiences distorted sensations that would not ordinarily exist in the natural world.

Halo effect An economic term used to explain why the popularity of one item might carry over to another, unconnected item.

Hard drugs A designation used by the Dutch government (and others) to distinguish highly potent drugs that are most susceptible to addiction and physical or psychological harm.

Harm reduction Any drug policy that seeks to reduce the harm of drug use and drug laws to both the individual and society. Usually used in conjunction with evidence-based programs associated with decriminalization and legalization efforts.

High Intensity Drug-Trafficking Area (HIDTA) A designation used by the federal government to identify regions where illegal drugs are most frequently transported through. Often also include points of high intensity manufacturing, sales, and use. These areas usually involve highways and multiple communities.

High-Density Drug-Trafficking District A designation used by governments to identify points within a community where the most illegal drug dealing and use occurs. These may only be as small as a single house, street corner, or maybe as large as several city blocks.

HIV/AIDS Human Immunodeficiency Virus that is associated most often with Acquired Immune Deficiency Syndrome. Patient's natural immunity systems do not operate at the levels necessary to prevent ordinary illnesses. The combination of virus and syndrome is treatable but is often deadly.

Human right A right that exists regardless of local, state, or national laws. In the United States, the most common human rights involve the rights to life, liberty, and private property (the last two are often described as "the pursuit of happiness").

Human trafficking A form of modern slavery. Victims are smuggled away from their homes and are used for sex work (prostitution) or for physical labor. Victims may be abused by family members, acquaintances, or strangers.

Ideology A set of deeply held beliefs that reflect a pattern of values related to politics, economics, morality, and faith.

Legalization A process by which a substance or behavior that once was prohibited by local, state, or national law is permitted. Legalization usually includes some regulations that still prohibit use under certain circumstances: age, location, quality, and fees.

Local option A legal practice instituted by the state of Alaska that grants rural villages the right to choose whether or not alcohol or other legalized substances be allowed in. Villages may choose to prohibit or regulate sales, transportation, and possession.

Medicaid A federal program under the Social Security Administration that is used to pay for medical services and materials for adults and children with limited income or other resources.

Medicare A federal program under the Social Security Administration that is used to pay for medical services and materials for adults aged sixty-five years or older and for people with disabilities.

Morality A system of principles and value judgments that is used to evaluate whether behaviors, intentions, or actions are right or wrong. Usually backed by a set of religious presumptions but may also be reinforced by nonreligious philosophical systems of ethics.

Narcotics A classification used to identify any drug that is derived directly or indirectly from the opium plant.

Nongovernment organization (NGO) An international organization that spans multiple countries but which is not recognized by any particular government. Usually developed to help society and usually not for profit.

Open-air drug market A term used by law enforcement to describe any district where buyers and sellers of illegal drugs are able to meet and transact deals without prior arrangement. Usually marked by high-intensity recreational drug use.

Opioids A class of narcotics that are most often characterized by their origin in chemical laboratories.

Opportunity cost That which is lost by the decision to pursue another option that cannot be pursued simultaneously.

Outreach worker A social worker who works outside in order to make the most contacts with people who may not have a permanent residence but who need some form of social service for medical, mental, or economic needs.

Overdose Prevention Site (OPS) A physical location where drug users consume their substances in the presence of others who are willing to help respond with medical assistance in cases of unintentional overdose.

Parole A condition when a prisoner is released before the end of the sentence, either temporarily or permanently.

Physical dependency A condition that occurs when a person has been taking a physical substance enough times that the removal of the substance produces harmful physical reactions (called withdrawal symptoms).

Plea bargain An agreement between the government and an indicted offender which promises a lesser charge or sentence recommendation if the offender agrees to plead guilty or agrees not to contest the charges. Plea bargains are intended to avoid criminal trials.

Polydrug use A practice of using more than one recreational drug to achieve intoxication, often leading to unexpected interactions that result in overdose or death.

Prescription drugs Therapeutic drugs that are legally produced to help treat a physical or mental condition and which are regulated through the oversight of a qualified medical professional.

Probation A condition when a convicted offender may avoid incarceration based on certain conditions that involve some supervision outside of a jail or prison. Often granted to first-time offenders and to prisoners who conduct themselves appropriately during detention.

Psychoactive A quality in a substance that impacts mental processes and perception.

Psychological dependency A condition that occurs when a person has been taking substances or engaged in behaviors enough times that ending the substance use or behavior results in strong emotional reactions that impact mood, motivation, concentration, and cognition. May also result in physical manifestations related to heart rate, sweating, and breathing.

Psychosis A psychological condition that occurs when the person no longer distinguishes between objective reality and perceived reality. Often associated with schizophrenia.

Psychotropic A characteristic of any substance that manipulates mental processes including mood, perceptions, and cognition.

Recreational use Refers to the intended use of any drug for purposes that do not primarily seek to treat a physical or mental disorder.

Red light district Any urban district that is recognized for its illegal activity.

Sanctuary city A designation by which a local government publicly declares that it will not enforce or prosecute certain kinds of crimes listed by state and federal authorities.

Selective enforcement (or nonenforcement) The formal or informal policy of law enforcement officials who make decisions to enforce particular laws with arrest, detention, or confiscation of illegal goods based on certain circumstances of the crime.

Sin taxes Any tax on an item or behavior that is traditionally judged to be immoral (wrong).

Sobriety The condition of not being intoxicated.

Social services Any service that is intended to help the physical, medical, psychological, or economic needs of someone who lives in a particular community. Usually these are tax-funded but may be funded through private donations.

Stigma The negative social pressure that is associated with certain actions or behaviors. Usually results in embarrassment or shame before others.

Supervised Consumption Site (SCS) A physical location where drug users may consume their substances in the presence of others who are willing to help respond with medical assistance in cases of unintentional overdose.

Supervised Injection Site (SIS) A physical location where users who inject drugs may obtain sterilized needles for free and often are permitted to inject their substances in the presence of others who are willing to help respond with medical assistance in cases of unintentional overdose.

Supply control Any drug policy that seeks to limit the access of certain recreational drug to users, through interdiction during transport or the elimination of drugs at the source of manufacture.

Synthetic drugs Any drug that was manufactured in a laboratory and which does not occur naturally as a plant or mineral.

Temperance Any movement that encourages the practice of individual moral self-restraint. Became most associated with groups that sought the limitation or prohibition of alcohol consumption.

THC Tetrahydrocannabinol, which is the primary psychoactive ingredient in cannabis (marijuana).

Therapeutic use Refers to the intended use of any drug for purposes that primarily seek to treat a physical or mental disorder and not for purposes of pleasure.

Tolerance (drugs) The condition (physical or psychological) when the pleasurable effects of a substance or behavior diminish after repetition. Usually leads to addiction.

Tolerance (police enforcement policy) The system of nonenforcement by law enforcement agents in the Netherlands (called *gedoogbeleid* in Dutch). Imitated by other cities and nations around Europe, the United States, and Canada.

Trafficking The transport of illegal goods.

Wet villages A designation used in Alaska to indicate a village that permits existing state laws that allow alcohol and other substances to be bought, sold, or possessed for consumption.

References

Alexandrova, Anna, ed. (2002), *AIDS, Drugs and Society*, New York: International Debate Education Association.

Babor, Thomas, Jonathan Caulkins, Benedikt Fischer, David Foxcroft, Keith Humphreys, Maria Elena Medina-Mora, Isidore Obot, Jürgen Rehm, Peter Reuter. (2018), *Drug Policy and the Public Good*, 2nd ed., Oxford: Oxford University Press.

Balkin, Karen F., ed. (2005), *Current Controversies: Drug Legalization*, Farmington Hills, MI: Greenhaven Press, 2005.

Ballotpedia Website (2020), "Oregon Measure 110, Drug Decriminalization and Addiction Treatment Initiative (2020)," accessed on October 5, 2024 at https://ballotpedia.org/Oregon_Measure_110,_Drug_Decriminalization_and_Addiction_Treatment_Initiative_(2020).

Barbour, Scott, ed. (2000), *Current Controversies: Drug Legalization*, Farmington Hills, MI: Greenhaven Press.

Barcott, Bruce (2015), *Weed the People: The Future of Legal Marijuana in America*, New York: Time Books.

Bates, Kristin A., and Richelle S. Swan (2014), *Juvenile Delinquency in a Diverse Society*, Thousand Oaks, CA: Sage Publications.

Bayer, Ronald, and Gerald M. Oppenheimer, ed. (1993), *Confronting Drug Policy*, New York: Cambridge University Press.

Bayers, Ronald, and Lawrence O. Gostin, Bruce Jennings, and Bonnie Steinbock, eds. (2007), *Public Health Ethics: Theory, Policy, and Practice*, New York: Oxford University Press.

Bean, Philip (2014), *Drugs and Crime*, 4th ed., New York: Routledge.

Beazley, Jonathan C., and Stephanie Field (2018), *Cannabis on Campus: Changing the Dialog in the Wake of Legalization*, New York: Routledge.

Becker, Gary S., and Richard A. Posner (2009), *Uncommon Sense: Economic Insights, from Marriage to Terrorism*, Chicago: University of Chicago Press.

Beilenson, Peter L., and Patrick A. McGuire (2012), *Tapping into the Wire*, Baltimore, MD: John Hopkins University Press.

Belenko, Steven, Matthew Hiller, and Leah Hamilton (2013), "Treating Substance Use Disorders in the Criminal Justice System," *Current Psychiatry Reports*, 15 (11) November. doi: 10.1007/s11920-013-0414-z; PMCID: PMC3859122NIHMSID: NIHMS532476PMID: 24132733, accessed on October 1, 2024.

Belgium Federal Research Programme on Drugs (2021), "Summary: An Evaluation of the Belgium Drug Policy," Belgium Science Policy Office (BELSPO).

Belgium Science Policy Office (BELSPO) (2021), Federal Research Programme on Drugs Summary, "Evadrug: An Evaluation of the Belgian Drug Policy" by nine professors, most of which are from the University of Ghent.

Benavie, Arthur (2009), *Drugs: America's Holy War*, New York: Routledge.

Benavie, Arthur (2016), *How the Drug War Ruins American Lives*, Santa Barbara, CA: Praeger.

Benjamin, Daniel K., and Roger Leroy Miller (1991), *Undoing Drugs: Beyond Legalization*, New York: Basic Books.

Berenson, Alex (2019), *Tell Your Children: The Truth about Marijuana, Mental Illness, and Violence*, New York: Free Press.

Beusekom, Ineke van, Mirjam van Het Loo, and James P. Kahan (2002), *Guidelines for Implementing and Evaluation the Portuguese Drug Strategy*, Santa Monica, CA: RAND Europe, .

Bjelopera, Jerome P. (2018), "Antia—Background," *Congressional Research Service*, January 3, accessed on September 30, 2024 at https://crsreports.congress.gov/product/pdf/IF/IF10839/2.

Boggs, Carl (2015), *Drugs, Power and Politics: Narco Wars, Big Pharma, and the Subversion of Democracy*, Boulder, CO: Paradigm Publishers.

Bohm, Robert, and Jeffrey Walker, ed. (2006), *Demystifying Crime and Criminal Justice*, Los Angeles: Roxbury Publishing.

Bollinger, Lorenz, ed. (1997), *Cannabis Science: From Prohibition to Human Right*, Frankfurt, Germany: Peter Lang, .

Bonevac, Daniel (2013), *Today's Moral Issues: Classic & Contemporary Perspectives*, 7th ed., New York: McGraw-Hill.

Branson, Richard, ed. (2016), *Ending the War on Drugs*, London: Virgin Books.

Byrnes, Chris (2009), "Injecting Drug Use, HIV, and AIDS in the Muslim World." In *Islam and AIDS: Between Scorn, Pity and Justice*. Edited by Farid Esack and Sarah Chiddy. Oxford: Oneworld, pp. 198–210.

Bugliosi, Vincent (1996), *The Phoenix Solution: Getting Serious about Winning America's Drug War*, Beverly Hills, CA: Dove Books.

Bureau of Justice Statistics Bulletin (1982), "Prisoners 1925–81," December, accessed on September 15, 2024 at https://bjs.ojp.gov/content/pub/pdf/p2581.pdf.

Cabot, Heather (2020), *The New Chardonnay: The Unlikely Story of How Marijuana Went Mainstream*, New York: Currency Press.

Califano, Joseph A. (2007), *High Society: How Substance Abuse Ravages America and What to Do about It*, New York: Public Affairs.

Canada Special Committee of the Senate on Illegal Drugs. Benjamin Dolin, Law and Government Division of Parliamentary Research Branch for Canadian Library of Parliament (2001), "National Drug Policy: The Netherlands," August 12, 2001 prepared for Special Committee of the Senate on Illegal Drugs, accessed on September 15, 2024 at https://sencanada.ca/content/sen/Committee/371/ille/library/dolin1-e.pdf.

Canada Website (2024), "Canadian Drugs and Substances Strategy: Overview," accessed on September 10, 2024 at https://www.canada.ca/en/health-canada/services/substance-use/canadian-drugs-substances-strategy.html.

Caulkins, Jonathan P., Beau Kilmer, and Mark A. R. Kleiman ([2012] 2016), *Marijuana Legalization: What Everyone Needs to Know*, 2nd ed., Oxford University Press: New York.

Caulkins, Jonathan P., Beau Kilmer, Mark A. R. Kleiman, Robert J. MacCoun, Gregory Midgette, Pat Oglesby, Rosalie Liccardo Pacula, Peter Reuter (2015), *Considering Marijuana Legalization: Insights for Vermont and Other Jurisdictions*, New York: RAND Corporation.

Centers for Disease Control, Marissa B. Esser, Adam Sherk, Yong Liu, Timothy S. Naimi (2024), "Deaths from Excessive Alcohol Use—United States, 2016–2021," *Morbidity and Mortality Weekly Report (MMWR)*, 73 (8) (February 29), pp.154–61.

Cole, George F. (1976), "Evolution of the New York Prison System." In *Criminal Justice—Law and Politics*, 2d ed., Washington, DC: Office Criminal Justice.

Connecticut Government Letter on European Drug Policies (1971), "Great Britain Misuse of Drugs Act (1971)"; Halsbury's Statutes §§ 28–1 to 28–40. In *Connecticut Govt Letter on European Drug Policies*, accessed on September 3, 2024 at https://www.cga.ct.gov/PS94/rpt/olr/htm/94-R-0015.htm.

Cooper, Wilbert L., and Christie Thompson (2020), "Will Drug Legalization Leave Black People Behind," *Marshall Project*, November 11, 2020, accessed on October 6, 2024 at https://www.themarshallproject.org/2020/11/11/will-drug-legalization-leave-black-people-behind.

Correction Research Associates (1967), "Community Work: An Alternative to Imprisonment (Principles and Guidelines)," published in Washington, DC, accessed on September 17, 2024 at https://www.ojp.gov/pdffiles1/Digitization/1722NCJRS.pdf.

Council of the European Union (2021), "EU Drug Strategy 2021–2025," accessed on September 3, 2024 at https://www.euda.europa.eu/drugs-library/eu-drugs-action-plan-2021-2025_en.

Council on Criminal Justice (2023). *The Footprint: Tracking the Size of America's Criminal Justice System*, accessed on September 23, 2024 at https://counciloncj.foleon.com/the-footprint-trends-in-crime-arrests-and-the-total-correctional-population/the-footprint/.

Cozic, Charles P. (1998), *Illegal Drugs: Current Controversies*, San Diego, CA: Greenhaven Press.

Czech Republic (2013), "Annual Report: The Czech Republic 2012 Drug Situation" accessed on September 12, 2024 at https://www.drogy-info.cz/data/obj_files/1345/629/2012_annual_report_drug_situation_czech_republic.pdf.

Czech Republic (2023), "Annual Reports on Illicit Drugs in the Czech Republic, 2023," accessed on September 12, 2024 at https://www.drogy-info.cz/en/publications/annual-reports/report-on-illicit-drugs-in-the-czech-republic-2023/.

Czech Republic (2024), "Government Council for Addiction Policy Coordination," ("Council") is established by law in accordance with Section 28, Paragraph 3 of Act No. 65/2017 Coll., accessed on September 12, 2024 at https://vlada.gov.cz/en/ppov/protidrogova-politika/government-council-for-the-coordination-of-addiction-policy-196563/.

Czech Republic and Manuel Cardoso (2017), "Integrated Drug Policy in Portugal: National Conference in Alcohol and Its Social Impacts in the Czech Republic 2017," Office of Intervention on Addictive Behaviors and Dependencies, Prague, September 27, 2017.

Decorte, Tom, Simon Lenton, and Chris Wilkins, ed. (2020), *Legalizing Cannabis: Experiences, Lessons and Scenarios*, Routledge: New York.

Derrickson, Jason, ed. (2014), *Marijuana Legalization: State Initiatives, Implications, and Issues*, New York: Nova Publishers.

Dervan, Lucian E. (2024), "Fourteen Principles and a Path Forward for Plea Bargaining Reform," *American Bar Association Journal* Vol. 38, No. 4, (Winter), accessed on October 5, 2024 at https://www.amer ican bar.org/gro ups/crimi nal_ just ice/publi cations/crimi nal-just ice-magaz ine/2024/win ter/fourt een-pri ncip les-path-forw ard-pleabargain ing-ref orm/.

Doweiko, Harold E. (2009), *Concepts of Chemical Dependency*, 7th ed., Belmont, CA: Brooks/Cole Cengage Learning.

Dufton, Emily (2017), *Grass Roots: The Rise and Fall and Rise of Marijuana in America*, New York: Basic Books.

Duke, Steven B., and Albert C. Gross (1993), *America's Longest War: Rethinking Our Tragic Crusade against Drugs*, New York: G. P. Putnam's.

Eldredge, Dirk Chase (1998), *Ending the War on Drugs: A Solution for America*, Bridgehampton, NY: Bridge Works.

European Monitoring Centre for Drugs and Drug Addiction (2011), "Drug Policy Profiles: Portugal," Luxembourg: Publication of Office of European Union.

European Monitoring Centre for Drugs and Drug Addiction (2023), "Drug-Induced Deaths—the Current Situation in Europe (European Drug Report 2023)," Luxembourg: Publication of Office of European Union.

European Union Drugs Agency (EUDA) (2024), "Penalties at a Glance," updated on February 16, 2024, accessed on September 5, 2024 at https://www.euda.europa.eu/publications/topic-overviews/content/drug-law-penalties-at-a-glance_en.

European Union Drugs Agency (2023), "Drug Policy Evaluation in Europe—Topic Overview," December, accessed on September 5, 2024 at https://www.euda.europa.eu/publications/topic-overviews/policy-evaluation_en.

European Union Drugs Agency (2003), "EU Action Plan to Combat Drugs (1995–1999)," accessed on September 5, 2024 at https://eur-lex.europa.eu/EN/legal-content/summary/action-plan-to-combat-drugs-1995-1999.html?fromSummary=23.

European Union Drugs Agency (2021), "EU Drugs Strategy and Drugs Action Plan 2021–25," accessed on September 5, 2024 at https://op.europa.eu/en/publication-detail/-/publication/fd218c19-c5d6-11ec-b6f4-01aa75ed71a1.

European Union Drugs Agency (2004), "Final Evaluation leading to EU Drugs Strategy 2005–12," Document (11/22/2004 in Brussels), accessed on September 9, 2024 at https://www.euda.europa.eu/document-library/eu-drugs-strategy-2005-2012_en.

European Union (1994), "Communication from the Commission to the Council and the European Parliament on a European Union Action Plan to Combat Drugs (1995–1999)," June 23, accessed on September 5, 2024 at https https://aei.pitt.edu/2955/.

European Union (1992), "Report from the European Committee to Combat Drugs (CELAD) to the European Council," December 11, accessed on September 5, 2024 at https://aei.pitt.edu/2955/1/2955.pdf.

European Union (2000), "EU-Action Plan to Combat Drugs 2000–2004," June 7, accessed on September 5, 2024 at https://eur-lex.europa.eu/legal-content/EN/TXT/?uri=legissum:l33092.

European Union (2004), "EU Drugs Strategy (2005–2012)," November 22, accessed on September 5, 2024 at https://eur-lex.europa.eu/LexUriServ/LexUriServ.do?uri=OJ:C:2005:226E:0233:0238:EN:PDF.

Evans, Rod L., and Irwin M. Berent (1992), *Drug Legalization: For and Against*, La Salle, IL: Open Court.

Falco, Mathea (1992), *The Making of a Drug-Free America: Programs that Work*, New York: Times Books.

Feiling, Tom (2009), *Cocaine Nation: How the White Trade Took Over the World*, New York: Pegasus Books.

Fish, Jefferson M., ed. (1998), *How to Legalize Drugs*, Northvale, NJ: Jason Aronson.

Fish, Jefferson M., ed. (2006), *Drugs and Society: U.S. Public Policy*, Lanham, MD: Rowman & Littlefield.

Fisher, Gary (2006), *Rethinking Our War on Drugs: Candid Talk about Controversial Issues*, Westport, CT: Praeger.

Fisher, Gary L., and Nancy A. Roget, eds. (2009), *Encyclopedia of Substance Abuse Prevention, Treatment, & Recovery*; volumes 1–3, Thousand Oaks, CA: Sage.

Flowers, R. Barri (1998), *The Prostitution of Women and Girls*, Jefferson, NC: McFarland.

Foucault Michel (1977), *Discipline and Punish: The Birth of the Prison*, New York: Pantheon Books.

France, Regional House and Territories of the State (2021), "The Implementation of the 'Crack Plan' in Paris," Audit Flash, December.

French Government Report (2021), "Entities and Public Policies the Implementation of the 'Crack Plan' in Paris," Audit Flash, December.

Gaines, Larry K., and Peter B. Kraska, eds. (1997), *Drugs, Crime, and Justice: Contemporary Perspectives*, Prospect Heights, IL: Waveland Press.

Gaines, Larry K., and Peter B. Kraska, eds. (2003), *Drugs, Crime, and Justice: Contemporary Perspectives*, 2nd ed., Prospect Heights, IL: Waveland Press.

Gerber, Rudolph (2004), *Legalizing Marijuana: Drug Policy Reform and Prohibition Politics*, Westport, CT: Praeger.

Gerdes, Louis I. (2001), *Legalizing Drugs: At Issue*, San Diego, CA: Greenhaven Press.

Gold, Mark S. (1993), *Cocaine*, New York: Plenum Medical Book Company, 1993.

Gonzales, Joaquin Jay, and Mickey P. McGee, eds. (2019), *Legal Marijuana: Perspectives on Public Benefits, Risks and Policy Approaches*, Jefferson, NC: McFarland.

Goode, Erich (1997), *Between Politics and Reason: The Drug Legalization Debate*, New York: St. Martin's Press.

Goode, Erich (2008), *Drugs in American Society*, 7th ed., New York: McGraw-Hill.

Government of Ireland, Department of Health, Department of Public Expenditure and Reform (2021), "Spending Review 2021: Focused Policy Assessment of Reducing Harm, Supporting Recovery: An Analysis of Expenditure and Performance in the Area of Drug and Alcohol Misuse," July.

Gray, James P. (2001), *Why Our Drug Laws Have Failed and What We Can Do about It*, Philadelphia: Temple University Press.

Greenwald, Glenn (2009), *Drug Decriminalization in Portugal: Lessons for Creating Fair and Successful Drug Policies*, Washington, DC: Cato Institute.

Grossman, Lewis A. (2021), *Choose Your Medicine: Freedom of Therapeutic Choice in America*, New York: Oxford University Press.

Haerens, Margaret, ed. (2014), *Doping: Opposing Viewpoints Series*, Farmington Hills, MI: Greenhaven Press.

Hamza Yusuf (2004), *Purification of the Heart: Signs, Symptoms, and Cures of the Spiritual Diseases of the Heart, Translation and Commentary of Imam Mawlud's Matharat al-Qulub*. Chicago: Starlatch.

Hardaway, Robert M. (2003), *No Price Too High: Victimless Crimes and the Ninth Amendment*, Westport, CT: Praeger.

Hardaway, Robert M. (2018), *Marijuana Politics: Uncovering the Troublesome History and Social Costs of Criminalization*, Santa Barbara: Praeger.

Hari, Johann (2015), *Chasing the Scream: The First and Last Days of the War on Drugs*, New York: Bloomsbury.

Hart, Carl (2021), *Drug Use for Grown-Ups: Chasing Liberty in the Land of Fear*, New York: Penguin Press.

Henne, Kathryn E. (2015), *Testing for Athlete Citizenship: Regulating Doping and Sex in Sport*, New Brunswick, NJ: Rutger's University Press.

Hesse, Josiah (2021), *Runner's High: How a Movement of Cannabis-Fueled Athletes Is Changing the Science of Sports*, New York: G. P. Putnam's.

Horowitz, David (2021), *I Can't Breathe: How a Racial Hoax Is Killing America*, Washington, DC: Regnery Press.

Huggins, Laura, ed. (2005), *Drug War Deadlock: The Policy Battle Continues*, Stanford, CA: Hoover Institution Press.

Husak, Douglas N. (1992), *Drugs and Rights*, New York: Cambridge University Press.

Husak, Douglas (2002), *Legalize This! The Case for Decriminalizing Drugs*, New York: Verso.

Husak, Douglas, and Peter de Marneffe, eds. (2005), *The Legalization of Drugs: For & Against*, New York: Cambridge University Press.

Inciardi, James (2008), *The War on Drugs IV: The Continuing Saga of the Mysteries and Miseries of Intoxication, Addiction, Crime, and Public Policy*, 4th ed., Boston: Pearson.

Inciardi, James A., ed. (1991), *The Drug Legalization Debate*, Newbury Park, CA: Sage. (Anthology that is mostly balanced, but includes slightly more libertarian arguments.)

Inciardi, James, and Karen McElrath, ed. (2011), *The American Drug Scene: An Anthology*, 6th ed., New York: Oxford University Press.

Ireland (2023), "Healthy Ireland Survey 2023," Ireland: Government Publications, Dublin.

Irish Government Website (2021), "Spending Review: Focused Policy Assessment of Reducing Harm, Supporting Recovery: An Analysis of Expenditure and Performance in the Area of Drug and Alcohol Misuse," July.

Jefferson, Thomas (1776),*The Declaration of Independence*, July 6, 1776 in Philadelphia: Pennsylvania Evening Post.

Johnson, Nick (2017), *Grass Roots: A History of Cannabis in the American West*, Corvalis: Oregon State University Press.

Jojarth, Christine (2009), *Crime, War, and Global Trafficking: Designing International Cooperation*, Cambridge, UK: Cambridge University Press: .

Jonnes, Jill (1996), *Hep-Cats, Narcs, and Pipe Dreams: A History of America's Romance with Illegal Drugs*, New York: Scribner.

Kallen, Stuart, ed. (2006), *Legalizing Drugs*, Farmington Hills, MI: Greenhaven Press.

Keys, David Patrick, and John E. Galliher (2000), *Confronting the Drug Control Establishment: Alfred Lindesmith as a Public Intellectual*, New York: State University of New York Press.

Kleiman, Mark, Jonathan Caulkins and Angela Hawken (2011), *Drugs and Drug Policy: What Everyone Needs to Know*, New York: Oxford University Press.

Klingemann, Harald, and Geoffrey Hunt, ed. (1998), *Drug Treatment Systems in an International Perspective: Drugs, Demons, and Delinquents*, Thousand Oaks, CA: Sage.

Kneeland, Timothy W. (2016), *Today's Social Issues: Democrats and Republicans*, Santa Barbara, CA: ABC-CLIO.

Krasner, Barbara, ed. (2019), *Harm Reduction: Public Health Strategies*, New York: Greenhaven.

Krauss, Melvyn B., and Edward P. Lazear (1991), *Searching for Alternatives: Drug-Control Policy in the United States*, Stanford, CA: Hoover Institution Press.

Kubeisy, Connor (2024), "The Drug Review Oregon's Measure 110 Has Been a Failed Policy Experiment," posted on February 26, accessed on October 5, 2024 at https://gooddrugpolicy.org/2024/02/the-drug-review-oregons-measure-110-has-been-a-failed-policy-experiment/.

Kuipers, Dean (2006), *Burning Rainbow Farm: How a Stoner Utopia Went Up in Smoke*, New York: Bloomsbury.

Kwitny, Jonathan (1992), *Acceptable Risks*, New York: Poseidon Press.

Langabeer, James R., Angela L. Stotts, Bentley J. Bobrow, Henry E. Wang, Kimberly A. Chambers, Andrea J. Yatsco, Marylou Cardenas-Turanzas, and Tiffany Champagne-Langabeer (2021), "Prevalence and Charges of Opioid-Related Visits to U.S. Emergency Departments," *Drug Alcohol Dependence*, April 1, 221:108568. doi: 10.1016/j.drugalcdep.2021.108568. Epub February 3, 2021.

Laslett, Peter (1963), ed., *John Locke Two Treatises of Government*, rev. ed., New York: Cambridge University Press.

League of Nations (1931), "Agreement for the Control of Opium Smoking in the Far East" (League of Nations Document, signed Bangkok, November 27,).

League of Nations (1931), "Convention for Limiting the Manufacture and Regulating the Distribution of Narcotic Drugs" (League of Nations Document, signed Geneva July 13,).

League of Nations (1936), "Convention for the Suppression of the Illicit Traffic in Dangerous Drugs" (League of Nations Document, signed Geneva, June 26).

Leavitt, Fred (1995), *Drugs & Behavior*, 3rd ed., Thousand Oaks, CA: Sage.

Leighton, Paul, and Jeffrey Reiman, ed. (2001), *Criminal Justice Ethics*, Upper Saddle River, NJ: Prentice Hall.

Leuw, Ed, and I. Haen Marshall, eds. (1994), *Between Prohibition and Legalization: The Dutch Experiment in Drug Policy*, New York: Kugler Publications.

Levinson, Martin H. (2002), *The Drug Problem: A New View Using the General Semantics Approach*, Westport, CT: Praeger.

Levinthal, Charles F., ed. (2003), *Point/Counterpoints: Opposing Perspectives on Issues of Drug Policy*, New York: Pearson Education Press.

Levitt, Steven D., and Stephen J. Dubner (2006), *Freakonomics: A Rogue Economist Explores the Hidden Side of Everything*, rev. ed., New York: William Morrow [Harper Collins Publishers].

Lewis, Michael, and Richard F. Hamm (2020), *Prohibition's Greatest Myths: The Distilled Truth about America's Anti-Alcohol Crusade*, Baton Rouge: Louisiana State University Press.

Lowinson, Joyce H., Pedro Ruiz, Robert B. Millman, and John G. Langrod, eds. (1997), *Substances Abuse: A Comprehensive Textbook*, 3rd ed., Baltimore, MD: Williams & Wilkins.

Lynch, Timothy, ed. (2000), *After Prohibition: An Adult Approach to Drug Policies in the 21st Century*, Washington, DC: CATO Institute.

MacCoun, Robert J., and Peter Reuter (2001), *Drug War Heresies: Learning From Other Vices, Times, & Places*, New York: Cambridge University Press.

Maine Office of Alcoholism and Drug Abuse Prevention (1979), *The Decriminalization of Marijuana and the Maine Criminal Justice System: A Time/Cost Analysis*, Augusta, ME: Maine Office of Alcoholism and Drug Abuse Prevention.

Mandelbaum, David Goodman (1965), "Alcohol and Culture," *Current Anthropology*, 6 (3), June 1965, pp. 281–293. The University of Chicago Press on behalf of Wenner-Gren Foundation for Anthropological Research.

Marion, Nancy E., and Joshua B. Hill, eds. (2019), *More on Legalizing Marijuana: Ongoing Shifts in American Politics*, Durham, NC: Carolina Academic Press.

Marion, Nancy E., and Joshua N. Hill, eds. (2019), *Marijuana 360: Differing Perspectives on Legalization*, Lanham, MD: Rowman & Littlefield.

Marshall, Eliot (1988), *Legalization: A Debate*, New York: Chelsea House.

Martin, Alyson, and Nushin Rashidian (2014), *A New Leaf: The End of Cannabis Prohibition*, New York: New Press.

McCaffrey, Barry R. (1999), *The Destructive Impact of Drugs on the United States: How the Legalization of Drugs Would Jeopardize the Health and Safety of the American People and Our Nation*, Washington, DC: US Government Printing Office.

Medford Oregon Police Department (2024), "MADGE/IMET Task Force," accessed on October 5, 2024 at https://www.medfordoregon.gov/Government/Departments/Police/MADGEIMET-Task-Force.

Meier, Robert, and Gilbert Geis (2006), *Criminal Justice and Moral Issues*, Los Angeles: Roxbury.

Merino, Noel (2014), *Drug Legalization*, Farmington Hills, MI: Greenhaven Press.

Merino, Noel (2014), *The Legalization of Marijuana: Opposing Viewpoints*, Farmington Hills, MI: Greenhaven Press.

Miller, Char, ed. (2018), *Where There's Smoke: The Environmental Science, Public Policy, and Politics of Marijuana*, Lawrence, KS: University Press of Kansas.

Miller, Richard Lawrence (1991), *The Case for Legalizing Drugs*, New York: Praeger.

Minnesota Department of Health (2021) pamphlet, "Estimates of Alcohol Poisoning Deaths," accessed on October 5, 2024 at https://www.health.state.mn.us/communities/alcohol/documents/alcoholpoison2021.pdf.

Mitchell, Chester Nelson (1990), *The Drug Solution*, Ottowa, Canada: Carleton University Press.

Moffitt, Athol, John Malouf, and Craig Thompson (1998), *Drug Precipice: Illicit Drugs, Organized Crime, Fallacies of Legalization, Worsening Problems, Solutions*, Sydney, Australia: University of New South Wales Press.

Moller, Verner (2010), *The Ethics of Doping and Anti-Doping: Redeeming the Soul of Sport?*, New York Oxon, UK: Routledge.

Moore, M. H., and Gerstein D. R, eds. (1981), *Alcohol and Public Policy: Beyond the Shadow of Prohibition*. Washington, DC: National Academies Press.

Mosher, Clayton J., and Scott Akins (2019), *In the Weeds: Demonization, Legalization, and the Evolution of U.S. Marijuana Policy*, Philadelphia, PA: Temple University Press.

Mosher, Clayton J., and Scott M. Akins (2014), *Drugs and Drug Policy: The Control of Consciousness Alteration*, 2nd ed., Thousand Oaks, CA: Sage Publication.

National Center for Health Statistics (2022), "National Health and Nutrition Examination Survey" housed within the Centers for Disease Control, and accessed on September 30, 2024 at https://www.cdc.gov/nchs/nhanes/index.html.

National Center for Health Statistics (2019), "National Ambulatory Medical Care Survey" housed within the Centers for Disease Control, and accessed on September 30, 2024 at https://www.cdc.gov/nchs/namcs/about/index.html.

National Health Statistics Reports, Merianne Rose Spencer, Donielle G. White, and Geoffrey Jackson (2023), National Hospital Care Survey Demonstration Projects: "Mortality Following Nonfatal Opioid Overdose Visits to the Emergency Department," U.S. Department of Health and Human Services, Centers for Disease Control and Prevention, National Center for Health Statistics, Number 187, May 23.

National Institute of Drug Addiction (NIDA) (2023), "Commonly Used Drug Charts," NIDA, accessed on September 15, 2024 at https://nida.nih.gov/research-topics/commonly-used-drugs-charts.

National Institute of Drug Addiction (NIDA) (2023), "Monitoring the Future (MTF) Report for 2023," accessed on September 15, 2024 at https://monitoringthefuture.org/wp-content/uploads/2023/07/mtfpanel2023.pdf.

National Institute of Justice (2019), "A Brief History of NIJ," posted October 24, 2019, appeared in *NIJ Journal* issue 281 (September) at https://nij.ojp.gov/topics/articles/brief-history-nij

National Institute of Justice (1997), *Preventing Crime: What Works, What Doesn't, and What's Promising*. Authors Lawrence W. Sherman, Denise Gottfredson, Doris MacKenzie, John Eck, Peter Reuter, and Shawn Bushway, NCJ Number 165366, accessed at https://nij.ojp.gov/library/publications/preventing-crime-what-works-what-doesnt-whats-promising-report-united-states

National Institute on Alcohol Abuse and Alcoholism (NIAAA) (2024), subset of National Institute of Health (NIH); "Understanding Alcohol Drinking Problems," accessed on September 15, 2024 at https://www.niaaa.nih.gov/alcohol-health/overview-alcohol-consumption/moderate-binge-drinking.

National Institute on Alcohol Abuse and Alcoholism (NIAAA), subset of National Institute of Health (NIH) (2022), "Age, Period, and Cohort Effects in Alcohol Use in the United States in the 20th and 21st Centuries: Implications for the Coming Decades," vol. 42 (1), January 13, accessed on September 15, 2024 at https://arcr.niaaa.nih.gov/volume/42/1/age-period-and-cohort-effects-alcohol-use-united-states-20th-and-21st-centuries.

National Institute on Drug Abuse, Carl G. Leukefeld, and Frank M. Tims, eds. (1992), *Drug Abuse Treatment in Prisons and Jails*, Washington, DC: US Department of

Health and Human Services, Public Health Service, National Institutes of Health, Government Printing Office [NIDA Research Monograph 118].

National Research Council (US) (1981) *Panel on Alternative Policies Affecting the Prevention of Alcohol Abuse and Alcoholism - Alcohol and Public Policy: Beyond the Shadow of Prohibition.* Edited by Moore M. H. and Gerstein D. R. Washington, DC: National Academies Press.

Netherlands Government Website (2024), "Drug Policies," accessed on September 24, 2024 at https://www.government.nl/topics/drugs.

Newton, David E. (2017), *Marijuana: A Reference Handbook*, 2nd ed., Santa Barbara, CA: ABC-CLIO.

Newton, David E. (1999), *Social Issues in Science and Technology: An Encyclopedia*, Santa Barbara, CA: ABC-CLIO.

Newton, David E. (2017), *Substance Abuse: A Reference Handbook*, 2nd ed., Santa Barabara, CA: ABC-CLIO.

Ninety-fifth Congress (1977), First Session, *Hearings Before Select Committee on Narcotics Abuse and Control*, Washington, DC: Government Printing Office.

NOVA-Information Management School (2021), *Executive Summary—External Evaluation of Portugal PNRCAD 2013–2020* [Plano Nacional para a Redução dos Comportamentos Aditivos e Dependências], Lisbon, Portugal.

Office of National Drug Control Policy, Executive Office of the President (2010), "FACT SHEET: Marijuana Legalization—a Bad Idea," October.

O'Hare, P. A., Newcombe R, Matthews A, Buning E C & Drucker E, eds. (1992), *The Reduction of Drug-Related Harm*, New York: Routledge.

Oki, G., N. Giesbrecht, P. J. Giffen, and S. Lambert (1976), *Decriminalization of Public Drunkenness: A Statistical Profile of Patterns and Trends*, Toronto, ON: Addiction Research Foundation.

One Hundred and Fourth Congress, Second Session (1996), *Hearing before the Committee on the Judiciary United States Senate: Examining the Newly Adopted Initiatives That Modify Arizona and California Law by Decriminalizing Drug Use in Some Circumstances*, Washington, DC: US Government Printing Office.

One Hundred Fifth Congress, First Session (1997), "Needle Exchange, Legalization, and the Failure of the Swiss Heroin Experiments: Hearing before the Subcommittee on National Security, International Affairs, and Criminal Justice, of the Committee on Government Reform and Oversight," House of Representatives, Washington, DC: US Government Printing Office.

One Hundred First Congress, First Session (1989), *Legalization of Illicit Drugs: Impact and Feasibility (A Review of Recent Hearings)*, Washington, DC: US Government Printing Office.

One Hundred Sixth Congress, First Session (2000), "Pros and Cons of Drug Legalization, Decriminalization, and Harm Reduction: Hearing before the Subcommittee on Criminal Justice, Drug Policy, and Human Resources, of the

Committee on Government Reform," Washington, DC: House of Representatives, US Goverment Printing Office.

One Hundred-Seventeenth Congress, Second Session (2022), "Developments in State Cannabis Laws and Bipartisan Cannabis Reforms at the Federal Level: Hearing before the Subcommittee on Civil Rights and Civil Liberties, of the Committee on Government Reform and Oversight," Washington, DC: House of Representatives, US Goverment Printing Office.

One Hundred-Seventh Congress, First Session (2001), "Medical Marijuana, Federal Drug Law and the Constitution's Supremacy Clause: Hearing before the Subcommittee on Criminal Justice, Drug Policy, and Human Resources, of the Committee on Government Reform," Washington, DC: House of Representatives, US Government Printing Office.

One Hundred-Sixteenth Congress, First Session (2019), "Challenges for Cannabis and Banking—Outside Perspectives: Hearing before the Committee on Banking, Housing, and Urban Affairs," Washington, DC: US Senate, US Goverment Printing Office.

One Hundred-Sixteenth Congress, First Session (2019), "Marijuana and America's Health—Questions and Issues for Policy Makers: Hearing before the Senate Caucus on International Narcotics Control," Washington, DC: US Senate, US Government Printing Office.

One Hundred-Sixteenth Congress, First Session (2019), "Marijuana Laws in America—Racial Justice and the Need for Reform: Hearing before the Subcommittee on Crime, Terrorism, and Homeland Security," Washington, DC: House of Representatives, US Government Printing Office.

One Hundred-Sixteenth Congress, Second Session (2020), "Medical Marijuana Research Act: Report from the Committee on Energy and Commerce," Washington, DC: House of Representatives, US Government Printing Office.

One Hundred-Sixth Congress, First Session (1999), "The Decriminalization of Illegal Drugs: Hearing before the Subcommittee on Criminal Justice, Drug Policy, and Human Resources, of the Committee on Government Reform," Washington, DC: House of Representatives, US Government Printing Office.

One Hundredth Congress, Second Session (1988), *Drug Legalization: Catastrophe for Black Americans—Hearings before the Select Committee on Narcotics Abuse and Control*, Washington, DC: US Printing Office.

One Hundredth Congress, Second Session (1988), *Hearing before the Select Committee on Narcotics Abuse and Control*, Washington, DC: US Government Printing Offices.

One Hundred-Thirteenth Congress, First Session (2013), "Conflicts between State and Federal Marijuana Laws: Hearing before the Judiciary," Washington, DC: US Senate, US Government Printing Office.

Osbeck, Mark K., and Howard Bromberg (2017), *Marijuana Law in a Nutshell*, St. Paul, MN: West Academic.

Panel on Alternative Policies Affecting the Prevention of Alcohol Abuse and Alcoholism, Committee on Substance Abuse and Habitual Behavior, Assembly of Behavioral and Social Sciences, and National Research Council (1981), *Alcohol and Public Policy: Beyond the Shadow of Prohibition*, National Washington, D.C.: Academies Press.

Parfitt, Jamie, and Pat Dooris (2023), "The Push to 'Fix and Improve' Measure 110," posted on KGW8 on September 19, accessed on October 5, 2024 at https://www.kgw.com/article/news/local/the-story/measure-110-fix-improve-coalition-ballot-measure-initiative/283-73b41ddd-2659-40ff-b20a-e5a93eab0476.

Police Executive Research Forum (2014), *New Challenges for Police: A Heroin Epidemic and Changing Attitudes Toward Marijuana*, Washington, DC: Police Executive Research Forum.

Portugal General-Directorate for Intervention on Addictive Behaviours and Dependencies (2021) Drug Plan Evaluation— – 2013–2020, "Evaluation of the National Plan for the Reduction of Addictive Behaviors and Dependencies 2013–2020," (from January 2021).

Portugal General-Directorate for Intervention on Addictive Behaviours and Dependencies (2013), "Plan for the Reduction of Addictive Behaviours and Addictions 2013-2020," accessed on October 1, 2024 at https://health.ec.europa.eu/document/download/1ba0ccb2-bed0-433b-841d-5c59d3d941e5_en.

Portugal General-Directorate for Intervention on Addictive Behaviours and Dependencies (2021), "Plan for the Reduction of Addictive Behaviours and Addictions 2021-2030," accessed on October 1, 2024 at https://www.icad.pt/Page/GetDocument/583.

Rahman, Fifa, and Nick Crofts, ed. (2013), *Drug Law Reform in East and Southeast Asia*, Lanham, MD: Lexington Books.

Reece, Albert Stuart Reece, and Gary Kenneth Hulse (2024), "Key Insights into Cannabis-Cancer Pathobiology and Genotoxicity," *Addiction Biology*, 29 (11), November 13, accessed on October 8, 2024 at https://doi.org/10.1111/adb.70003.

Regan, Trish (2011), *Joint Ventures: Inside America's Almost Legal Marijuana Industry*, Hoboken, NJ: John Wiley.

Reilly, Wilfred (2019), *Hate Crime Hoax: How the Left Is Selling a Fake Race War*, Washington, DC: Regnery Press.

Research Briefing for the House of Commons Library UK Parliament (1971), "UK Misuses of Drugs Act," by William Downs and Grahame Allen, "Illegal Drug Use and Organised Crime," accessed on March 4, 2024 at https://commonslibrary.parliament.uk/research-briefings/cdp-2024-0050/

Reznicek, Michael (2012), *Blowing Smoke: Rethinking the War on Drugs without Prohibition and Rehab*, Lanham, MD: Rowman & Littlefield.

Rhodes, Rosamond, Leslie P. Francis, and Anita Silvers, eds. (2007), *The Blackwell Guide to Medical Ethics*, Malden, MA: Blackwell.

Richards, David A., *Sex, Drugs, Death, and the Law: An Essay on Human Rights and Overcriminalization*, Totawa, NJ: Rowman & Littlefield.

Roleff, Tamara L., ed. (2004), *Opposing Viewpoints: The War on Drugs*, Farmington Hills, MI: Greenhaven Press.

Roleff, Tamara L., ed. (2005), *Drug Abuse: Opposing Viewpoints*, Farmington Hills, MI: Greenhaven Press.

Room, Robin, Benedikt Fischer, Wayne Hall, Simon Lenton, and Peter Reuter, eds. (2010), *Cannabis Policy: Moving Beyond Stalemate*, Oxford, UK: Beckley Foundation Press.

Rosenthal, Ed, and Steve Kubby (2003), *Why Marijuana Should Be Legal*, New York: Thunder's Mouth Press.

Rosenthal, Franz (1971), *The Herb: Hashish Versus Medieval Muslim Society*, Leiden: E.J. Brill.

Rowe, Thomas C. (2006), *Federal Narcotics Laws and the War on Drugs: Money Down a Rat Hole*, New York: Haworth Press.

Rudi Matthee (2005), *The Pursuit of Pleasure: Drugs and Stimulants in Iranian History, 1500–1900*, Princeton, NJ: Princeton University Press.

San Francisco Department of Health (2017), "Safe Injection Services Task Force, 2017 (Sept) Final Report," accessed on September 23, 2024 at https://www.sfdph.org/dph/files/SIStaskforce/SIS-Task-Force-Final-Report-2017.pdf.

Schaler, Jeffrey, ed. (1998), *Drugs: Should We Legalize, Decriminalize, or Deregulate*, New York: Prometheus Books.

Schick, Tony, and Conrad Wilson (2024), "Oregon's Drug Decriminalization Aimed to Make Police a Gateway to Rehab, Not Jail. State Leaders Failed to Make It Work," *OPB*, February 14, 2024, accessed on October 5, 2024 at https://www.opb.org/article/2024/02/14/oregon-drug-decriminalization-plan-measure-110-leadership-failures/.

Seattle Chamber Website (2023), "Drug Possession and Public Use Laws—a Timeline," by Lilly Hayward on August 4, 2023, accessed on September 24, 2024 at https://www.seattlechamber.com/news/2023/08/04/policy-advocacy/drug-possession-and-public-use-laws-a-timeline/.

Shohov, Tatiana, ed. (2003), *Medical Use of Marijuana: Policy, Regulatory and Legal Issues*, New York: Nove Science.

Shroder, Tom (2014), *Acid Test: LSD, Ecstasy, and the Power to Heal*, New York: Plume Book.

Smith, Benjamin T. (2021), *The Dope: The Real History of the Mexican Drug Trade*, New York: W. W. Norton.

Sowell, Thomas (1987), *A Conflict of Visions: Ideological Origins of Political Struggles*, New York: William Morrow, 1987.

Sowell, Thomas (1985), *Civil Rights: Rhetoric or Reality*, New York: William Morrow.

Sowell, Thomas (1990), *Preferential Policies: An International Perspective*, New York: William Morrow.

Sowell, Thomas (1994), *Race and Culture: A World View*, New York: Basic Books.

Sowell, Thomas (1983), *The Economics and Politics of Race: An International Perspective*, New York: William Morrow.

Stares, Paul B. (1996), *Global Habit: The Drug Problem in a Borderless World*, Washington, DC: Brookings Institute.

State of Oregon (2020), "Voter's Pamphlet: Oregon General Election," November 3, 2020.

Stone, Jason, and Andrea Stone (2003), *The Drug Dilemma: Responding to a Growing Crisis*, New York: International Debate Education Association: .

Sullum, Jacob (2003), *Saying Yes: In Defense of Drug Use*, New York: Tarcher/Putnam.

Swisher, Karin L., ed. (1991), *Drug Trafficking: Current Controversies*, San Diego, CA: Greenhaven Press.

Swisher, Karin L., ed. (1996), *Legalizing Drugs: Opposing Viewpoints*, San Diego, CA: Greenhaven Press.

Szasz, Thomas (1992), *Our Right to Drugs: The Case for a Free Market*, Westport, CT: Praeger.

Takahashi, Saul (2016), *Human Rights and Drug Control: The False Dichotomy*, Portland, OR: Hart Publishing.

Tate, Katherine, James Lance Taylor, and Mark Q. Sawyer, eds. (2014), *Something's In the Air: Race, Crime, and the Legalization of Marijuana*, New York: Routledge.

Tenaglia-Webster, Maria, ed. (2009), *Drugs: Opposing Viewpoints*, Farmington Hills, MI: Greenhaven Press.

Thompson, Stephen P., ed. (1998), *The War on Drugs: Opposing Viewpoints*, San Diego, CA: Greenhaven Press.

Trebach, Arnold S., and James A. Inciardi, eds. (1993), *Legalize It? Debating American Drug Policy*, Washington, DC: American University Press.

Trebach, Arnold, and Kevin B. Zeese, eds. (1990), *Drug Prohibition and the Conscience of Nations*, Washington, DC: Drug Policy Foundation.

Trebach, Arnold S., and Kevin B. Zeese, eds. (1992), *Milton Friedman and Thomas Szasz on Liberty and Drugs: Essays on the Free Market and Prohibition*, Washington, DC: Drug Policy Foundation Press.

United Nations (1972), "Commentary on the Protocol Amending the Single Convention on Narcotics Drugs, 1961," at Geneva March 25, Under UN Office of Drugs and Crime, after 1972 Amendments, accessed on September 20, 2024 at https://www.unodc.org/documents/treaties/organized_crime/Drug%20Convention/Commentary_on_the_protocol_1961.pdf.

United Nations (1962), "Commentary on the Single Convention on Narcotic Drugs, 1961," prepared by the Secretary-General, August 3, 1962, Under UN Office of Drugs and Crime, accessed on September 20, 2024 at https://www.unodc.org/documents/commissions/CND/Int_Drug_Control_Conventions/Commentaries-OfficialRecords/1961Convention/1961_COMMENTARY_en.pdf.

United Nations (1971), "Convention on Psychotropic Substances of 1971," UN Office of Drugs and Crime, accessed on September 20, 2024 at https://www.unodc.org/pdf/convention_1971_en.pdf.

United Nations (1946), "Protocol Amending the Agreements, Conventions and Protocols on Narcotic Drugs from 1912, 1925, 1931, and 1936" (UN Document, signed at Lake Success, December 11,), accessed on September 20, 2024 at https://digitallibrary.un.org/record/552019?ln=en&v=pdf/.

United Nations (1948), "Protocol Bringing Under International Control Drugs Outside the Scope of the Convention of 13 July 1931 for Limiting the Manufacture and Regulating the Distribution of Narcotic Drugs (as amended by Lake Success Protocol of 1946)" (UN Document, signed Paris, November 19), accessed on September 20, 2024 at https://digitallibrary.un.org/record/666805/files/?ln=en.

United Nations (1953), "Protocol for Limiting and Regulating the Cultivation of the Poppy Plant, the Production of International and Wholesale Trade in, and Use of Opium" (UN Document, signed New York June 23), accessed on September 20, 2024 at https://www.unodc.org/unodc/en/Resolutions/resolution_1954-07-12_3.html .

United Nations (1972), "Single Convention on Narcotic Drugs of 1961 as Amended by the 1972 Protocol," UN Office of Drugs and Crime, accessed on September 20, 2024 at https://www.un-ilibrary.org/content/books/9789210555845s002-c005 .

United Nations (2020), "UN Commission on Drugs Statements on WHO Five Recommendations, After Deleting Cannabis from Schedule IV List," UN Office of Drugs and Crime, accessed on September 20, 2024 at https://www.unodc.org/documents/commissions/CND/CND_Sessions/CND_63Reconvened/ECN72020_CRP24_V2007524.pdf.

United Nations (2005), "UN Convention against Corruption (2002 & 2003)—a Tool to Enforce the Organized Crime Convention against Corrupt Nations" (adopted October 31, 2003 and entered into force December 14, 2005 [140 signatories and 190 parties]), accessed on September 20, 2024 at https://www.unodc.org/unodc/treaties/.

United Nations (1988), "UN Convention against Illicit Traffic in Narcotic Drugs and Psychotropic Substances of 1988," UN Office of Drugs and Crime, accessed on September 20, 2024 at https://www.unodc.org/pdf/convention_1988_en.pdf.

United Nations (2000), "UN Convention against Transnational Organized Crime and Protocols Thereto," UN Office of Drugs and Crime, 2000 (adopted 2000, by resolution 55/25; set into force September 29, 2003 [147 signatories and 192 parties]), accessed on September 20, 2024 at https://www.unodc.org/unodc/treaties/.

United Nations, Office on Drugs and Crime (2008), "A Century of International Drug Control," chapter 2 in *World Drug Report 2008*, accessed on September 20, 2024 at https://www.unodc.org/unodc/treaties/.

United Nations, Office on Drugs and Crime (2007), "Drug Dependence Treatment: Interventions for Drug Users in Prison," accessed on September 20, 2024 at https://www.unodc.org/unodc/treaties/.

United Nations, Office on Drugs and Crime (2021), "Executive Summary: Policy Implications of World Drug Report 2021," UNODC Research, accessed on September 20, 2024 at https://solid-exceed.org/resources/publication/world-drug-report-2021.

United Nations, UN Office on Drugs and Crime (2009), brief article on "1912 Hague Opium Convention," posted on January 23 by the UN ODC, accessed on September 20, 2024 https://www.unodc.org/unodc/en/frontpage/the-1912-hague-international-opium-convention.html.

United Nations, UN Office on Drugs and Crime (2021), "Horizon Europe strategic plan (2021–2024)," accessed on September 20, 2024 at https://research-and-innovation.ec.europa.eu/system/files/2021-03/ec_rtd_horizon-europe-strategic-plan-2021-24-analysis.pdf.

US Census (2021), "Data on State and Local Government Expenditures for 2021," accessed on October 1, 2024 at https://www2.census.gov/programs-surveys/gov-finances/tables/2021/2021alfinsummarybrief.pdf.

US Census (2024), "Legal Sports Betting?," accessed on October 1, 2024 at https://www.census.gov/library/stories/2024/02/legal-sports-betting.html.

US Department of Justice (2020), "DOJ Drug Fact Sheet on Vaping and Marijuana Concentrates," accessed on August 25, 2024 at https://www.dea.gov/sites/default/files/2020-06/Vaping%20and%20Marijuana%20Concentrates-2020.pdf.

US Department of Justice, Drug Enforcement Administration (2025), "DEA: DEA Drug and Crime Fact Sheets," *stopped being updated in 2021*, accessed on September 1, 2024 at https://www.dea.gov/factsheets.

US Department of Justice, Drug Enforcement Administration (2024), "National Drug Threat Assessment 2024," accessed on September 1, 2024 at https://www.dea.gov/documents/2024/2024-05/2024-05-24/national-drug-threat-assessment-2024.

US Department of Justice, Drug Enforcement Administration (2003), "Speaking Out against Drug Legalization," accessed on August 30, 2024 at https://www.ojp.gov/ncjrs/virtual-library/abstracts/speaking-out-against-drug-legalization.

US Department of Justice, Federal Bureau of Prisons (1996), "Federal Prison Residential Drug Treatment Reduces Substance Use and Arrests after Release," accessed on October 2, 2024 at https://www.bop.gov/resources/research_projects/published_reports/recidivism/orepramjalcd.pdf.

US Department of Justice, National Drug Intelligence Center (2010), "Center Valley California High Intensity Drug Trafficking Area: Drug Market Analysis 2010," accessed on October 1, 2024 at https://www.justice.gov/archive/ndic/pubs40/40384/40384p.pdf.

US Department of Justice, National Drug Intelligence Center (2008), "Oregon High Intensity Drug Trafficking Area Drug Market Analysis 2008," June (anonymous), accessed on October 5, 2024 at https://www.justice.gov/archive/ndic/pubs27/27508/markets.htm.

US Department of State (2021), "International Narcotics Control Strategy 2021," accessed on September 5, 2024 at https://www.state.gov/wp-content/uploads/2021/02/International-Narcotics-Control-Strategy-Report-Volume-I-FINAL-1.pdf.

US Department of State, Bureau of International Narcotics and Law Enforcement Affairs (2021), "International Narcotics Control Strategy Report," vol. 1: Drug and Chemical Control, March.

US Dept of Health and Human Services (2022), "What Are Drug Courts," accessed on September 5, 2024 at https://www.hhs.gov/opioids/treatment/drug-courts/index.html.

US Government Accountability Office (2015), "State Marijuana Legalization: DOJ Should Document Its Approach to Monitoring the Effects of Legalization," December 30, 2015 accessed on October 1, 2024 at https://www.gao.gov/products/gao-16-1.

Vallance, Theodore R. (1993), *Prohibition's Second Failure: The Quest for a Rational and Humane Drug Policy*, Westport, CT: Praeger.

Vallee, Alexandre (2024), "Heavy Lifetime Cannabis Use and Mortality by Sex," *JAMA Network Open*, 7 (6), e2415227. doi:10.1001/jamanetworkopen.2024.15227.

Ventura, Marne (2018), *Pros and Cons: The Debate about Legalizing Marijuana*, Lake Elmo, MN: Focus Readers.

Vitale, Alex S. (2017), *The End of Policing*, New York: Verso.

Vitale, Alex S. (2017), *The End of Policing*, London: Verso,.

Vysotsky, Stanislav (2020), *American Antifa: The Tactics, Culture, and Practice of Militant Antifascism*, New York: Routledge.

Wainwright, Tom (2016), *Narco-Nomics: How to Run a Drug Cartel*, New York: Public Affairs.

Widener, Michael N. (2018), *Joint Tenancies: Property Leasing in Cannabis Commerce*, Chicago: American Bar Association.

Williamson, Kevin (1997), *Drugs and the Party Line*, Edinburgh, Scotland: Rebel.

Wilson, H. W., ed. (2014), *The Reference Shelf: Marijuana Reform*, Ipswich, MA: Grey House.

Wodak, Alex, and Ron Owens (1996), *Drug Prohibition: A Call for Change*, Sydney, Australia: University of New South Wales Press.

World Health Organization, Commission on Narcotic Drugs (2020), "Statements Following the Voting on the WHO Scheduling Recommendations on Cannabis-Related Substance," December 15. 2020, accessed on September 30, 2024 at https://www.unodc.org/documents/commissions/CND/CND_Sessions/CND_63Reconvened/ECN72020_CRP24_V2007524.pdf.

Ying Wong, and Jeanne Tsai (2007), "Cultural Models of Shame and Guilt." In *Handbook of Self-Conscious Emotions*. Edited by Jessica Tracy, Richard Robins, and June Tangney. New York: Guilford Press, pp. 209–23.

Young, Mitchell (2007), *Issues on Trial: Euthanasia*, Farmington Hills, MI: Greenhaven Press.

Zorea, Aharon (2000), *In the Image of God: A Christian Response to Capital Punishment*, Lanham, MD: University Press of America.

Zorea, Aharon (2005), "Plurality and Law: The Rise of Law Enforcement in Organized Crime Control," PhD Dissertation, St. Louis University.

Zorea, Aharon (2012), *Birth Control (Health and Medical Issues Today)*, Westport, CT: Greenwood Press2012.

Zorea, Aharon (2014), *Steroids (Health and Medical Issues Today)*, Westport, CT: Greenwood Press.

Zorea, Aharon (2017), *Finding the Fountain of Youth: The Science and Controversy Behind Extending Life and Cheating Death*, Westport, CT: Greenwood Press.

Zorea, Aharon (2022), *Marijuana: Your Questions Answered (Q&A Health Guides)*, Westport, CT: Greenwood Press.

Index

About the Author

Aharon W. Zorea, PhD, is professor of history at the University of Wisconsin–Platteville. His published works include many Greenwood and Bloomsbury titles, *Marijuana: Your Questions Answered* (Q&A Health Guides) (2022), *Finding the Fountain of Youth: The Science and Controversy behind Extending Life and Cheating Death* (2017), *Steroids* (Health and Medical Issues Today) (2014), and *Birth Control* (Health and Medical Issues Today) (2012), as well as *In the Image of God: A Christian Response to Capital Punishment* (2000). He has been teaching at the university level for more than twenty years and has written more than sixty articles on politics and legal and social policy. Zorea holds a master's degree from Purdue University and a doctorate from Saint Louis University. His articles and recorded lectures can be found through a variety of outlets online.